TREASURE
SEEKERS

Project Editor: Camilla MacWhannell
Project Art Direction: Diane Spender
Design: Mary Ryan
Picture research: Sharon Southren
Production: Janette Davis
Map illustrator: Vanessa Card

Printed in Dubai

TREASURE
SEEKERS
THE WORLD'S GREAT FORTUNES
LOST AND FOUND

DR. JANE MCINTOSH

CONTENTS

INTRODUCTION

The thought of treasure and seeking it out stirs the blood and fills most of us with the spirit of adventure. But what is treasure? If you asked people today, most would probably say it is gold, silver and precious stones. When we look at peoples of the past or at other cultures in the modern world we find that these same materials have been treasured by many societies. Why? And why have some cultures placed their highest value on other materials, such as jade, textiles, obsidian or even feathers?

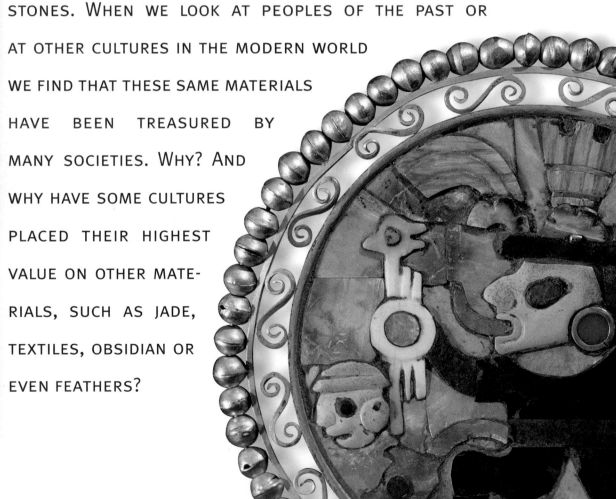

WHAT IS TREASURE?

Introduction

Treasured materials have many features in common. They are almost without exception attractive – who is not thrilled, for example, by the sparkle of gems or the brilliance of gold? Treasures stir powerful aesthetic feelings. For many cultures the emotions go beyond this: the magnificence of precious materials inspires feelings of awe and reverence, so that, for example, the Incas regarded gold as the sweat of the sun and silver as the tears of the moon, both sun and moon being gods. Many cultures have attributed supernatural powers to such materials, regarding them as protective or healing or even life-giving – the ancient Chinese, for example, believed that jade conveyed immortality.

Another element that most treasures have in common is rarity. The first treasures that we know of were rare and curious objects picked up as long as 120,000 years ago by Neanderthal people in their travels and treasured by their finders: things such as fossils. Objects produced as little as 50 years ago and available then for a modest price become modern treasures because so few of them remain – and this has always been true: the Romans, for example, collected Greek antiquities and the Aztecs those of the earlier Toltecs, though in these and other cases there were also other considerations, such as reverence for the skill of the earlier craftsmen and respect for ancestral cultures. In the same way heirlooms mean more to people than other pieces of equal absolute value: they are invested with sentimental value as well as intrinsic worth.

Thus rarity adds an extra dimension to the aesthetic value of materials. Quartz may shine with the brilliance of diamonds, or iron pyrites glitter like gold, but we accord little value to common quartz and pyrites compared with the highly prized diamonds and gold. Rarity, especially when combined with the great distance over which a material has to travel between source and ultimate owner, has always enhanced the prestige of certain materials. In the ancient Near East, for example, one of the most highly valued materials was lapis lazuli, a beautiful stone of the most brilliant blue, which for many centuries could only be obtained from a remote source at Badakshan in Afghanistan. However, the people of the Indus valley

ABOVE: Dazzled by their gleaming splendour, Howard Carter and Lord Carnarvon open the gilded wooden shrines containing the stone sarcophagus and golden coffins of the young Egyptian king, Tutankhamun.

LEFT: This Peruvian ear ornament is made of gold, highly valued by most societies and lapis lazuli, a rare stone of brilliant blue much prized in antiquity, but also shell, regarded by the ancient Peruvians as the food of the gods.

ABOVE: An old map may be the starting point for a lifetime's quest for lost or hidden treasures. The Caribbean hides many wrecks of Spanish treasure ships and pirate hoards.

the glass-like obsidian, often in beautiful dark shades of green or blue; rarity, since obsidian was only available in a few localities; and the skilled craftsmanship that could work this fragile material into elaborate shapes, often creating three or four faces in profile around the edge of a piece.

Treasure-hunting

Two emotions motivate the majority of treasure-hunters. One is the desire to get rich quick: the same feeling that drives people to bet on sporting events or buy lottery tickets, week after hopeless week. This is generally not greed: more the fulfilment of dreams. Who does not wish to be rich? The mere thought of it allows us to indulge in happy speculation about what we might do, without any real expectation of achieving these dreams. Treasure-hunters sometimes do strike lucky, just as some people win the lottery, but often the time, effort and money invested are greater than the material rewards.

So why do it? Probably because of the excitement. Treasure-hunting is an adventure, a searching for clues and following of trails, along paths often richly littered with the earlier adventures of others. There is mystery, the search for something known or suspected but lost. There is the mystique of the treasure, most often based on the stories that go with its original acquisition or deposition – for example, the history of those whose burials were filled with valuables, such as the young Egyptian king Tutankhamun or the cruel Chinese emperor Shi Huangdi, buried with his terracotta army; the plight of those caught up in natural disasters from which they sought vainly to escape, such as the victims of the eruption of Vesuvius at Pompeii or the unfortunate people who went down with the *Titanic*; the mysteries of treasure hidden when danger threatened and never recovered because of the death of the owner – pirate gold, for example.

Mysteries and murders inevitably seem to be associated with treasure believed to have been hidden by pirates. Stolen after years of

civilization, who gained a monopoly over its supply and who may also have found another source in the Chagai Hills of Baluchistan, prized lapis lazuli only for its commercial value in trade with the Near East. They themselves were much more interested in harder gemstones, such as jasper and agate, which would hold a high polish.

This leads to a further ingredient in what constitutes treasures: their properties. Materials are valued for qualities that set them apart and make them strange, mysterious or seemingly supernaturally efficient. Exceptional hardness is one such quality, found in jade, for example. Incorruptibility is another. Gold does not tarnish or corrode but emerges from the ground as pristine as when it was buried, even after thousands of years. Obsidian, the natural glass formed by volcanoes, can be chipped like flint to make tools, but the edge so formed is much sharper – it is, in fact, the sharpest edge that can be produced by human hands, far sharper than metal, and it is used today in brain surgery. In the past, in areas as far apart as the Near East and Mesoamerica, obsidian was traded over enormous dis-

tances by early farming communities.

These values are inherent in the materials themselves. But treasured value also comes from the skill, craftsmanship and labour of the creator. A piece of jewellery from a high-street store may contain gold and gems of no less original value than those used in a piece created by Fabergé, but the price attached to the latter item is infinitely higher. The Incas and other South American cultures placed a very high value on finely woven textiles of alpaca wool, and reserved those of vicuña wool for the emperor himself. The elongated carnelian beads made by the Indus people 4,000 years ago were both superlative works of skill and extremely time-consuming to make: a necklace represented as much as a year's work for an ancient craftsmen.

Most treasures have several or all of these features. Wonderful carved items of obsidian were highly valued by the Maya, for example. These combine the aesthetic qualities of

careful planning or taken on the spur of the moment when an opportunity seemed too good to pass up, treasure acquired illegally has to be hidden and the pirate's tracks covered before it can be recovered and enjoyed. Often death overtakes the thief before he can return and the secret details are passed on, shrouded in ever-greater obscurity.

Even the hint of treasure can inflame the imagination. Take the Money Pit, for example: a mysterious shaft discovered over 200 years ago and carefully booby-trapped by its makers. There is no information that this hole in the ground may yield treasure but people have spent millions trying to penetrate its secrets. Why? Because they reason

that there would have been no point in creating such an elaborate arrangement if it doesn't contain treasure.

But before the adventure comes the preparation. There is more to treasure-hunting than going out with a metal detector. Careful planning is essential: finding out what to look for and where, obtaining appropriate licences and permissions and researching the laws on different kinds of treasure – both looking for it and dealing with it if you strike lucky. Some people become so absorbed in their hobby of treasure-hunting that they end up devoting their lives to it. For others it is an absorbing pastime. But for all there is the heady thrill of the quest.

ABOVE: Obsidian – natural glass created in volcanoes – has been prized by many cultures for its attractive appearance and rarity and for the sharpness of the cutting edges that can be created from it.

TOP LEFT: Searching in places where people are likely to have accidentally dropped coins or small personal valuables can be very rewarding for the metal detector enthusiast.

Tanis●

Valley of the Kings●

Hartwell

Witte Leeuw

Great Zimbabwe●

Doddington

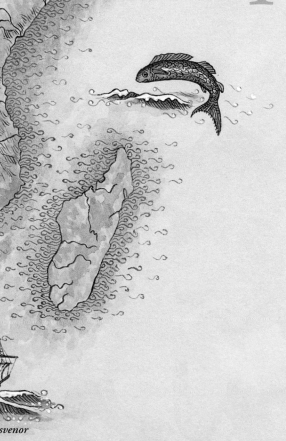

AFRICA

Grosvenor

THE ANCIENT EGYPTIANS BELIEVED THE BODIES OF THE DEAD HAD TO BE PRESERVED FOR ALL ETERNITY AS THE HOME OF THEIR SPIRIT AND SO THEY MUMMIFIED THEM. THEY ALSO CONSIDERED IT NECESSARY TO FURNISH THE DECEASED WITH EVERYTHING THAT THEY WOULD REQUIRE IN THE OTHER WORLD: MODELS AND PAINTINGS OF THEIR SERVANTS AND MANY OF THEIR POSSESSIONS.

ABOVE: The intact tomb of the obscure Egyptian king, Tutankhamun, was discovered in November 1922. The king's spectacular grave offerings drew large crowds of fascinated spectators who watched as the workmen gradually brought the treasures from the tomb.

LEFT: The back of Tutankhamun's throne shows the young king with his wife, Ankhesenamun, their robes inlaid with silver. Sheet gold covers the throne, with decorative inlays of coloured glass, terracotta and stone.

GOLD OF THE PHARAOHS

Valley of the Kings

In the case of pharaohs (kings) many of these offerings were made of gold and jewels. Traditionally pharaohs were buried within pyramids placed near the mortuary temple, where offerings were made for the benefit of their spirits. These conspicuous monuments attracted tomb robbers who, despite elaborate precautions, often succeeded in penetrating the burial chamber, carrying off the valuables on which the pharaoh depended for his eternal comfort and in many cases damaging the royal mummy in the process.

Amenhotep I (1525–1504 BC) made the first break with this tradition, being buried at some distance from his mortuary temple, and his successor, Thutmose I (1504–1492 BC), began the new practice of creating a tomb in the hills overlooking the traditional necropolis at Thebes. Here in the Valley of the Kings most pharaohs of the New Kingdom (fifteenth to late thirteenth century BC) were buried. Their tombs took the form of long, rock-cut corridors and chambers, many elaborately painted.

The new system proved no more effective than the old in guarding against robbers. During the troubled period of the Twenty-first Dynasty (1069–945 BC) the royal mummies were moved to a place of safety in an older tomb at Deir el-Bahri, to prevent further desecration.

Rediscovering the pharaohs

Interest in ancient Egypt never really died and for many centuries mummies were ground up to make a medicine thought to have powerful properties. By the eighteenth century there was considerable scholarly and popular interest in ancient Egypt and travellers began to visit the Valley of the Kings, by this time the stronghold of bandits.

Giovanni Belzoni went to Egypt in 1815 and spent five years investigating ancient

ABOVE: The towering cliffs of the Valley of the Kings were riddled with complexes of chambers carved to provide eternal accommodation for Egypt's rulers.

Egyptian remains, hunting for papyrus manuscripts and collecting other antiquities. He explored the Valley of the Kings and satisfied himself that he had discovered every tomb it contained. Among these was the magnificently decorated tomb of Seti I (1294–1279 BC), which contained the pharaoh's alabaster coffin. All the graves Belzoni explored had been plundered in the past, and wooden statues and broken pieces of funerary equipment were their only remaining contents.

Several other explorers investigated the Valley of the Kings during the nineteenth century and in 1898 Victor Loret discovered a cache of 13 royal mummies that had been placed for safety in the tomb of Amenhotep III (1390–1352 BC). Like other tombs in the Valley, it had been thoroughly looted of everything saleable. Many of the Valley's tombs had also suffered from flooding which had damaged and disturbed their contents. In 1902 an official permit allowing exclusive exploration of the Valley of the Kings was granted to a wealthy American, Theodore

M. Davis, with Howard Carter (representing the Egyptian government's Antiquities Service) undertaking excavations on his behalf. Carter located and explored several tombs, uncovering many broken treasures and wonderful tomb paintings. Davis struck lucky when his explorations revealed the well-preserved tomb of Tuyu and Yuya, parents of Queen Tiy, wife of the pharaoh Amenhotep III. By 1914, however, Davis had decided that the Valley had yielded all its secrets and that no unplundered tomb could be found.

By this time Carter was working with another wealthy patron of Egyptology, the Englishman Lord Carnarvon. They were not convinced that the Valley of the Kings was exhausted. Over the years a few things had been found bearing the name of King Tutankhamun, including objects from his funerary feast and mummification rites. This

pharaoh, who had ruled between 1336 and 1327 BC, had come to the throne at the age of eight. He had been born during the revolutionary period when Akhenaten had abandoned the traditional gods of Egypt and introduced the monotheistic worship of the Aten, the orb of the sun. Akhenaten's successor, Smenkhara, had continued this heretical cult but when Tutankhamun succeeded him the Aten cult was swept aside and monuments bearing references to the Aten, Akhenaten or his wife Nefertiti were mutilated. Little was known of Tutankhamun and his grave had never been found. Could it still lie concealed in the Valley?

Last chance

Carter and Carnarvon secured the concession to work in the Valley of the Kings in 1914, but war broke out almost at once and it was not until 1917 that Carter could start substantial investigations here. Over the following years he looked at a number of places in and around the Valley, returning at intervals to an area he considered very promising, a triangle of uninvestigated ground between three tombs that had previously been emptied, those of Merneptah, Ramses II and Ramses VI. This area had been used as a dumping ground for debris removed in clearing the adjacent tombs and had therefore been ignored. When Carter cleared the debris he came upon the remains of a little village of stone slab huts, the home of the workmen who constructed the tomb of Ramses VI. Its survival made it clear that beneath it lay a patch of the Valley of the Kings that had been untouched since the twelfth century BC. Might this undisturbed area conceal a tomb?

Carter was very hopeful. He therefore saved this patch of ground until 1922, when Carnarvon began to tire of work in Egypt, using the slim possibility of an undiscovered tomb to revive Carnarvon's flagging interest. Carnarvon decided it was worth trying, as a final piece of work before relinquishing his concession in the Valley. So on November 1,

1922 Carter began the excavation and removal of part of the workmen's village. Three days into the excavation his workmen came upon a step: the entrance to a tomb. Was it a completed tomb or merely the abandoned beginning of one? If it was a finished tomb, had it been looted by the ancient robbers?

To find out, Carter and his workmen cleared the stairway down to the twelfth step – and came upon a sealed doorway. Carter examined it and realized that it had been broken into. But it had been resealed by priests at the time and not subsequently damaged. What lay behind the sealed door? Carter made a small hole and squinted in – a tunnel full of rubble blocking the passage met his eye.

Suspense

Carter now knew he was facing the strong possibility of an undisturbed tomb. Carnarvon was in England and not due at the site for some months. Restraining his impatience and excitement, Carter filled in the staircase again, posted a guard on the tomb and telegraphed Carnarvon, who said he would come soon. For three anxious and nail-biting weeks Carter waited for him to arrive by boat.

On November 23 Carnarvon reached Luxor and work recommenced the following day. The staircase was cleared and the doorway fully exposed, revealing a seal bearing the name of Tutankhamun. But mixed debris in the rubble also contained the names of other kings and the door seemed small for a genuine tomb entrance. Would this prove to be merely a cache of material collected from disturbed tombs?

Excited but apprehensive, the two men cleared the debris from the passage and came to an inner door. The door seals showed again that the chamber had been disturbed but resealed by priests of the necropolis. The excavators fully cleared this door, then Carter made a tiny hole in it, inserted a candle and peered in. As his eyes adjusted to the dim light he was struck dumb by what

he saw. Behind him, Carnarvon waited impatiently; to his anxious enquiry, Carter could only manage to reply that he saw "wonderful things".

Royally furnished

They had discovered an intact tomb: one whose contents have never ceased to astonish the world since then. So many wonderful things were indeed there that it was ten years before Carter and his many helpers could complete the work of investigating and recording the objects in the tomb, and conserving and removing them.

The door to which they had come opened into an antechamber containing three gilt couches, a golden throne, four dismantled chariots and a beautiful chest decorated with a scene of Tutankhamun hunting, as well as many other splendid objects, their orderly arrangement slightly upset by the activities of tomb robbers. The priests who resealed the tomb had managed to tidy this chamber, but in the adjacent annexe there was utter chaos: the jumbled, smashed mess left by the robbers in their haste.

Beyond the antechamber was the door to another chamber, flanked by two life-size statues of Tutankhamun. On February 17, 1923 Carter opened it and saw a breathtaking sight. The small chamber was entirely filled by a gilded shrine. Within this was a nested arrangement of further shrines containing a magnificent stone sarcophagus. This contained three nested coffins, two of gilded wood and the third of solid gold. Over the face of the young pharaoh was a mask made of gold inlaid with lapis lazuli.

Beyond this chamber lay another, packed with treasures that had belonged to the young ruler. The room was dominated by an exquisite gilded shrine within which was an alabaster chest containing Tutankhamun's embalmed viscera. There were also gilded boxes full of "shabti" figures, model people deposited there to work for their king in the afterworld. In this chamber too there were signs of disorder caused by the robbers.

ABOVE: Every one of the treasures in Tutankhamun's tomb was painstakingly recorded and lifted with the utmost care. Many pieces were fragile and had to be carefully packed before they were removed from the tomb.

No stone unturned?

Tutankhamun's tomb was poorly furnished by comparison with those of his more important predecessors and successors. But the chances of finding another tomb intact are almost non-existent, so Tutankhamun's treasures are likely to remain the most splendid ever to be found on Egyptian soil.

Had the Valley of the Kings now yielded its last secret? It seems not. In the 1990s an American team headed by Professor Kent Weeks relocated a tomb which had been slightly explored in 1825, and discovered that the known portion actually led into an enormous complex of chambers, the largest discovered in the Valley of the Kings, containing the burials of about fifty sons of Ramses II – robbed but still fascinating. But as modern survey and reconnaissance techniques are brought into play, the chances of there still being unknown remains in the Valley itself are steadily decreasing.

However, this is not the only place in

ABOVE: The silver coffin of the ninth century BC king Sheshonq II was found in the antechamber of Psusennes' tomb at Tanis. It contained his mummy, wearing this golden mask.

Egypt with rich burials. The Valley of the Kings is only a small part of a much larger New Kingdom necropolis at Thebes, with the tombs of royal ladies in the adjacent Valley of the Queens and noble burials elsewhere within it. Earlier Egyptian royalty were interred in pyramid complexes at Giza, Abusir, Dashur and elsewhere. Before the discovery of Tutankhamun one of the most spectacular finds was a cache of gold jewellery belonging to Twelfth Dynasty princesses found in 1894 by Jacques de Morgan at Dahshur. This jewellery may have been abandoned by tomb robbers or deliberately concealed by the priests to outwit them. The following year de Morgan discovered the unplundered grave of Princess Khnemit, replete with jewellery of gold, carnelian and lapis lazuli, including two magnificent golden crowns inlaid with gems.

Overshadowed by Tutankhamun's splendours and later by the outbreak of the Second World War, the excavations by Pierre Montet in the 1920s to 1950s at Tanis, capital of some of Egypt's late pharaohs, are often overlooked. Within the precinct of the temple of Amen these kings were entombed in small chambers, modestly furnished by comparison with former glories. Here in 1939 Montet found the unplundered graves of six pharaohs, that of Psusennes (1039–991 BC) being the most impressive: the king wore a gold mask and was interred in a silver coffin placed inside a granite coffin and sarcophagus, and was accompanied by many gold and silver vessels.

Although the mummies and graves of many pharaohs have been found, there are still many other rulers whose last resting place we do not know. These include Alexander the Great, who died in Babylon in 323 BC, but whose embalmed body was finally laid to rest in a magnificent golden tomb in Egypt. Occasionally people claim to have discovered it but none has yet been proved right.

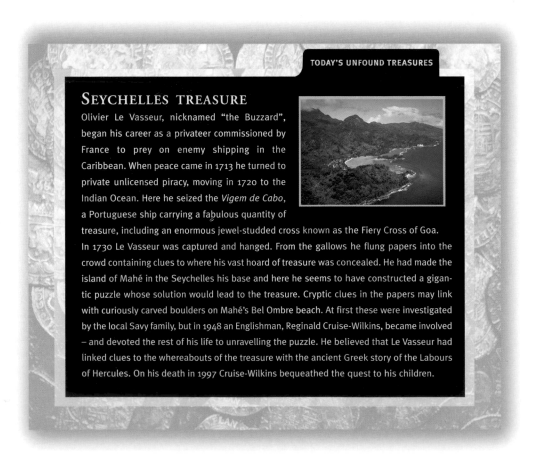

TODAY'S UNFOUND TREASURES

SEYCHELLES TREASURE

Olivier Le Vasseur, nicknamed "the Buzzard", began his career as a privateer commissioned by France to prey on enemy shipping in the Caribbean. When peace came in 1713 he turned to private unlicensed piracy, moving in 1720 to the Indian Ocean. Here he seized the *Vigem de Cabo*, a Portuguese ship carrying a fabulous quantity of treasure, including an enormous jewel-studded cross known as the Fiery Cross of Goa. In 1730 Le Vasseur was captured and hanged. From the gallows he flung papers into the crowd containing clues to where his vast hoard of treasure was concealed. He had made the island of Mahé in the Seychelles his base and here he seems to have constructed a gigantic puzzle whose solution would lead to the treasure. Cryptic clues in the papers may link with curiously carved boulders on Mahé's Bel Ombre beach. At first these were investigated by the local Savy family, but in 1948 an Englishman, Reginald Cruise-Wilkins, became involved – and devoted the rest of his life to unravelling the puzzle. He believed that Le Vasseur had linked clues to the whereabouts of the treasure with the ancient Greek story of the Labours of Hercules. On his death in 1997 Cruise-Wilkins bequeathed the quest to his children.

Tutankhamun's innermost coffin, in which his mummy lay, was made of solid gold. It represented the youthful king in the guise of Osiris, god of death and resurrection. The king holds the crook and flail, symbols of royalty.

THE GOLD OF AFRICA

West African gold

Herodotus, the fifth-century BC Greek ethnographer and historian, tells of a curious ancient trade in gold dust. Carthaginian sea-farers would come ashore at traditional places of exchange on the West African coast and set out the goods they had to offer. After lighting a signal fire they would return to their ships. The natives would appear, lay down gold in exchange and then retire. The Carthaginian traders would return to assess the quantity of gold. This process continued

RIGHT: The kingdoms of West Africa produced magnificent bronze and brass sculptures and reliefs like this 17th-century Benin warrior.

BELOW: At the heart of the southern African town of Great Zimbabwe lies a complex of impressive stone-walled enclosures where the king lived with his family and important rituals were performed.

but when he found the first of the site's bronze treasures someone attempted to steal it from under his bed as he slept. His work revealed the richly endowed burial of a local chief who died in the ninth century AD. The chief had been interred in a wooden chamber, seated on a stool dressed in his regalia. With him were buried three magnificent ivory tusks and many bronze objects, including a beautiful shell with intricate geometric patterns over its entire surface.

Several West African states manufactured superb bronze and brass sculptures, of which the most outstanding works were created by the Ife and the Benin. Their neighbours the Asante were the richest in gold and produced fine goldwork, especially crowns for their kings. When European traders first came to this coast in the fifteenth century, they were anxious to acquire both slaves and gold, for which they traded not only manufactured luxuries but also guns and ammunition. Initially the African kingdoms had the whip hand, for their centres lay inland and European traders penetrated there only with official permission and backing.

Eastern traders

Arab merchants traded by sea with East Africa. Coastal towns here imported spices, fine pottery and textiles and in return exported slaves, ivory and gold obtained from the interior. The gold came mainly from the Zimbabwe plateau, where, in the eleventh century AD, the Shona state established its capital on top of a steep hill at Magungubwe on the Limpopo River. Around 1250 the capital was moved further north to Great Zimbabwe. Here, to house the king and his court, a series of magnificent stone-walled enclosures was constructed, surrounded by a substantial town which flourished into the fifteenth century.

By the seventeenth century, when Europeans began to establish bases in southern Africa, the equality of earlier trading

THE *GROSVENOR*

The British East India Company ship the *Grosvenor* left Sri Lanka on June 13, 1782, laden with Company goods, including a considerable quantity of diamonds and the private property of its officers: tidy sums in gold and silver. After nearly two months of open sea, on August 4 several seamen thought they glimpsed land, but their observations were ignored and the *Grosvenor* ran aground on rocks off the mouth of the River Tezani in southern Africa. About 100 people drowned as the ship sank and, of the 123 who managed to scramble ashore, only nine survived the long, gruelling trek to the nearest settlement.

In 1880 gold and silver coins on the beach alerted Sydney Turner, a shipowner, to the location of the wreck, and he attempted to obtain more by using dynamite, but with little success. As time passed both the reputed size of the treasure and the ambitious designs of the treasure-seekers grew – among these were proposals to construct a breakwater around the wreck site or to bring in a special large crane. To date all attempts to recover the treasure have failed, often costing the prospective salvors substantial sums of wasted money. For the lucky beachcomber, coins or trinkets occasionally still wash ashore, but the wreck is too inaccessible for ordinary exploration.

until both sides were satisfied but at no time did they ever meet.

In later times Arab traders from North Africa employed camel caravans to cross the Sahara desert and obtain gold, ivory and slaves, in exchange for manufactured goods. From the tenth to the sixteenth century AD, West Africa was Europe's main source of gold. The wealth of West African kingdoms became legendary, with reports that even the kings' dogs wore collars of gold. Many prosperous inland towns developed as a result of trade links across the Sahara, and their riches can be gauged by the occasional discovery of wealthy burials.

Bronzes and gold

In 1959 the archaeologist Thurstan Shaw was invited to excavate at Igbo Ukwu, a site in southern Nigeria where superb bronzes had been previously discovered. The excavation proved a nerve-racking experience for Shaw. Not only was he suffering ill health

ABOVE: This gold head was probably the death mask of an Asante ruler.

ABOVE AND FAR LEFT: Graves at the early Shona capital of Mapungubwe contained a number of wooden artefacts plated in gold.

TOP LEFT: Royal burials uncovered recently at the 15th–16th century town of Thulamela in southern Africa were richly furnished with gold jewellery.

relations was gone, a victim of the degrading effect of the slave trade. Africans were now viewed as culturally and intellectually inferior to Europeans, incapable of great artistic or architectural works. By the nineteenth century missionaries, explorers and prospectors were penetrating many parts of the African interior. One, a young geologist called Carl Mauch, learned of impressive ruins: the massive fortified settlement at Great Zimbabwe. Visiting them, he published an account of what he had seen. In the climate of nineteenth-century thought it was not considered possible that Great Zimbabwe had been erected by natives. Instead Mauch and his contemporaries speculated that it represented the remains of some kingdom known in antiquity – perhaps the palace of the Queen of Sheba. This was an exciting prospect, for it was thought that the ancient gold mines of King Solomon in Ophir should lie nearby.

King Solomon's Mines

Solomon (c.1015–977 BC), King of Israel, made his capital, Jerusalem, a place of great splendour, reserving his most magnificent efforts for the Temple. He is said to have obtained 120 talents of gold for these works from the distant land of Ophir, to which he sent a naval expedition. When the Queen of Sheba heard of Solomon's glory, she decided to pay him a state visit and was apparently greatly impressed both by the city and by the king himself. Her gifts were themselves splendid in the extreme, and included spices, gems and tons of gold.

Where were Sheba and Ophir? Clearly they lay to the south of Israel. The discovery of Great Zimbabwe seemed to raise the possibility that Sheba and Ophir lay in southern Africa. The idea rapidly developed and many Europeans embarked on expeditions to southern Africa, searching for the legendary mines of gold and diamonds, both of which were eventually found. The legend inspired literature such as Rider Haggard's influential novel *King Solomon's Mines* (1885), and this development in turn fed the quest for gold and treasure.

Excavations by Gertrude Caton-Thomson in the 1930s demonstrated that Great Zimbabwe was the creation of local Shona people. The 1930s also saw the discovery of rich burials at Magungubwe, containing many valuable imported glass beads, along with copper and gold ornaments and wooden vessels and animals plated in gold. This cemetery, now protected by law, is still under investigation. Occasionally other similarly rich graves are discovered in southern Africa.

SHIPS WRECKED OFF AFRICA

THE *WITTE LEEUW*

In 1613 the galleon *Witte Leeuw* (*White Lion*), owned by the VOC (Vereenigde Oost-Indische Compagnie, or Dutch East India Company), was returning home from a successful trading expedition to Indonesia, in consort with three other VOC merchantmen and two English ships. They rounded the Cape of Good Hope and put in at St Helena for provisions, anchoring in Jamestown Bay. While they were there, two Portuguese carracks were sighted.

A novel procelain drinking vessel.

At this time the Portuguese and Dutch were in conflict over rights in the East Indies. The Dutch therefore gave battle, while the neutral English ships stood by watching. The Portuguese captain, seriously outnumbered but commanding a disciplined and efficient crew, held his position and battered the Dutch ships with his guns. Suddenly something went wrong on the *Witte Leeuw* – perhaps a gun exploded over the magazine. The ship blew apart and sank. One of the other Dutch ships had been sadly mauled and the remaining ships fled.

The Belgian diver Robert Stenuit's researches on post-medieval wrecks kept turning up references to the *Witte Leeuw*. Intrigued, in 1976 he decided to search for it. Investigating places in Jamestown Bay marked as foul anchorage sites, where obstructive debris lay on the seabed, Stenuit and his collaborators found a group of six cannons. Raising one to the surface, they were gratified to discover that it bore the insignia of the VOC – their investigation was on the right lines.

The wreck proved to be deeply buried beneath a substantial deposit of more recent debris of all sorts. When finally they uncovered remains of the *Witte Leeuw* they received a big surprise. Stenuit had seen the ship's manifest and was expecting a cargo of spices and gems – 15,171 bags of pepper and 1,311 diamonds were listed. But instead the first thing they found was fine porcelain, which obviously had been included in the cargo unknown to the company officials back home.

During a seven-month season Stenuit and his colleagues recovered a considerable quantity of porcelain, much of it undamaged,

An airlift was used in the excavation of the *Witte Leeuw*.

due to the cushioning effects of peppercorns which had also survived. But they found no diamonds. These would have been kept secure in the captain's cabin and when the ship blew up they were all dispersed beyond any hope of recovery.

THE *DODDINGTON*

Robert Clive had gone out to Madras in 1743 as an impoverished clerk with Britain's East India Company, but his military genius soon brought him to prominence in his country's hostile encounters with the French on Indian soil. In 1753 he returned to Britain an extremely wealthy man and was commissioned as a lieutenant colonel. He was sent out to India again to take command of the British trading station at Fort St David and to lead a combined naval and army expedition against the French.

The expeditionary force was a substantial one. Seven ships sailed from Britain in April 1755, loaded with hundreds of soldiers as well as munitions and food for the troops. One vessel, the *Doddington,* was carrying a company of 200 Royal Artillery soldiers and a quantity of valuables, including Clive's own treasure chest containing around £3,000 in gold, an enormous sum at the time.

After the convoy had rounded the Cape of Good Hope, the *Doddington* became separated from the other ships. Navigation in the area was dangerous as the coast was not at that time properly charted. During a serious storm on July 16 the *Doddington* ran on to rocks forming part of Bird Island, which appeared on charts of that time as "Chaos Island" or "Confused Island" because its location was uncertain. Many men were washed overboard at once and as the ship broke up more were drowned. Only 23 managed to reach the island.

Fortunately many of the stores from the ship were washed ashore. Along with fresh fish and eggs, these enabled the men to survive on the island for seven months. Some of the valuables from the ship were also saved: mainly silver plate belonging to a Mr Boddam. Several earlier ships had been wrecked here, and the castaways were able to gather enough smashed timber to construct a boat in which to escape, which they called the *Happy Deliverance.* In this they finally came to shore in Mozambique.

SHARK-INFESTED WATERS

There was talk at the time of salvaging the *Doddington,* but nothing came of it. It was not until 1977 that two South African brothers, David and Gerry Allen, began seriously to search for the wreck. They had a detailed account by the *Doddington's* mate, Evan Jones, to guide them to the site, but his directions were not clear and the island had been the scene of a number of shipwrecks, making it more difficult to pinpoint an individual wreck. Huge swells impeded work and made positional recording virtually impossible with the technology of the time. (Modern equipment and techniques have recently enabled the wreck of the *Doddington* to be surveyed in detail.) In addition, the waters around the island are full of fish and therefore support many seals, which in turn attract large numbers of Great White sharks. Although not usually aggressive towards humans, the sharks can easily mistake divers for seals and attack them, inevitably inflicting very serious wounds.

Working in great secrecy to avoid the problematic publicity and competition that they had previously suffered during salvage work, but keeping in touch with the director and the historian of the Port Elizabeth Museum, the brothers and their teammates explored these waters until they located promising remains, including guns that finally identified the wreck as the *Doddington*. From it they salvaged a quantity of copper, silver "pieces of eight" coins and one of the guns, leaving the iron cannon on the site. Of Clive's gold, however, there was no trace.

SALVAGING THE *HARTWELL*

The *Hartwell* was on its maiden voyage to China in 1787, laden with British East India Company silver for buying eastern porcelain, tea and spices, and with consignments of private merchandise. Conditions on board were not happy and the men eventually mutinied. Deprived of sleep during the three days it took to bring the mutiny under control, the captain made fatal navigational errors and the ship was driven on to a reef in the Cape Verde islands. No one died but nothing was saved of the ship's valuable contents.

The East India Company soon engaged the services of William and John Braithwaite to salvage the cargo, nearly 6,000 kilograms (13,230lb) of silver. This proved a difficult task as the packing chests had broken open, widely scattering the coins. Nevertheless, over two years the brothers managed to raise a considerable quantity, worth 11,000 Spanish dollars – only to be attacked by pirates who carried off the lot.

The Braithwaites began again, using the latest diving equipment brought out from Britain. This time they were more successful and within the year they had brought up a great quantity of silver coins – to a value of nearly 100,000 dollars. At this point they decided to stop, although by no means all the treasure had been recovered. The rest must still lie under the sea.

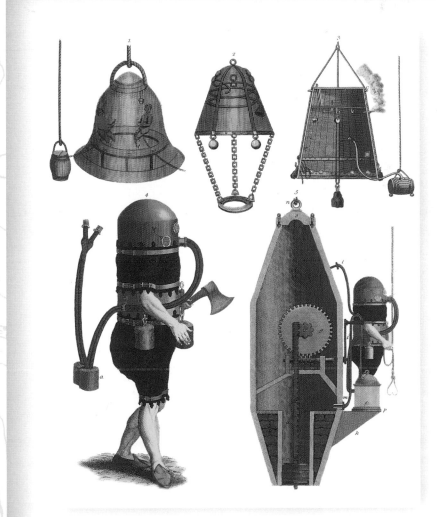

The latest in diving equipment was employed by the 18th-century salvors of the *Hartwell*.

Soloha

Kul Oba

Pazyryk

Troy

Oxus Treasure

Ulu Burun

Marlik Tepe

Dunhuang

Byblos   Nimrud

Qumran

Chang'

Masada

Tepe Nush-i Jan

Tell el-'Ajjul

Susa

Begram

Taxila

Tillya Tepe

Mohenjo Daro

Allahdino

Souttoukeny

Geldermalsen

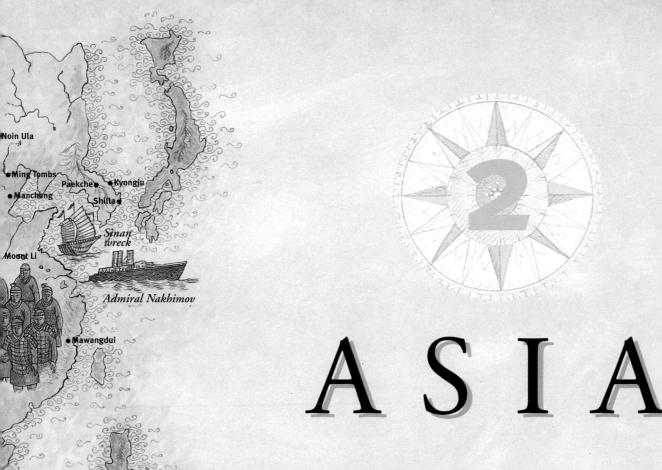

Noin Ula

Ming Tombs

Mancheng

Mount Li

Paekche

Shilla

Kyongju

Sinan wreck

Admiral Nakhimov

Mawangdui

2

ASIA

IN 1922 SIR LEONARD WOOLLEY BEGAN EXCAVATIONS IN THE ANCIENT CITY OF UR IN SOUTHERN MESOPOTAMIA (IRAQ), FAMOUS AS THE BIRTHPLACE OF THE BIBLICAL PATRIARCH ABRAHAM. HE STARTED WORK IN THE AREA WHERE AN EARLIER EXCAVATOR HAD UNCOVERED PART OF THE WALL OF THE SACRED PRECINCT AND AT ONCE FOUND BURIALS, WITH POTTERY, BRONZE OBJECTS AND STONE BEADS.

ABOVE: Every detail of king Meskalamdug's typical early Mesopotamian hairstyle – plaited, twisted into a bun and fastened with a headband – has been lovingly recreated in his helmet.

TOP: Woolley's excavations uncovered much of the ancient city of Ur. Here he is painstakingly uncovering a terracotta figurine.

ROYAL TOMBS OF UR

The gleam of gold

Woolley was expecting gold beads too, but the workmen found none. He therefore offered baksheesh (a bribe) for every gold bead found. The next day suddenly many gold beads appeared. The workmen had been selling them to the local goldsmith, but had bought them back as Woolley was offering a much better price.

The cemetery, on which Woolley began serious work in 1927, was dug into the soft ground where rubbish had been dumped in the early days of the city. People were buried here in the period from 2600 to 2400 BC, when Ur was one of the principal cities of Mesopotamia, for a while being regarded as the city in which the gods had vested supreme authority.

Several thousand individuals were buried in the cemetery during this period. Most were placed in a wooden coffin or wrapped in a mat and their personal possessions buried with them – a few pots, some pieces of jewellery, a knife or a dagger and sometimes a cylinder seal bearing their own name or symbol, to be rolled on clay sealings or tablets as their "signature".

One grave stood out. The burial pit contained a large number of pots, bronze vessels and weapons, including a number of spears stuck into the ground in a row at the head of the grave, and some of these objects were of gold. When the earth was removed from the coffin, it revealed that the body was covered in jewellery of gold and lapis lazuli, along with golden bowls. Two of these bore a name – Meskalamdug, one of Ur's early kings. The finest object was an exquisite helmet in the shape of a wig, made of beaten electrum (an alloy of gold and silver). Each strand of hair had been carefully delineated in the decoration on its surface.

Royally furnished

Meskalamdug's grave had been richly furnished but was otherwise like the others in the cemetery. Woolley also discovered 16 other royal burials that had been treated much more elaborately. Although there was considerable variation in detail, all followed a similar form. The cemetery had been expertly plundered in ancient times, and many graves were badly disturbed. The best-preserved was that of Queen Puabi, probably the wife of an unidentified king whose burial chamber lay just below her grave pit.

When the workmen dug the queen's grave, a pit more than 12 metres (39 feet) long, they could not resist the temptation to plunder the king's burial chamber below. They concealed their nefarious activity by placing the large chest of the queen's clothes over the tell-tale hole.

At the end of the grave pit they constructed a stone chamber. The dead queen was decked in all her finery – a beautiful gold headdress in the form of three gold wreaths ornamented with flowers, a cloak of beads made of gold and precious stones, gold pins and amulets, and a golden cup in her hands. Lying on her bier, she was carried down the ramp of the grave pit and placed within the chamber. Around her were arranged a number of her valued possessions – a second headdress of lapis lazuli beads decorated with small figures in gold, several cockle-shells containing valuable green cosmetics, and many vessels of gold and silver.

Other valuable objects were placed in the grave pit outside the chamber. These included a wooden sledge decorated with small lions' heads in gold and silver, drawn by a pair of oxen who had been killed once the sledge was in place. A wooden gaming board inlaid with lapis lazuli, shell and other

ABOVE: Beautiful necklaces, earrings and hair ornaments of gold, carnelian and lapis lazuli adorned many of the women who accompanied Queen Puabi into her grave.

BELOW: Modelled in wood, this magnificent figure of a goat was covered with silver, gold, shell and lapis lazuli.

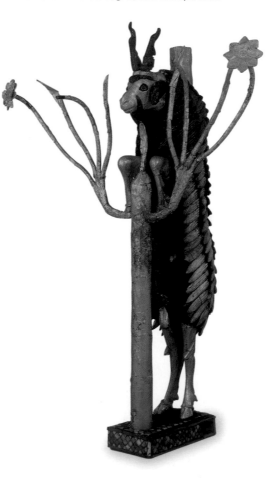

colourful materials was placed, with its playing counters, near the sledge, and many gold tools and weapons, and vessels of alabaster, silver and other precious materials, were added.

Stepping into eternity

The grooms who led the oxen into the pit remained with them. A dozen young women also made their way into the grave, wearing fine headdresses and necklaces of gold, lapis lazuli and carnelian. One carried a lyre exquisitely decorated with a bull's head made of lapis lazuli and gold. Three other maidens made their way into the queen's burial chamber, and two crouched by the royal bier. Five soldiers took up their station in the ramp leading down into the grave pit.

Each of these attendants carried a cup which must have contained a drugged drink. Lying down, they composed themselves for death and drank the draught. Dead or unconscious, they never moved as mats and earth were piled over them and the grave was then sealed.

The same scene took place within the other royal graves. In one, called by Woolley the Great Death Pit, six soldiers and 68 court ladies gave up their lives. One lady, perhaps arriving late, had not had time to put on her silver hair ribbon. Woolley found it, still rolled up, at her side.

All the graves that had not been plundered contained objects equally as wonderful as those in Puabi's tomb. Lapis lazuli, a stone of brilliant blue, was one of the most precious materials at the time, since it had to be imported over thousands of kilometres from the only source known to the Mesopotamians, in Afghanistan. Two statues in the Great Death Pit had been made of large quantities of lapis lazuli, gold and silver. They depicted a goat standing on his hind legs to eat a golden bush. Lapis lazuli also formed the background on a mosaic showing two scenes, war and peace, that decorated an object known as the "Standard of Ur", perhaps the soundboard of a musical

instrument. A number of instruments, mainly lyres, were found in the graves, all as richly decorated as that in Puabi's grave.

TREASURE OF KING PRIAM

A dream of heroes

The story of the Trojan War, fought by the Greeks to recover their stolen Greek princess Helen, the most beautiful woman in the world, and immortalized by the great Greek epic poet Homer, has fired the imagination of many down the ages. Alexander the Great (356–323 BC), beginning his amazing conquest of the Persian Empire, turned aside at

Troy to honour the heroes of that ancient conflict. In Germany in the early nineteenth century a small boy who drank up the tales of Homer's heroes from his clergyman father grew into a teenage grocer's assistant, spellbound one day by the incomprehensible but impassioned recitation of Homer's words by a drunken customer. Young Heinrich Schliemann vowed then that he would learn to understand Homer's epics in their original Greek and that one day he would seek the lost city of the Trojan War, which many people believed to have been only a creation of fiction.

Born in 1822, Schliemann showed a remarkable flair for both languages and business. By the age of 25 he was already established as a prosperous merchant in

ABOVE: The fabled "Treasure of King Priam" discovered by Schliemann at Troy included both gold jewellery and vessels of bronze, silver and gold. The bottle and fluted cup are translations into gold of shapes familiar in Near Eastern pottery, but the double-spouted, double-handled "sauceboat" is unique.

Heinrich Schliemann was a man with a mission that sustained him for more than 30 years – to prove the historical truth of the story of the legendary Trojan War.

St Petersburg in Russia and was fluent in eight languages. When he visited the USA in the 1850s, his financial acumen enabled him to accumulate a substantial fortune and his business ventures elsewhere were similarly successful. By 1863 Schliemann was wealthy enough to abandon commerce and pursue his dream.

He prepared himself by travelling widely and studying at the Sorbonne in Paris. In 1868 he visited the Troad – the area of Turkey in which the legendary Trojan War took place – and here he met Frank Calvert, the US vice-consul. At the time, those who believed that Homeric Troy had really existed identified it with a place in the Troad called Bunarbashi, but Calvert was convinced that the mound of Hisarlik was the true location. He had purchased a part of the mound, but lacked the resources to excavate it. Schliemann shared Calvert's view and possesed the funds. In 1870, too impatient to await an official permit to excavate, the German began a trial investigation of the Hisarlik mound.

Trojan gold

Official permission caught up with Schliemann and in 1871 he began major excavations in the mound. This was massive, representing many centuries of occupation, and he had decided that the Troy of the Trojan War lay at the bottom, so he wantonly removed walls, houses and other debris from the deposits above. Later, when experience, criticism from the scientific community and his own discoveries had taught him greater caution and respect for the material he was uncovering, he regretted his first destructive enthusiasm and conducted his excavations more systematically, particularly from 1882, when he was assisted by Wilhelm Dörpfeld, who became one of the finest archaeologists of the age.

By 1873 Schliemann's excavations had revealed the remains of nine superimposed cities on the site of Hisarlik and had convinced many that he had indeed discovered Troy. There were, however, many professional doubters, who were moved by both jealousy and serious reservations about Schliemann's methods, results and honesty. In this they were to some extent justified, for he was a ruthless romantic, given to embroidering the truth and dishonest when it served his ends.

Schliemann identified one of the early levels, Troy II, as the city of King Priam and the Trojan War, partly because it had been destroyed by a conflagration. Here he uncovered the remains of massive walls and gates and many objects that had served the people of the time, such as pottery. As the 1873 season approached its end the excavations took a dramatic turn. As was his habit, Schliemann was watching his men at work. Suddenly he dismissed them all, telling the foreman that he had just remembered that it was his birthday and that the men should take an extended break to celebrate. When they had all left, he jumped down to where they had been working – where his sharp eyes had spotted the glint of gold. Working feverishly with a knife and regardless of the masonry of the wall hanging above him, Schliemann rapidly cut out the treasures and hastily concealed them in his wooden hut. When he came to write his account of the discovery, he recorded that his wife had shared the adventure, but in fact she was in Athens at the time.

Later Schliemann was able to examine the treasure more closely. All the objects had been packed tightly together, with many pieces of gold jewellery placed inside a massive silver jar, and this suggested to him that they had been hidden as Troy fell to the Greeks. Their magnificence left him in no doubt that he had found the personal treasure of King Priam and his family – the golden rings, necklaces, bracelets and earrings of Helen, of the Trojan Queen Hecuba and of Prince Hector's wife Andromache, as well as golden cups and silver knife blades. One particularly fine headdress was made of hundreds of tiny gold leaves hung on linked vertical chains.

ABOVE: Sophia, the Greek girl whom Schliemann had chosen as his wife, was photographed wearing the gold necklaces, earrings and headdress that Schliemann identified as the treasure of King Priam.

Suspicion and deceit

Schliemann's uncharacteristic behaviour that morning had alerted the suspicions of the government agent, Effendi Amin, whose job it was to watch the excavation, and he demanded to search the excavator's storage chests and cupboards. When Schliemann refused, Amin went off to obtain official support. Schliemann lost no time in enlisting the help of Frank Calvert's brother to smuggle away the gold, without, it seems, revealing what it was – his letter to Calvert refers to broken pottery. The treasure was carried safely to Greece, where Schliemann exhibited it in his house. He took photographs of his young Greek wife, Sophia, dressed in the golden jewellery. The Turks were justifiably outraged, particularly as Schliemann's excavation permit required that he divide his finds equally with the Turkish authorities. They demanded that he pay a fine of 10,000 francs – but Schliemann succeeded in turning away their wrath by handing over 50,000 francs instead, in exchange for outright ownership of the treasure.

Winning respect

Schliemann next turned his attentions to the home of the Greek heroes, excavating at Mycenae (see p.93), where he was even more spectacularly successful. His methods, amateur even by the standards of the time (although they improved), his showmanship and his lack of transparency made other archaeologists suspicious of his findings, and the fact that he was uncovering new, previously unknown civilizations meant that there was no established material against which to prove that his finds were as ancient as he claimed. Gradually, however, scholars were won over and the Bronze Age civilizations he had discovered were accepted – but throughout his life Schliemann remained touchy about his finds and easily enraged by criticism.

"King Priam's treasure", along with other lesser hoards of gold and silver from Troy, and many other objects such as pottery, had become internationally famous. Many countries vied for the honour of acquiring them from Schliemann. He was torn – Greece was the country of Homer and his dreams; Russia had been his home in the days of his youthful rise to wealth; England had welcomed him with open arms when German scholars had been hostile; but Germany was his native land. Germany began to accord him the acclaim he had always sought, presenting him with honours, and eventually Schliemann chose Berlin as the final home of his treasures.

The treasures vanish

Schliemann's Trojan collections were installed in Berlin in 1881 with lavish ceremony, and remained there until 1945. During the Second World War the Germans looted a vast number of art treasures and antiquities from the countries that they invaded. In 1945, when the tide of war turned against Germany, many of these looted valuables, along with Germany's own art treasures, were hidden or taken to places of comparative safety (see p.134). The finds from Troy were dispersed – the lesser pieces were concealed in various places, and after the war some were recovered, while others seem to have disappeared for ever. "King Priam's treasure" and the other Trojan gold was packed, with other treasures from Berlin's Museum for Pre- and Early History, in three boxes and taken to the well-fortified flak-tower in the city's zoo, where they were jealously guarded and cared for by Wilhelm Unverzacht, the museum's director. In the final days of the flak-tower's siege, he even slept on the boxes.

On May 1, 1945, the defenders of the flak-tower surrendered to the Russians. Concerned by the looting all around, Unverzacht worked hard to hand over his treasures intact to the Russian authorities. The three boxes were taken with other objects of particular importance and flown to Moscow – where they disappeared.

Nothing was known about their subsequent fate, although it was much discussed. The Cold War made international investigation impossible. However, the collapse of communism in the 1980s brought many things to light, including archives which revealed that for half a century Schliemann's gold had been resting in the vaults of the Pushkin Museum in Moscow. In 1996 they at last saw the light again, in a magnificent exhibition in the museum.

Not Priam's gold

Schliemann had resumed excavations at Troy in 1878 and in 1882 was joined by Dörpfeld; they worked together until Schliemann's death in 1890. By this stage much more was known about Greek and Anatolian prehistory than had been in 1870, when Schliemann made his first discoveries. In the final season it became clear to both men that Troy II, which Schliemann had identified as Priam's city, was in fact much earlier. Dörpfeld regarded Troy VI as the city of the Trojan War, around 1200 BC. Later the eminent American archaeologist Carl Blegen was able to pin down finally the Troy of Homer's epic – Priam, if he had existed, had ruled the city of Troy VIIA.

Schliemann's spectacular gold finds belonged to a far earlier age – the later third millennium BC. Metallurgy was at that time in its infancy and many cultures of Europe and West Asia created lavish works of gold for their kings and chiefs (see pp.27 and 91). Troy had been a major centre of trade during that period, part of a network of towns that grew wealthy through the exchange of local resources and, in particular, metal ores. The extraordinary goldwork uncovered by Schliemann at Troy was part of the wealth of its rulers and included a number of pieces assembled by a craftsman to be melted down to make something else.

RICH CITIES OF THE LEVANT

An exciting discovery

George Bass is a pioneer of marine archaeology who has spent his life investigating ancient wrecks. In 1960, early in his career, he excavated the remains of the oldest shipwreck then known – a Bronze Age Syrian cargo boat carrying copper ingots and scrap metal which was wrecked around 1200 BC on Cape Gelidonya off Turkey's southern coast. That wreck had been spotted by sponge divers and Bass kept in close contact with the sponge divers of the region, whose daily work gives them ample opportunities to discover ancient wrecks. To ensure that the sponge divers knew what to watch out for, Bass and his team would give slide shows in the divers' villages to show them what the remains might look like.

One day in 1982 a young sponge diver named Mehmet Çakir noticed some strange objects on the seabed near Ulu Burun off Turkey's southern coast – they looked like "metal biscuits with ears". Recognizing this as a description of ancient copper ingots, the diver's captain reported the find to the Museum of Underwater Archaeology at Bodrum, who contacted Bass. Could this be another early trading vessel? Bass and his team investigated. What they found surpassed their wildest dreams. Not a humble cargo boat, this time, but a ship carrying a royal gift of Bronze Age treasures from the Levant coast to some prince in the Aegean – and at least 100 years earlier than the Cape Gelidonya wreck, making it the earliest shipwreck discovered in the world.

Preliminary survey work in 1983 revealed the remains of a ship 9 metres (30 feet) long, outlined by her cargo – hundreds of neatly stacked ox-hide-shaped copper ingots that were typical Bronze Age products of Cyprus,

ABOVE: Schliemann rapidly published reports on his excavations at Troy, well illustrated with drawings of the remains that he had uncovered, like this view of the city walls from the south-east.

ABOVE: A diver labels and catalogues the amphorae, copper ingots and other objects in the ancient shipwreck at Ulu Burun – a time-consuming process.

surface after a deep dive can suffer from the "bends", a painful and potentially crippling condition, so, as a precaution, Bass's team initially dived for only five minutes at a time. They learned that they could build up to two 20-minute dives per day as long as they had long periods of decompression using pure oxygen.

In the sandy area around the ship's keel, excavation was relatively easy – the sediments could be sucked away with an airlift. But in the upper portion the archaeologists had laboriously to chisel away the concretions that had welded the ship's cargo into a solid mass. Once exposed, the position of every one of the thousands of items in the cargo had to be painstakingly mapped, using stereo-photography and hand-held tapes. The slope of the ground made this a difficult task. Some of the finds were small enough for the divers to carry to the surface. But to lift the massive and heavily encrusted storage jars and stone anchor weights, something stronger than people was required, and for this operation the excavators used nets attached to balloons.

The ancient mariners' loss

Copper – 354 ox-hide ingots and 130 round "bun" ingots – formed the major part of the cargo, more than 10 tonnes (10 tons) in all. Tin ingots added another tonne – tin was essential for alloying with copper to form bronze, from which most tools and weapons of the time were manufactured, including the swords, daggers, axes, knives, razors and cauldrons found on the ship. Equally valuable at the time was the consignment of more than 145 Canaanite jars containing the yellow resin of the terebinth shrub (*Pistacia terebinthus*), used in Egypt as incense and by the Mycenaeans of Greece for making perfume. The ship was probably Canaanite, although some of the personal possessions on board show that the crew also included Mycenaeans. The Canaanites, predecessors of the Phoenicians, lived in the Levant and traded a wide range of raw materials, many of

the main exporter of copper at that time. Bass and his team began the arduous business of excavating the wreck in 1984 – but it was not until 1994 that the task was completed. The wreck lay in 43 metres (140 feet) of water, sloping steeply downwards to 52 metres (170 feet) – a dangerous depth at which to work. Because of the difference in pressure, divers rising too rapidly to the

which have been recovered from the wreck. This included ivory from hippos and small Syrian elephants (these later became extinct) and blue glass, probably manufactured to a secret recipe known only to the Canaanites. About 175 glass ingots were found in the cargo. These would have been used by their Egyptian and Mycenaean customers to manufacture glass vessels.

The cargo also included some scrap metal to be melted down and reused, including part of a gold ring, bits of gold pendants and twisted pieces of silver bangles. A surprising item among the scrap was a gold scarab bearing the name of the Egyptian Queen Nefertiti, wife of the heretical pharaoh Akhenaten and Tutankhamun's mother-in-law. Not all the gold was scrap, however. There were several gold amulets and pendants, perhaps worn for good luck by members of the crew. A fine example shows a goddess holding a gazelle in each

hand. One of the most valuable items in the cargo was a magnificent gold chalice. Along with five ram's-head drinking vessels made of faience, the raw ivory and a number of fine cylinder seals, these may have been diplomatic gifts intended for the ruler of the Aegean lands for which the ship was bound when it was wrecked on the treacherous rocks at Ulu Burun.

Trading cities

This was a time of particular prosperity for the cities of the Levant coast. In the early centuries of the second millennium BC, many were strongly influenced by their neighbour, Egypt, which either controlled or claimed to control many of them. Byblos in particular had close ties with Egypt. The tombs of its rulers, excavated in the cliffs along the city's shores, contained many fine objects that may have been diplomatic gifts from the rulers of Egypt. Other objects, such

ABOVE: Golden treasures from the Ulu Burun shipwreck included a pendant of Syrian manufacture which showed a naked goddess holding a gazelle in each hand.

BELOW: This gold pectoral from a royal tomb at Byblos depicts the Egyptian god Horus but was made locally.

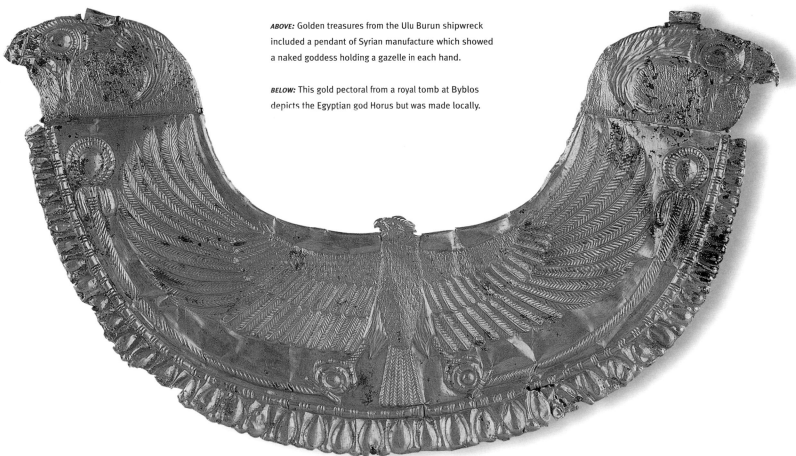

as a beautifully wrought gold pectoral (chest ornament) bearing an image of a hawk (the form in which the Egyptian god Horus was usually depicted), were probably locally made by craftsmen heavily influenced by Egyptian art styles and ideas.

For about a century (c.1650–1550 BC) Egypt was ruled by a dynasty, the Hyksos, who came from the Levant or who were related to inhabitants of that region. During this time close diplomatic links existed between Egypt and independent Canaanite cities of the Levant. Trade flourished, the city states trading with their neighbours in Egypt, Mesopotamia, Anatolia and the islands of the eastern Mediterranean. The prosperity enjoyed by these cities was vividly demonstrated by discoveries at Tell el-'Ajjul in southern Palestine, which was under Hyksos control.

In 1933 the eminent British Egyptologist Flinders Petrie uncovered five substantial hoards of goldwork from the houses of Tell el-'Ajjul and from the city's palace. Further gold treasures were found in the graves of warriors in the cemetery, buried with their horses. Many of the pieces found were simple gold pendants in the basic shape of women, with face, breasts and vulva but no limbs. These represented Astarte, the goddess of fertility. Other pendants took the form of a star and there were also rings with gemstones and toggle pins for fastening clothing, objects that were likewise relatively simple in design. The greater part of the jewellery, however, shows the amazing skill and versatility of the craftsmen of this time. Elaborate earrings, pendants and pectorals were created using granulation, a technique in which tiny balls of gold are attached to the surface of a gold object with a glue that contains copper hydroxide. The object is then heated, carbonizing the glue and reducing the copper hydroxide to metallic copper, which then bonds with the gold. In this way the Tell el-'Ajjul goldsmiths produced

ABOVE: Layard used methods similar to those of the Assyrians who had originally brought the winged stone bulls to Nimrud when he removed the statues from the site to transport them to London.

RIGHT: This finely carved ivory plaque, inlaid with gold, carnelian and lapis lazuli, found in the Assyrian king's treasure-house, was probably of Phoenician workmanship.

beautiful objects, decorated with figures of birds or geometric patterns.

SPLENDOURS OF THE PALACE AT NIMRUD

Winged beasts

In 1842 Paul-Émile Botta, French consul at Mosul in Iraq, began desultory investigations of several ancient mounds near the city and found remarkable sculptured reliefs depicting warfare and processions. The French government, impressed by his finds, sponsored excavation and recording of the sites, which were none other than two successive capital cities of the Assyrians, Dur-Sharrukin (modern Khorsabad) and Nineveh.

In 1845 Austen Henry Layard, a young

diplomat at Constantinople, began work on his own account on a third mound, Nimrud, with financial backing from the British ambassador, Sir Stratford Canning. Tunnelling into the Nimrud mound and following the line of ancient walls, Layard uncovered the spectacular remains of the ancient Assyrian city of Kalhu. He revealed enormous statues of winged bulls flanking the entrance to the throne room of a royal palace, its walls carved with scenes showing the military and sporting achievements of King Ashurnasirpal II (reigned 883–859 BC) – lion and bull hunts, campaigns and sieges. Fired by the magnificence of Layard's discoveries, the British government belatedly began to sponsor his efforts. In subsequent years he uncovered the remains of a second palace, built by a later king, Tiglath-Pileser III (reigned 744–727 BC) and successfully arranged for the monumental statues and reliefs to be shipped to England, where they still dominate the Assyrian collection in the British Museum. The French were less fortunate – many of the sculptures that they had excavated were lost or destroyed while being transported to France.

The conquering kings

In the tenth century BC, Assyria began to expand its power over Mesopotamia and adjacent areas of West Asia. Ashurnasirpal II pushed the boundaries of the Assyrian Empire still further, boasting that he had washed his weapons in the Great Sea (the Mediterranean). He decided to found a new capital city, Kalhu, which he peopled with displaced inhabitants from many of the lands he conquered. Work was begun in 878 BC on the massive city walls and the king's palace, which took about 15 years to complete. Ashurnasirpal gave a great feast that lasted 10 days to mark the inauguration of the palace, inviting nearly 70,000 guests, who consumed, among other things, 14,000 sheep, 1,000 deer, 10,000 loaves of bread

and 10,000 skins of wine. To the magnificence of the royal palace, with its throne room, public halls and private chambers, Ashurnasirpal added other splendid public buildings – temples to the goddess Ishtar and to other deities, a ziggurat and impressive government offices. A large central square was decorated with trophies collected during the king's successful campaigns and monuments commemorating them. The king also had a canal dug from the Upper Hab River to provide water for the orchards and botanic garden that he constructed to adorn his city.

The annual campaigns of Ashurnasirpal and his successors yielded huge quantities of plunder and the defeated peoples were also compelled to pay tribute – gold, silver and other metals, linen and other textiles, timber, ivory, exotic creatures and many other goods. The king's son and successor, Shalmaneser III (reigned 858–824 BC), began work soon after his accession on a new palace to act partly as a treasure-house for all the wealth that was accumulating. Completed in 846 BC, the new palace was also a fortress and an arsenal. Three great courtyards enabled the king to muster and view his troops, complete with chariots. Workshops for making and replacing armour, weapons and other military equipment flanked the parade ground. The royal residence formed another wing of the complex, and consisted of a great throne room with a massive dais on which stood the king's throne, public ceremonial rooms and private apartments, including a harem.

Royal treasures are in most cases carefully preserved unless they are carried off by conquering enemies, but when Sir Max Mallowan excavated Shalmaneser's palace he uncovered a number of wonderful objects that had never been removed. These included exquisite ivory carvings, some made by local craftsmen, others imported from many lands, including Egypt and Phoenicia. Some pieces were ornaments, such as a procession of tribute bearers leading animals. Others were elements from furniture such as chests,

CAPTAIN KIDD'S TREASURE

Captain William Kidd was a Scot, born around 1645, who by 1690 was sailing in American waters with an English letter of marque, an official licence to use his ship as a private man-of-war, capturing the ships of England's enemies. In effect he was a government-sponsored pirate, and in 1695 he received a further government commission, to deal with Indian Ocean pirates who were preying on English shipping. Four years later Kidd seized the *Quedagh Merchant*, a merchant ship operating under a French pass. He did not bring the ship in to a legitimate port and on his return to America he was arrested for piracy. Sent back to England, he was tried and hanged. But was he guilty? Were his acts of piracy forced on him by a mutinous crew, as he claimed, or was this a cover? Had he been a pirate in his younger days? While awaiting execution, he claimed to have buried a substantial treasure but did not reveal the location. Many spots around the globe are rumoured to be the hiding place. In the 1930s a chest bearing Kidd's name was found, with a treasure map of an unidentified island in the China Sea. A number of similar charts have been discovered.

chairs and beds, or ornamental plaques to decorate them, depicting people, plants and animals – sphinxes were a popular motif. Fragments of gold scattered on the floor of the storeroom show that originally many of the ivory pieces had been gilded.

Mallowan found other treasures in about 100 pottery jars at the base of a deep well. These included an exquisite carved ivory head of a woman which he called "Mona Lisa", her face bearing an enigmatic smile like that of the famous painting. The same well produced a pair of ivory plaques, only 10 centimetres (4 inches) long, showing a lioness killing a young man. Gold covers the loincloth worn by the young man and highlights his hair and the red and blue lotus flowers in the background are made with lapis lazuli and carnelian inlays.

Golden princesses

Assyrian texts describe the splendours of their royal burials, but the majority were looted in the past. However, in 1988 excavations beneath the floor of Ashurnasirpal's

throne room uncovered an amazing find – three intact royal tombs, complete with their priceless grave furnishings.

One tomb contained the burial of a man, laid to rest with 200 pieces of gold jewellery and a variety of other fine objects. The most impressive was the tomb of Ashurnasirpal's queen. The queen's body itself was not found and her great stone coffin was empty. But in three bronze coffins placed beside it, more than 400 pieces of gold jewellery had been deposited, including a crown.

A second tomb contained the remains of two princesses, who had been buried at a somewhat later date with gold necklaces, earrings and anklets in abundance. Their clothes had been sewn with hundreds of gold ornaments in the form of stars and flowers. Food for the afterlife had been placed with them, in jars and bowls of gold and precious alabaster. An inscription identified one as the wife of Sargon II (reigned 721–705 BC), who abandoned Nimrud and founded a new capital, Dur-Sharrukin, in 717 BC.

HIDDEN TREASURES OF THE HOLY LAND

THE OLD OLD TESTAMENT

In 1947 Muhammad adh-Dhib, a shepherd boy of the Beduin Ta'amireh tribe, was searching for a lost sheep among the hills west of the Dead Sea. Idly he tossed a pebble into a cave, to rouse the animal if it had strayed inside. He heard the chink of the stone against pottery – could it be treasure? He fetched two friends and they went in to investigate.

To their disappointment, the cave contained only a series of large storage jars. Smashing these, the boys found they were full of old manuscripts. They took seven away with them, hoping they might be worth a little, and were able to sell them to a shoemaker in Bethlehem named Kando, who dealt in antiquities.

It was not long before the significance of the find became apparent. These seven scrolls were part of an ancient library which had belonged to a religious community, the Essenes, who had lived at Qumran from the second century BC. In AD 67, when the Holy Land was under Roman rule, the Jews revolted against their oppressors. The Essene community hastily hid their precious manuscripts, at first wrapping them carefully and placing them in large storage jars which they secreted in caves, and then, as the tide of Roman reprisals swept closer, stowing them loose in hiding places near at hand.

In 1949 an expedition was mounted to investigate the area where the scrolls had been found. This and later explorations have revealed a large number of manuscripts from a number of caves, as well as the settlement of the Essenes themselves at Qumran. This was a strict and austere Jewish community whose members renounced worldly riches. Among the scrolls recovered was one detailing the rules by which they lived. Others included copies of books of the Bible – an exciting find because, until these were discovered, the earliest surviving copies of the Bible were only around 1,000 years old. These were twice that age. The texts also included a number of commentaries and other works of scholarship written by the Essenes.

THE COPPER SCROLL

One scroll, however, was completely different. Instead of parchment, it was inscribed on copper. The text was written in archaic language and in a script unlike those in the other Dead Sea scrolls. Why? Because, it seems, the Copper Scroll was a copy of an earlier manuscript, transferred on to copper because that was a more durable material than parchment or whatever the original had been written on. Much of the text is difficult to read, partly because of the obscurity of the language but also because its

The unique Dead Sea Scroll inscribed on copper.

The Qumran caves, where the Dead Sea Scrolls were discovered.

writers deliberately made it cryptic

But despite the problems, and the differing opinions of scholars on the detail of its meaning, there is no doubt overall about what it is. The Copper Scroll is a list of hidden treasures, giving information about where they were hidden. Most of the treasures were gold and silver bars and vessels but there were also precious oils and unguents, ritual robes and other valuable materials. There has been considerable debate about the quantities, but even the lowest reading of the figures in the text puts them around 100 kilograms (220lb) of precious metals.

The presence of the Copper Scroll among the austere Essenes is a mystery. Was it inscribed by them or not? If so, to what did it refer? Some scholars suggest the scroll gives the hiding place of treasures taken from the Temple in Jerusalem before it was sacked by the Romans in AD 68. But the Essenes were on bad terms with the Temple priests so it seems unlikely that they would have been chosen to hide the Temple's wealth. On the other hand, the Essene community was remote from civilization and might seem an ideal place to conceal treasure. One recent suggestion, by the metallurgist Robert Feather, is that the treasure belonged to the Temple of Aten in the city built by Egypt's heretical monotheistic king, Akhenaten. When he died, the traditional Egyptian priesthood quickly destroyed his monuments. Feather is not alone in linking the monotheism of Akhenaten with that of the Jews and particularly with the Essenes, whom he sees as the repository of the information on where the Aten treasure was hidden.

Who knows? Obviously the identity of the treasure is important in determining where lie the locations cryptically described in the Copper Scroll – Egypt? Palestine? Somewhere else? So far, no one has broken the code and found any of the treasures, so they remain as well hidden as on the day they were deposited.

HEROD'S PALACES

The Romans became involved in the affairs of the Holy Land in 64 BC when the two rival claimants to the throne each appealed to Rome for support against the other. Their dispute became caught up in the civil wars between Pompey and Caesar, Antony and Cleopatra and Octavian (Augustus), and eventually Antipater, chief minister of the kingdom, rose to power. In 40 BC the Roman Senate appointed Antipater's son, Herod (74–4 BC), as king of Judaea; he married Mariamne, a daughter of the Judaean royal house, to strengthen his position. When the dust of Rome's own affairs settled, Herod, a skilful politician, was confirmed by Augustus as king.

A cruel and suspicious ruler, who executed many members of his own family, Herod was nevertheless a cultured man, with a passion for building. His personal wealth and substantial state revenues gave him the means to indulge his passion, and being on good terms with the Romans, he was able to make use of Roman skills and knowledge in civil engineering. He rebuilt the Temple in Jerusalem, turned a small town into the fine port city of Caesarea, and constructed a number of palaces for himself.

His most ambitious residence was the palace that he had built on the side of the massive rock at Masada. He surrounded the top of the rock with a casemate wall and built storerooms, baths and reservoirs. His palace was constructed on three terraces built out from the northern end of the rock and was lavishly decorated with paintings and mosaics.

Equally unusual in form was the palace complex that Herod built in the Judaean desert and which he named Herodium after himself. A series of palatial buildings, bathhouses and other structures were laid out at ground level, while a small mound was built up to form a conical hill on and into which a circular fortress was constructed. This contained a palace on a grand scale, with a pillared courtyard and gardens as well as luxurious private apartments.

When Herod died in 4 BC, the historian Josephus recounts that he was borne on a solid-gold bier adorned with precious stones, wrapped in crimson cloth and wearing a golden crown and diadem. He was laid to rest at Herodium, which he had designed also as his mausoleum. Modern investigations of the fortress-palace, however, have failed to reveal the king's tomb.

The ruins of the Herodium, one of Herod's palaces.

THE WEALTH OF PERSIA

Elam and Susa

While cities and empires rose and fell on the plains of Mesopotamia, another civilization flourished on the Iranian plateau. Its chief city was Susa, home of the Elamite kings, who were often in conflict with the peoples of the plain. Many of the finest works of Mesopotamian sculpture were found at Susa, to which they had been taken as the spoils of war. The city had many temples, to a variety of gods but particularly to Susa's patron deity, Inshushinak. Among the votive offerings associated with the shrine is a gold figure of a bearded man carrying a goat, presumably as a sacrificial offering. A matching statuette in silver was found with it. Susa was a major city for thousands of years, still important under the Persian Achaemenid Empire (529–330 BC) and continuing as a key centre into much later times.

The tombs of Susa's kings may have been sited somewhere away from the city. Brick-vaulted tombs discovered at Haft Tepe (ancient Kabnak) are thought to be those of Susa's fourteenth-century BC kings, while underground vaulted chambers containing cremated remains found at Choga Zambil (ancient Al-Untash-Napirisha) are likely to have been the resting place of the Elamite kings in the thirteenth century BC. Little remains of the grave offerings that must once have accompanied these burials, owing to the activities of looters. Among these the chief was probably Ashurbanipal, King of Assyria, who sacked the city in 647 BC, breaking open royal tombs and removing not only the treasures but also the bones of the Elamite kings.

Marlik Tepe

In contrast to these plundered graves, intact burials of great splendour, dated around 1200 BC, were discovered by chance in 1961 at Marlik Tepe near the Caspian Sea. A

ABOVE: This 12th-century BC statue of a worshipper was a votive offering in the Temple of Inshushinak at Susa.

BELOW: A beaker decorated with winged bulls from Marlik displays the great skill of the ancient goldsmiths.

mound thought at first to be natural was found to cover a series of royal graves, some cut into the rock and others constructed of stone slabs. Vessels of pottery, gold and silver, bronze figurines, a great variety of weapons and jewellery of precious stones and metals abounded in the graves, particularly those of royal women and children. Nature had provided inspiration for the local craftsmen, who had created golden jewellery in the shape of pomegranates, pottery vessels in the form of animals, including a charming bear, and gold vases decorated with trees as well as imaginary creatures such as unicorns and winged bulls.

Tepe Nush-i Jan

While the Assyrians and Elamites were locked in conflict in the west, eastern Iran saw the emergence on to the international stage of two related Indo-Iranian tribes, the Medes and Persians. In 614 BC the Medes made common cause with the Babylonians and together they sacked the Assyrian capital, Nineveh, in 612. Following this success the Medes spread into Anatolia, coming to control a huge empire. Few of their sites have been excavated. One exception is the religious centre at Tepe Nush-i Jan. Here two temples with a pillared hall and courtyards were constructed around 800 BC. The central temple had a fire altar, suggesting that the Medes' beliefs were related to Zoroastrianism, which became the main religion of later Iranian empires. Around 600 BC, a complete reorganization of the site was initiated and the central temple was filled with stones in preparation. The project was abandoned, however, perhaps due to troubled circumstances. A hoard discovered in one of the buildings would support this theory. Hidden around 600 BC and never recovered, it consisted of 321 pieces of silver packed into a bronze bowl. These included rings and pendants as well as small silver bars for use as "money". Some of the pieces had been manufactured much earlier, as far back as 2000 BC.

GOLDEN TOMBS OF THE SCYTHIAN HORDES

Robbers frustrated by falling rubble

Paul Dubrux was a Frenchman who had been driven from his homeland by the French Revolution of 1789. In 1797 he entered the Russian Civil Service. After being posted to Kerch in the Crimea in the 1810s, he took a lively interest in the numerous local funerary mounds of the Scythian nomads who had lived in the region during the first millennium BC. In September 1830 the military in the area were ordered to acquire and transport several hundred stones to build a barracks. Dubrux was invited by Kerch's governor to visit the scene of their labours and recognized that the mound at Kul Oba, from which they were moving a large number of stones, was a Scythian burial tumulus. So the officer in charge was detailed to keep an eye on their work here.

On September 19 a massive entrance passage made of cut stone was revealed in the side of the mound, leading into a vaulted chamber. Originally the stonework had been held up by wooden posts but these had disintegrated, leaving the stones barely supported by the surrounding earth. The dangers of the excavation seemed likely to deter any tomb robbers, but Dubrux was still concerned that the chambe rmight be looted after work hours. Rightly so, for the minute he had left the site the guards also deserted their post and local villagers moved in to pillage the tomb. As Dubrux had had the tomb entrance blocked with stones, they were

unable to do much damage on the first night, but, although a guard was posted on subsequent nights, the robbers got in and removed a quantity of small gold objects. On the fifth night, however, collapsing stones injured some of the robbers and frightened them off. Dubrux was later able to recover some of the gold that the pillagers had stolen.

A royal burial

The mound contained four burials, only one of which had been robbed by the villagers. This burial had been placed at a separate level from the rest and was probably not

related to them. Of the other three, one was a slave or groom and one was a woman who was probably the wife of the principal individual in the grave. This man, who must have been a king or nobleman of the Scythians, was decked with golden finery – a torc around his throat, its ends decorated with figures of Scythian horsemen, a felt cap decorated with gold, rings and bracelets. He had been buried in one side of a large timber coffin. In the other compartment of the coffin were his treasures – a massive sword with a gold hilt, golden leg guards, a golden-handled whip, a gold bowl and five figurines made of gold.

His wife's coffin was also well furnished, containing a bronze mirror with a gold handle and a magnificent electrum vase decorated with scenes of Scythian daily life. She too wore a gold torc and bracelets as well as gold necklaces and pendants and a headdress of electrum. Elsewhere in the tomb were horse bones, bronze and silver cauldrons and drinking vessels, knives with handles of

ABOVE: A golden belt buckle from a nomad tomb depicts a tiger fighting with a fabulous beast – a fine example of the vibrant art of the steppes.

BELOW: This gold chest-ornament has scenes of nomad life, such as milking sheep, in the upper register and fights between mythical beasts in the lower.

ivory or gold and the remains of ivory inlay from a coffin, exquisitely decorated. Numerous gold plaques scattered over the floor must have fallen from textiles which had covered the tomb's walls.

Nomads

The grave at Kul Oba is by no means the wealthiest of the Scythian burial mounds found in the Eurasian steppes. Unfortunately, however, these mounds were often ransacked in antiquity, so many have lost their treasures. We know a great deal about the Scythians who inhabited the area around the Black Sea during the first millennium BC, not only from the graves which have been excavated but also from their neighbours, the Classical Greeks. The great Greek historian and ethnographer Herodotus gave a detailed description of their way of life. Some Scythians, he said, had settled down to farm, living in permanent villages, but the majority of them were nomads who grazed large herds of sheep

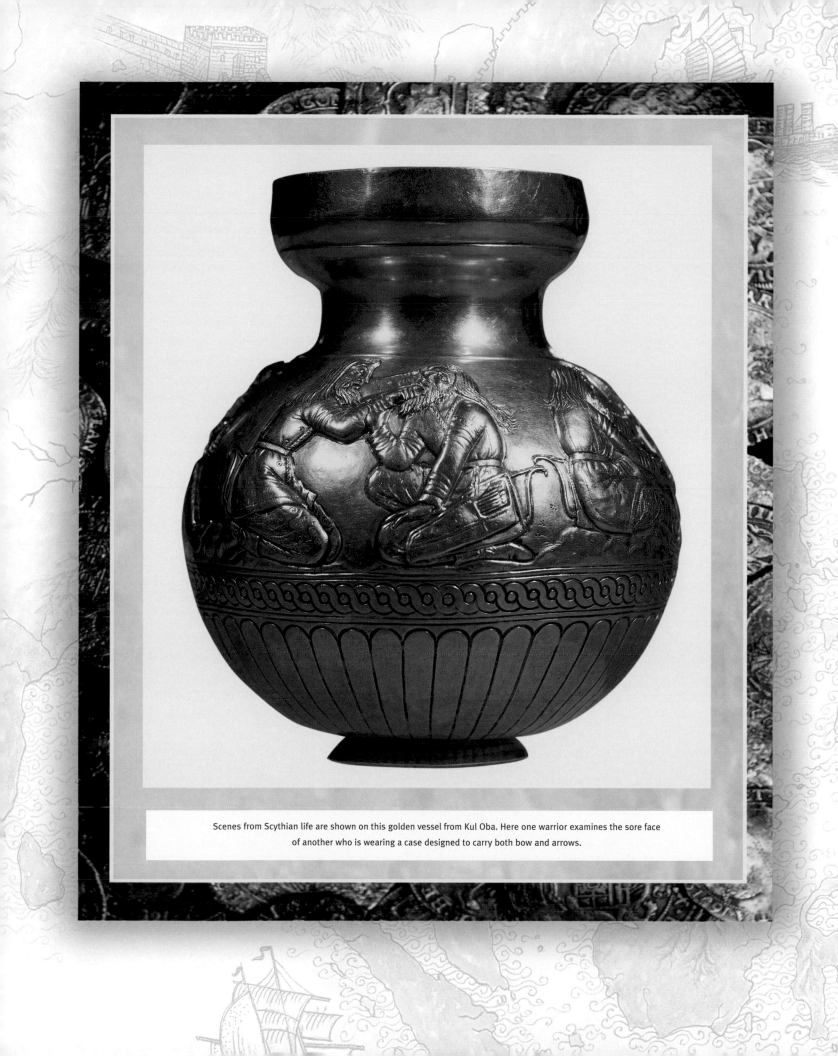

Scenes from Scythian life are shown on this golden vessel from Kul Oba. Here one warrior examines the sore face of another who is wearing a case designed to carry both bow and arrows.

on the scattered pastures of the steppe. Similar groups lived and moved through the entire steppe region, which stretches to the border of China.

These nomads rode horses and travelled in horse-drawn wagons, living either in the wagons or in tents. Fine artists, they produced colourful woollen clothing, saddlecloths, rugs and carpets, elaborate wooden carvings, including headdresses for themselves and their horses, and exquisite gold and silver jewellery and vessels. Many were decorated in what has become known as the "Animal Style": swirling designs of real or imaginary beasts, often engaged in combat with one another. One famous example depicts a panther attacking a yak which has seized an eagle which is pecking the panther. Much Scythian goldwork seems to have been made by Greeks working to Scythian specifications – there was considerable trade between these two very different nations.

Immense sacrifices

Herodotus also described Scythian royal burial practices. Dead kings were first mummified, their guts removed and replaced with herbs and frankincense and their bodies

ABOVE: A wall hanging of coloured felt found at Pazyryk depicts a warrior riding a saddled and bridled horse, in front of a goddess seated on an elaborate chair.

coated in wax. They were then taken in procession on a wagon throughout the Scythian lands before being buried in huge pits with their golden treasures and a number of sacrificed attendants. After a year 50 attendants and 50 fine horses were sacrificed and displayed on wheels supported by stakes around the funerary mound.

No excavated nomad burials have revealed remains of this gruesome arrangement, but there is plenty of evidence of sacrifices, both of people and horses. A huge barrow at Arzan in southern Siberia contained the burials of 23 individuals besides the man and woman at the centre, and 160 sacrificed horses. Even the relatively modest burial of a woman recently found on the Ukok plateau in the Altai mountains was accompanied by six horses.

Deep freeze

The Altai mountains have many nomad burial mounds and these have been plun-

dered by treasure-seekers almost from the moment when the mourners left. In 1924 a Russian archaeologist, Sergei Rudenko, led a reconnaissance expedition to the Pazyryk region, where he found a number of promising mounds. In 1927 he began excavations here and in 1947 returned to the region to excavate further mounds.

The task Rudenko's team faced was extraordinarily difficult. During the severe winters in this region, the ground becomes frozen to a considerable depth. The nomads had dug their grave shafts during the summer, but after they filled in the graves water had accumulated within them. The following winter this had frozen, sealing the graves in a permanent block of ice. Now the archaeologists were faced with the problem of unfreezing them. Nineteenth-century archaeologists had experimented with lighting fires on the graves. Rudenko's team tried a different approach: they poured buckets of boiling water over the ground.

Robbers had dug into the mounds within a few decades of the burials being made, so all were disturbed. They must have carried off many precious objects of gold and silver, but they left behind a great wealth of other treasures. Because the tombs had remained frozen a great many organic artefacts were preserved – an extremely unusual situation.

Textiles and tattoos

In one grave was found the mummified body of a man aged about 60 who had been furnished with a false beard made of human hair. His limbs and torso had been tattooed with designs of animals, including lively horses kicking up their heels and imaginary monsters. In more recent years other tattooed bodies have been found in burials in the Altai mountains and it was clearly a common decoration favoured by both men and women.

This man had been buried in a coffin made from a hollowed-out larch tree trunk decorated with pieces of leather cut out in the shape of deer. A woman of about 40, her hair in pigtails, was also buried in this tomb. Many of their clothes had survived – soft leather boots for indoor wear, decorated with gold leaf and beads sewn on to the soles; caftans of squirrel skin and sable fur; a shirt of woven hemp with red woollen braid; and stockings made of felt.

Like other grave mounds doscovered in the region, the burials had been placed inside a chamber constructed of wooden logs set in the bottom of a deep shaft. Sacrificed horses were placcd in the shaft around the chamber and these also were furnished with richly decorated textiles, including saddles and other pieces of harness made of wood and leather, woollen saddle cloths and elaborate headdresses with felt decorations.

Another grave yielded the earliest Persian carpet to have survived, showing a line of horsemen and a frieze of elks, set between geometric bands of decoration. The nomads were linked by trade with both east and west, for the grave also contained a fine Chinese silk cloth embroidered with phoenixes. A large felt wall hanging decorated with a repeating design of a goddess on a throne and a moustached warrior on his horse before her was made by the nomads themselves.

A lucky find

We can only guess what treasures the graves contained before they were looted by the ancient robbers. Luck gave one team of archaeologists a glimpse of the original magnificence of such tombs when, in 1913, an expedition from the Russian Imperial Archaeological Commission entered its fourth season of excavating a massive Scythian burial mound at Soloha on the River Dnieper. The central chamber on which the team had been working over the previous years had been plundered not long after the burial was made. Before starting work, the director of the excavation, Professor Wesselowsky, had carefully examined the burial mound and had come to the

ABOVE: A Scythian tomb yielded a twisted bracelet of gold and turquoise with elaborate decorations in relief on each end.

conclusion that it probably also covered a second, less substantial burial chamber placed to one side. Investigations revealed that he was right and that the robbers had failed to make this deduction, for the chamber proved to be undisturbed.

In the tomb's outer chamber, five horses, decked in gold and bronze finery, were laid in a row, with their groom beside them. Beyond these was a guard armed with bow and arrows. Another soldier, with a sword and clad in a coat of mail, lay at the king's feet. All around the king lay his weapons and splendid armour, including a bronze helmet, a coat of mail and a sword in a wonderful gold sheath. A great gold torc was around his neck and gold bracelets on his arms. Five magnificent silver vases stood beside him, decorated with scenes of Scythians hunting, picked out in gilt, while a vast gold dish was concealed in a niche at the king's head along with a woodcn bow and arrow case covered with a beautiful silver and plaster scene depicting a battle.

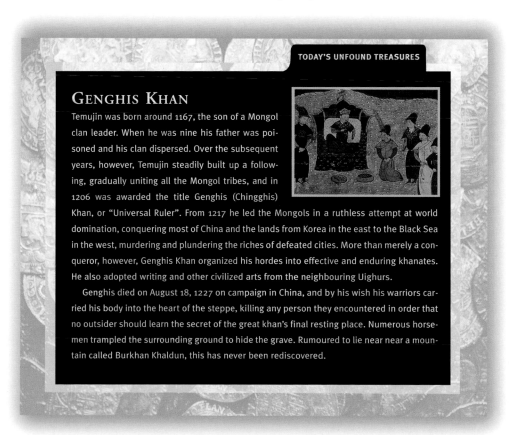

TODAY'S UNFOUND TREASURES

GENGHIS KHAN

Temujin was born around 1167, the son of a Mongol clan leader. When he was nine his father was poisoned and his clan dispersed. Over the subsequent years, however, Temujin steadily built up a following, gradually uniting all the Mongol tribes, and in 1206 was awarded the title Genghis (Chingghis) Khan, or "Universal Ruler". From 1217 he led the Mongols in a ruthless attempt at world domination, conquering most of China and the lands from Korea in the east to the Black Sea in the west, murdering and plundering the riches of defeated cities. More than merely a conqueror, however, Genghis Khan organized his hordes into effective and enduring khanates. He also adopted writing and other civilized arts from the neighbouring Uighurs.

Genghis died on August 18, 1227 on campaign in China, and by his wish his warriors carried his body into the heart of the steppe, killing any person they encountered in order that no outsider should learn the secret of the great khan's final resting place. Numerous horsemen trampled the surrounding ground to hide the grave. Rumoured to lie near near a mountain called Burkhan Khaldun, this has never been rediscovered.

INDUS CIVILIZATION

A forgotten people

The nineteenth century was a great age of discovery in West Asia and by the early twentieth century the riches of Assyria and Babylonia, and of their third-millennium predecessors the Akkadians and Sumerians, were well known. In India, however, no civilization was known prior to the first millennium BC and the region was thought to be a backwater.

But in 1924, when Woolley was beginning to reveal the marvels of Ur (see p.27), Sir John Marshall, Director-General of the Archaeological Survey of India, announced the remarkable discovery of an unsuspected civilization in the Indus valley, contempo-

rary with that of Mesopotamia. It soon became apparent that the two had traded with each other, senior partners in a mercantile network that linked all the countries bordering the Persian Gulf.

These two great powers could not have been more different. Mesopotamia had long been a region of warring city states, eventually united in 2350 BC when King Sargon of Agade conquered his rival rulers. The Indus civilization seems to have been always a land of peace, united into a single state from the time of its sudden emergence around 2600 BC. Sumerian and Akkadian cities were composed of unplanned residential areas that sprang up around the temples which had dominated urban life from the earliest times. Palaces housed the élite, both priests and royalty, and the latter were buried with lavish offerings. In the Indus region the towns were made up of planned residential

ABOVE: The great city of Mohenjo Daro on the Indus was one of the world's first planned cities, constructed of baked brick. Most houses had bathrooms – a welcome facility in this hot environment.

areas with streets orientated north–south and east–west but there were few structures that can clearly be identified as public buildings. The Great Bath at Mohenjo Daro is the closest thing to an identifiable religious structure and there are no obvious temples; nor are there palaces or royal graves. Even the personal possessions of the Indus people gave little clue to social hierarchy: most city dwellers seemed to have had similar fine pottery and stone or metal tools. Figurines depicting Indus people showed that women wore bangles, elaborate headdresses and necklaces of beads. Many pieces of jewellery were also found, in houses or in graves – bangles of shell or stone and thousands of

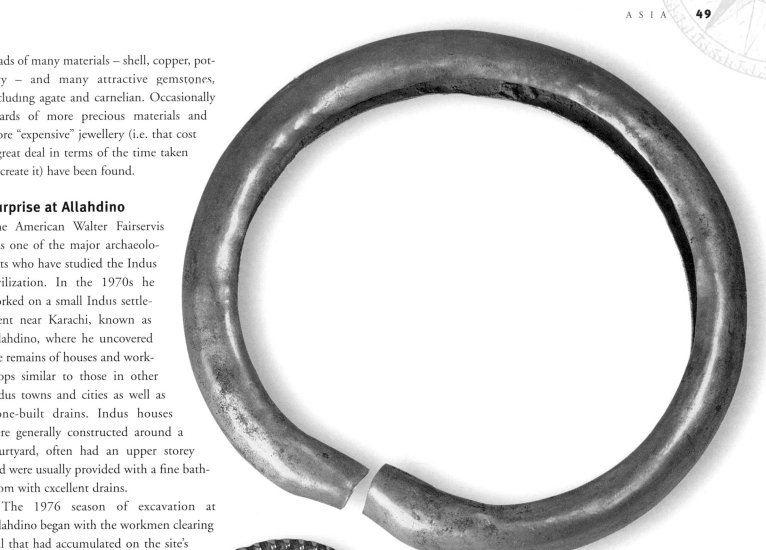

beads of many materials – shell, copper, pottery – and many attractive gemstones, Including agate and carnelian. Occasionally hoards of more precious materials and more "expensive" jewellery (i.e. that cost a great deal in terms of the time taken to create it) have been found.

Surprise at Allahdino

The American Walter Fairservis was one of the major archaeologists who have studied the Indus civilization. In the 1970s he worked on a small Indus settlement near Karachi, known as Allahdino, where he uncovered the remains of houses and workshops similar to those in other Indus towns and cities as well as stone-built drains. Indus houses were generally constructed around a courtyard, often had an upper storey and were usually provided with a fine bathroom with excellent drains.

The 1976 season of excavation at Allahdino began with the workmen clearing soil that had accumulated on the site's surface since the end of the previous year's work. Suddenly Fairservis stopped his workmen and sent them away – it was his wife's birthday, he told them, and he had decided to give them a holiday. In fact Fairservis's eagle eye had spotted gold and he was taking no chances. While the workmen moved off, his assistant, Elizabeth Walters, carried on her work, calmly cleaning round a small pot that was beginning to show up – the spot where Fairservis had seen the gold. When they were alone the pair carefully removed the pot and its contents. The excavation driver, Tahir Hussain Khan, could be relied on, so Fairservis had him drive them back to their hotel. Safely ensconced in Karachi's Hotel Metropole, Fairservis and Walters examined their find.

ABOVE: Gold jewellery uncovered at Mohenjo Daro included a bangle – an important article of female attire even in present-day India – and an ear ornament with a central depression that once held an inlay of some precious material.

The puzzling hoard

Within the pot they found a hoard of Indus jewellery. There were silver rings made of coiled wire that may have been worn on fingers or toes. Pieces of gold were stored to be made into jewellery in the future and there were several thin bands of gold that might have been headbands. Numerous silver beads made up three strings, held apart by spacer beads. Eight large silver discs were part of another necklace, along with a half-moon-shaped centrepiece. The most impressive object was a massive belt made out of beads, similar to those worn by the women depicted in many Indus figurines. Bronze spacer beads held together six strings of carnelian beads, each bead 6–10 centimetres (2½–4 inches) long. These beads were superb works of craftsmanship, requiring a specially

THE *SÃO PAULO*

The *São Paulo* was a Portuguese carrack, a huge vessel weighing more than 1,524 tonnes (1,500 tons), plying the trade route to the East Indies. She set sail from Belém in Portugal in April 1560, carrying coin, rich trade goods such as tapestries and many passengers, but illness and adverse weather slowed her journey and a storm brought it to an end the following January, wrecking the ship on a small island just off Sumatra. The passengers and crew managed to recover some goods, including food, and were able to survive while they constructed and repaired boats to take them off the island – though some of their number were captured and eaten by neighbouring cannibals. When they left, the boats were overcrowded since some of the merchants had packed in salvaged goods, but they seized a junk and sailed down the Sumatra coast. Putting in at the River Menencabo, they were deceived by apparently friendly natives who fell on them in the night, capturing or killing around 70 of them. The survivors managed to reach Java, where, weakened, some of them died of overeating. The remaining 250 eventually reached their destination, the trading post of Malacca (Melaka) in July.

hard and fine drill to make the central perforation down their length and each may have taken a week or 10 days to drill. It would also have taken days to make the bead from the original lump of stone. So the 36-bead belt represented about a year and a half's work for a skilled craftsman.

The pot therefore contained a substantial treasure at the time it was hidden. It was presumably the property of the principal family in Allahdino, local landowners or major government officials. What threat caused them to hide their treasure and what prevented them from retrieving it, we shall never know.

BELOW: This elaborate ornament of six rows of gold beads with spacer bars and semicircular terminals would have been worn as a choker by a lady at Mohenjo Daro 4,000 years ago.

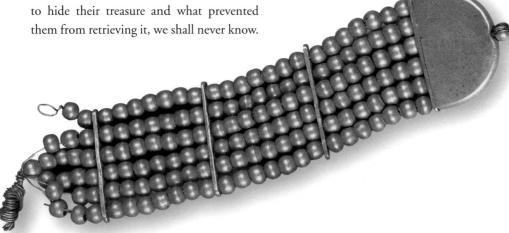

GOLDWORK FROM THE MYSTERIOUS MEGALITHS OF SOUTHERN INDIA

Similar to European structures

Megalithic monuments – large structures built of massive stones – are among the most impressive and most prominent remains of the prehistoric past in western Europe. Men sent out from Britain in the early nineteenth century to work in southern India were amazed to discover similar megalithic monuments scattered about the landscape. Some were low mounds enclosed by circles made of massive boulders. Within the mound, and often partly exposed by erosion, there was frequently a cist, a rectangular stone box built of dressed slabs or uncut boulders. The most impressive were massive cromlechs, free-standing structures built of enormous undressed rocks.

The similarities with European megaliths were striking. Was there a connection, despite the great distances involved and the general absence of such monuments in the intervening lands? What were the megaliths built for and was the reason the same in both areas? Many antiquarians connected the European megaliths with the Celts and their priests, the Druids. They suggested that the megaliths might be temples with altars upon which human sacrifices were made. Some antiquarians in India adopted the same theory.

When local southern Indians were asked about the megaliths, they produced unsatisfactory answers. The structures dated back to a time when people lived for hundreds of years, they said. When they became really elderly, they were quite unpleasant to have around, so their relatives built megaliths in which to shut them up, giving them plenty to eat and drink but keeping them out of the

ABOVE: The earrings found in the grave at Souttoukeny were made by inserting many small elongated gold cones into a gold disc. Equally elaborate were the floral pendants.

home. Alternatively, they said that the megaliths were the homes of ancient pygmies of superhuman strength or of the monkey-people who helped Rama, hero of the Hindu epic poem the *Ramayana*.

Some antiquarians took these stories at face value. They excavated some of the megaliths and recorded seriously that there was no evidence that the skeletons they found inside had been those of either pygmies or monkeys. Nor did the megaliths seem to be houses. They certainly contained some domestic objects, such as pottery and tools, but lacked normal features of houses such as hearths, proper doors and furniture.

Iron Age graves

Judging by the number of bones found in those that were excavated, it seemed very likely that these magnificent structures were graves. More recent investigations have proved this suggestion to be right in most cases – although there are still some mysterious megaliths that were not graves, such as

the standing stones erected alone or in lines. Some individuals were buried lying on their back or side; others were cremated and their remains collected in an urn placed in the grave. In many cases the graves contained the collected remains of a number of people – skulls and long bones in particular, sometimes neatly sorted by type and stacked in heaps.

The majority of these megalithic graves contained grave goods – attractive black-and-red pottery was very common and often the deceased were wearing beads. Most of the tools and weapons – knives, daggers, chisels, axes, swords and the like – were made of iron, for unlike the European megaliths, those of India have turned out to be of Iron Age date, from around 700 BC until the early centuries AD. Similar grave goods have been found in other kinds of graves that clearly belong to the same period, such

as burials in urns of various sizes, some surrounded by a small stone circle, others packed close together in urn fields. The most unusual are burials placed in curious terracotta sarcophagi in the shape of bathtubs standing on multiple pairs of legs.

Horse-riders and princes

Although most of the offerings in these burials are of ordinary, everyday objects, some are more elaborate. The people in the most northerly group of graves, in Maharashtra, were horse-riders and were buried with the horse harness they had used, such as stirrups and bits. Sometimes the horses were also sacrificed to accompany them. These graves often contained copper or bronze decorations for horses, bronze bells and bronze dishes, bowls and lids decorated with figures of animals.

Similar bronzes were found in a few graves further south, at Adichanallur in southern Tamil Nadu, where an enormous urn cemetery was discovered. Some of the urns also contained diadems made of sheets of beaten gold. Gold or silver beads were found occasionally in graves elsewhere in the south.

But the most spectacular burial was uncovered in the French toehold in southern India, Pondicherry district. A massive stone circle at Souttoukeny surrounded a large cist grave in which a "bathtub" sarcophagus had been placed, along with the bodies of a man and a woman. A splendid sword accompanied the burials, along with magnificent and elaborate gold jewellery showing superb craftsmanship. This included earrings in the shape of a flower with radiating petals and pendants in the form of lotus flowers dangling on gold chains. There were also gold bangles and many beads of gold and silver. Surely this was the burial of a prince and princess. Was she sacrificed to accompany him into death? Sati (wife immolation) was an Indian practice of later times and perhaps we see it here.

ABOVE: Small naturalistic carvings of animals like this panther were among the decorations fashioned in ivory that were discovered at Begram.

INDO-GREEKS AND KUSHANS

Bactria and Gandhara – lands of the north-west

In 533 BC the first Persian emperor, Cyrus the Great, overran north-west India. This gold-rich area became the twentieth satrapy (province) of the empire – and its richest, providing 360 talents of gold dust in tribute. The Gandhara region saw many changes of master in the centuries that followed. Alexander the Great held the north-west briefly after conquering the Persian Empire, but in the chaos and civil war that followed his death, Chandragupta Maurya (reigned 321–297 BC) incorporated Gandhara into his expanding Indian empire, which reached its greatest extent under his grandson, Ashoka (reigned 268–232 BC), around 260 BC. When the Mauryan Empire declined, the north-west came under the rule of petty Greek kingdoms that had grown up in Bactria from colonies founded by Alexander

the Great. The Indo-Greeks in turn were succeeded as rulers of the area by Central Asian nomads, the Shakas (Scythians) and later the Kushans, who controlled the region until it fell in AD 460 to the merciless invasion of the Huns.

City of monks and merchants

Taxila, the capital city of Gandhara, developed over the years into a major centre of trade, art, learning, industry and religion. It moved at least three times, the Mauryan city on the Bhir Mound being superseded by a planned Indo-Greek city, Sirkap, and later a Kushan foundation in Central Asian style, Sirsukh, replaced Sirkap. The crossroads of routes leading from the west into Central Asia and India, cosmopolitan Taxila was open to influences from many cultures. While the Mauryans ruled the region, Buddhism became established here, and many fine monasteries were built in the valley. Wealthy merchants and princes made rich offerings in the Buddhist shrines – the Kushans were particularly generous patrons. A fine hybrid art style developed under the Indo-Greek rulers, Indian motifs and themes from both Buddhism and folk religion being combined with Classical realism. Western religions also flourished under the Indo-Greeks and their successors: shrines erected in Taxila included a probable Zoroastrian fire temple.

From Taxila merchants and missionaries set out along the dangerous and difficult Silk Road to China through Central Asia, a route that developed from the late second century BC and which prospered particularly under the Kushans who controlled the western portion of the regions through which it ran. Wealth flowed into and through the city. Gold, silver and gems were used to make exquisite jewellery and reliquaries for holding holy remains of the Buddha and of Buddhist saints, while imported luxuries included elaborately decorated tableware and Classical statuary from Alexandria and the Roman world and silks from China.

The carved panels found at Begram show a mixture of styles, reflecting the cosmopolitan nature of this region. The traditional art of the Indian dynasties to the south was the source of inspiration for this panel.

ABOVE: Elaborate golden diadems decorated with pendant discs were among the rich ornaments found with the six individuals buried in the mound at Tillya Tepe.

RIGHT: A golden chariot carrying two men and drawn by four horses formed part of the hoard found in 1880 on the bank of the River Oxus (Amu Darya).

Taxila's wealth made it a target for invaders. Defensive walls were erected around many of the monasteries to protect the monks and their treasures against the frequent attacks on the valley. Sometimes the people of the city received enough warning to give them time to hide their treasures. However, when they fell at the hands of the intruders, the secret of their hidden wealth died with them – to be rediscovered by the archaeologists who excavated the houses and monasteries of the city almost 2,000 years later.

Gold and silver coins, silver dishes, gold and silver bracelets, earrings and necklaces, small Buddhist stone sculptures, soapstone toilet trays for mixing cosmetics, gold figurines of Indian goddesses, ivory combs and many other personal treasures were recovered from the successive cities and religious foundations at Taxila.

Royal treasure-house or customs shed?

Ivories were also foremost among the treasures discovered from the town of Kapisha (modern Begram), which lay to the northwest of Taxila, near the western end of the Silk Road. In 1938 a Belgian archaeological team excavating the town came across a bricked-up room which they opened to reveal a wealth of treasures from east, west and south. Chinese lacquer vessels lay alongside goblets of Roman alabaster and painted glass, one depicting the famous Pharos lighthouse at Alexandria. Bronze statuettes were also imports from the Mediterranean, and these included figures that had been used as weights on a steelyard balance. Decorative plaques depicting Buddhist scenes were among the beautifully carved ivories from India found in the Begram treasure. A statue of a goddess personifying the holy River Ganges was one of many ivory pieces that had once formed elements of carved furniture. Pieces of ivory with finely inscribed decoration in the Parthian style were also found.

The objects in the Begram hoard had been made at different times from the first century BC until the mid-third century AD. Since the town was a major trade entrepôt, some people have suggested that the storeroom contained customs tolls collected from merchants journeying through the area. More probably, however, these treasures were accumulated by successive Indo-Greek and Kushan kings of the ancient state of Kapisha and were hidden here when the city was threatened. The building in which they were stored was destroyed in AD 241 when the town was invaded by the Sassanian King Shapur I (reigned 241–272), and their owners never returned to dig their treasures from the ruins.

Golden burials

The lands along the River Oxus (Amu Darya) had enjoyed considerable prosperity in the Bronze Age and in later times, under Indo-Greek and Kushan rulers, they were involved in the lucrative Silk Road trade network. The riches that could be accumulated by noble families in this region are shown by a chance discovery at Tillya Tepe, a small mound on the Oxus in southern Bactria.

The Russian archaeologist Victor Sarianidi was excavating a Bronze Age settlement on this site in the late 1980s when he suddenly came upon six burials of the Kushan period (early centuries AD) that had been cut down into the earlier deposits. He and his team worked against the clock to excavate these six graves, which were stuffed with treasures, determined to recover all there was to find before treasure-seekers moved in to plunder the site.

The six individuals buried here, men and women, were placed first in a simple wooden coffin and this was wrapped in a shroud decorated with discs of gold and silver. Like the nomad inhumations of the steppe, these burials were placed in a deep shaft and covered by a wooden roof. Despite the relative simplicity of the graves, they contained a remarkably rich set of grave goods – some 20,000 items in all. The greater part consisted of gold clothing and jewellery worn by the deceased –

THE *DOURADO*

Louis Dominic de Rienzi had spent many adventurous years exploring and travelling in the Americas, the Mediterranean and much of Asia. He had also taken part in many famous conflicts – Waterloo, the Greek fight for independence from the Turkish Ottoman Empire and Italy's struggles for freedom. He had discovered several important archaeological sites, including Petra (above), and had visited many others, assembling a great collection of antiquities. This he had with him when in 1829 he embarked from Macao in the East Indies on the *Dourado*, bound for Bombay. Within a week, however, the ship was in serious difficulties. Everyone took to the boats, and Rienzi, by his own account, played a heroic part in rescuing drowning companions. Abandoning the doomed ship, the boats headed for Singapore, not far distant. On arrival, the captain persuaded the authorities to send an immediate salvage team, with armed guards, for the ship contained $500,000 in gold. The salvage ships failed to find the *Dourado*, but within a few days she was reported to have sunk off the island of Bintan. Divers were soon at work but their success was limited to recovering a few small objects. Rienzi returned to Europe, lamenting his loss.

headdresses decorated with hundreds of pendant discs, rings, necklaces, earrings and the like as well as weapons decorated with gold and ivory. The lively decoration on many of the pieces shows the many influences at work in Kushan society at the time – traditional themes from West Asian art going back millennia; motifs and styles introduced by the Hellenistic Greeks; and ideas brought in by steppe nomads, including the nomadic Kushan forebears of the settled people of this region.

Plundered hoard

In 1880 three merchants were journeying across Afghanistan when they were set upon by bandits and robbed. Their servant escaped and reached the local British political officer, a Captain Burton, who at once began a search. The bandits were caught around midnight and made to hand over a large proportion of what they had stolen. This included a number of fine gold pieces from a hoard that had apparently been discovered on the banks of the Oxus at Takht-i Kuwad. Burton purchased one piece from the merchants, a gold bracelet with terminals in the form of griffins. Originally this had been inlaid with precious stones. In both shape and style, this bracelet was similar to examples known from the Persian Empire.

This hoard, which the merchants eventually sold to Sir Alexander Cunningham, Director General of the Archaeological Survey of India at the time, was said to have contained about 1,500 coins and 150 other objects, all of gold or silver. As the pieces belong to various different periods, it is likely that the hoard was made up of offerings accumulated through time in a temple treasury. Other pieces from the

ABOVE: This massive gold bracelet from the Oxus treasure is companion to the one purchased by Captain Burton.

BELOW: A sheet gold plaque from the Oxus treasure shows a Zoroastrian priest with rods used in religious rites.

period of the Persian Empire included a magnificent repoussé gold sheet plaque depicting a priest clad in tightly fitting trousers, a short-sleeved tunic and a hood. A number of gold signet rings included some that were Persian in style and others that were Greek. One of the most elaborate pieces was a gold model of a chariot drawn by four horses. Within it stood the charioteer, his hands on the reins, a gold torc at his neck and wearing a simple tunic, while at his side on a bench sat a more sumptuously dressed figure wearing a long, decorated robe.

THE CAVE OF 1,000 BUDDHAS

A Chinese adventurer

The Silk Road link between east and west was opened up by the Chinese in the years after 128 BC, when general Zhang Qian returned from a perilous mission. He had been sent out 11 years earlier, by the Han emperor Wu Di, to make contact with the Yuezhi nomads, enemies of the Xiongnu nomads who were causing considerable trouble to the Han Empire. After being captured by the Xiongnu and kept prisoner for 10 years, Zhang Qian escaped and reached the borders of India. Further misadventures followed, but he eventually managed to return home. Although Zhang Qian failed in his mission to win Yuezhi support for joint military activity, he brought back a

great deal of useful information about the west and opportunities for trade which Wu Di was swift to act upon. He and his successors established military outposts in oasis towns along the routes skirting the fearsome icy wastes of the Taklamakan desert and opened up trade with the west. For many centuries caravans travelled along this route, carrying Chinese silk and lacquer, furs imported from the steppe nomads, glass and alabaster wares and statuary from the Mediterranean, spices and cotton textiles from India, incense from Arabia and the fabulous "horses that sweat blood" from Ferghana on the Silk Road itself.

Buddhist missionaries also travelled the Silk Road from west to east, taking Buddhism to China, Korea and Japan, where it rapidly won adherents. Buddhist shrines and monasteries were established in many of the oasis towns along the Silk Road,

often decorated with impressive sculptures and paintings. By the fifth century AD Chinese pilgrims were travelling west to study and worship in the Buddhist centres and shrines of India and Sri Lanka and to obtain copies of sacred manuscripts. One, Xuan Zang, who undertook this difficult and hazardous journey in the seventh century AD, left a vivid account of his travels.

Into Central Asia's icy wastes

Xuan Zang's writings were a constant and inspiring companion to Sir Aurel Stein, a scholar who intrepidly explored the Silk Road and its towns in the early years of the twentieth century. And, by good fortune, they also provided the key that unlocked the door to Stein's greatest discovery.

Stein, accompanied by his Chinese secretary, Jiang Siye, his little dog Dash and a small team of native helpers, visited and

ABOVE: The numerous cave shrines at Dunhuang were richly decorated with stucco sculptures and paintings in tempera, depicting the Buddha and his followers, processions of Buddhist saints and scenes illustrating parables from former lives of the Buddha.

Jiang to examine them. The following day he opened up the hidden recess and allowed Stein to examine some of the texts. And eventually he agreed to Stein removing some of the hoard, on condition that nothing should be said of this publicly until Stein had left Chinese soil.

Priceless manuscripts

The hidden cache was a find of exceptional importance. It contained a huge number of perfectly preserved manuscripts on wood, bark, silk and other materials. There were Buddhist and other sacred texts, official documents, poetry, books on geography, philosophy and many other subjects, dating from between the fifth and eleventh centuries AD and written in a number of different languages. One was the earliest printed work to survive – a copy of the "Diamond Sutra" text, dating from AD 868. In addition, the cache contained many beautiful silk painted banners. These, which were in themselves a treasure without price, had probably been hidden when the area was threatened by barbarian hordes in 1135.

Wang permitted Stein to remove 24 cases of manuscripts in 1907. These eventually reached the British Museum, where they kept an army of scholars busy for decades. The following year Stein's friend and colleague Paul Pelliot also visited the "Cave of 1,000 Buddhas" and was permitted to take away 15,000 more manuscripts.

However, news of the find had now trickled out and the authorities began to take an interest. They ordered that the remaining manuscripts be sent to Peking, and in compensation made a large payment to the shrine. The money never reached the shrine – it was diverted into many pockets on the way instead – and the manuscripts similarly dwindled away on their journey, only a small proportion reaching Peking. Fortunately, Wang had kept back some of the texts, carefully hidden away, and when Stein paid a final visit in 1914 he was able to give him a further 600 manuscripts.

investigated a number of ruined oasis towns along the Silk Road. Here he found the remains of fruit trees, an indication that the inhabitants had maintained efficient irrigation systems there many hundreds of years earlier. He excavated houses, uncovering rubbish that revealed a fascinating picture of life – discarded clothing, a mousetrap, musical instruments and documents which include the homesick musings of Chinese officials doing garrison duty in lonely outposts like Dunhuang.

While he was working on these sites, Stein heard rumours that interesting manuscripts had been found at Dunhuang. He therefore paid a visit to this former town and religious centre. Here he found rocks riddled with artificial caves in which Buddhist monks had created monastic cells and shrines, often beautifully painted.

The Daoist monk who took care of the complex was absent at the time of Stein's first brief reconnaissance visit, but a Tibetan monk was able to show him a manuscript from the supposed hoard. This had apparently been discovered by accident during repair work a few years earlier. The monk, anxious for the safety of the precious manuscripts, had sealed them behind a wooden door.

A few weeks later Stein returned to Dunhuang. A meeting with the Daoist

ABOVE: The valley of Dunhuang was riddled with caves excavated into the laterite cliffs. These were used as Buddhist shrines and as dwellings for monks over many centuries.

guardian, Wang Daoshi, quickly convinced him that extreme care would be needed in handling this timorous and indecisive character. Stein sent his secretary Jiang to open negotiations, promising to make a substantial donation to the shrine if he himself were allowed to look at the manuscript collection. Wang seemed interested though uncertain and likely to shy off at any minute. At this point Xuan Zang came to the rescue. Stein asked to be shown around the shrine, of which Wang, who had restored it personally, was very proud. As they looked about, Stein began to talk about Xuan Zang. Immediately Wang lit up. Not only was he familiar with the story of Xuan Zang's travels but he had even commissioned a set of pictures illustrating his life on the cave temple wall. One scene showed Xuan Zang crossing a river with the precious collection of Buddhist manuscripts he had obtained in India. This provided an opening that Stein did not let slip, and gradually he coaxed Wang to allow him to follow this eminent example.

On the first night, Wang brought out some manuscripts with great secrecy and allowed

TOMB OF THE FIRST CHINESE EMPEROR

AN EFFICIENT TYRANT

Wars between rival Chinese states had been a way of life for centuries when Prince Zheng ascended the throne of the Qin state in 246 BC, aged just 13. One of the first things that he did was to begin work on his tomb, which was to be of unprecedented splendour. Qin had been gradually winning the fight since 316, conquering its rivals or taking them over by diplomacy, and the new king continued its expansion. Between 230 and 221 BC, Qin's armies defeated the remaining six rival states and Zheng became ruler of the first united Chinese state.

Shi Huangdi, First Emperor, as Zheng now styled himself, was a man of extreme contrasts and later opinions of him are very mixed. Aided by his able first minister, Li Si, and his chief eunuch, Zhao Gao, he reorganized China's administration, reformed and codified the laws, standardized the script, coinage, weights and measures and even axle lengths on chariots, improved agriculture and created an efficient network of roads and canals for transport and irrigation. He also extended the empire and provided it with effective defences against the hostile barbarians on its northern fringes by joining the walls that rival states had erected on their borders to form the first Great Wall, a massive earthen rampart.

But his advances were paid for in great suffering. Thousands of peasants died while undertaking compulsory labour to construct the Great Wall – many of their skeletons lie crushed beneath its foundations. The emperor dealt ruthlessly with opposition, both actual and potential. He ordered the burning of all books on history, philosophy and other subjects that could give people the opportunity to compare his reign unfavourably with former times and to develop rebellious thoughts, and he put to death 460 scholars who might similarly have fomented rebellion. Harsh punishments were laid down for any who might dare rebel. His wars and massive building programmes (including work on his tomb, where 700,000 people

A later painting of Shi Huangdi burning books and executing scholars.

were employed) were achieved by taxing the peasants unmercifully and by excessive forced labour and conscription, so that the economic and social fabric of the state crumbled.

PREY TO FEAR AND SUPERSTITION

Not surprisingly, there were many who wished to see Shi Huangdi dead. One plot nearly succeeded. Jing Ke, a scholar and warrior, was granted an audience with the emperor to present him with the head of a slain opposing general and a map of the kingdom of Yan. Hidden inside the rolled-up map was a poisoned dagger and when Jing Ke was within range he snatched this out and grabbed the emperor by the sleeve. Before the assailant's blow could land, however, Shi Huangdi had torn himself away, ripping off the sleeve, and had darted behind a pillar. While the emperor struggled to draw his long sword, the court physician hit Jing Ke with his medicine bag. Within seconds Shi Huangdi freed his sword and set upon Jing Ke, stabbing him eight times and killing him.

The emperor lived in daily fear of his life and devised elaborate precautions to protect himself. He had many palaces throughout his realms, furnished with everything he could need, including concubines, and he travelled constantly, often incognito, so that no assassin could predict his whereabouts from day to day. Constantly seeking a way to prolong his existence, he sent out expeditions in search of the Elixir of Life and employed scholars, quacks and magicians to devise a life-preserving potion. One scholar caused him extreme fury by fleeing while in his service, claiming that the emperor was unworthy of having his life extended.

Shi Huangdi's obsession worked to the advantage of his trusted Li Si and Zhao Gao. When the emperor died suddenly in 210 BC, they hid the news and continued the royal progress as if nothing had happened, disguising the smell of his rotting corpse by placing his chariot near a cart of decaying fish. This gave them time to arrange the death of the crown prince and other impediments in their path to power, which they seized in the name of the emperor's youngest and weakest son. But their success was short-lived. Within four years the massive revolts that followed the emperor's death had swept them from power and a peasant called Liu Bang had seized the throne as first emperor of the Han Dynasty, which was to rule China for more than 400 years.

A massive artificial hill marks the burial place of Shi Huangdi.

No one knows if, as in this reconstruction, the rebel armies managed to penetrate the interior of the emperor's tomb.

THE EMPEROR'S TOMB

For 36 years an army of 700,000 conscripted labourers had been working to construct Shi Huangdi's final resting place at Mount Li. Details of the tomb were recorded by the Han historian Sima Qian. A vast complex was built above ground, with palaces and pavilions set within massive walls with splendid guard towers. In its centre was erected a mound more than 100 metres (330 feet) high, covering the chamber in which the emperor was to be buried. The chamber itself was a model of the world – the ceiling showed the pattern of the heavens with stars picked out in precious stones, while the floor was laid out with models of palaces, temples and other important buildings. The courses of the Yangtse River and the Yellow River were cut into the floor and filled with mercury which by some cunning mechanical means was made to flow perpetually into a miniature mercury ocean.

In the centre was the massive sarcophagus of cast copper in which the emperor was to be buried. All manner of treasures were to be placed with him. To prevent the impious disturbing his eternal peace, many booby traps were installed, including crossbows that would fire automatically if the tomb was broken into. When the emperor's body had been laid in the tomb, the jade entrance doors were sealed, trapping inside the pall-bearers who had passed the booby traps and therefore knew too much.

Others of the emperor's goods and treasures were buried in pits around the funerary complex. These included bronze model chariots, the emperor's horses and the animals from his menagerie.

ETERNAL GUARDIANS OF THE EMPEROR

Sima Qian did not describe all that was deposited around the emperor's tomb, however. In 1974 some peasants drilling for water discovered an underground chamber filled with terracotta statues. Archaeologists were called in to investigate – and have been working there ever since. Their excavations have revealed an amazing funerary offering – an entire army, more than 8,000 strong. Whereas earlier custom had been to sacrifice servants to accompany the royal dead into eternity, by the time of emperor Shi Huangdi models were being substituted for real people.

Four pits had been dug by the emperor's workforce. One was not completed by the time of his unexpected death and remains empty. Of the other three, one is quite small and represents the army's headquarters, housing life-size statues of the chief officers. The other two contain serried ranks of thousands of life-size terracotta soldiers, drawn up in battle order and eager to fight. There are spearmen and archers, horses and charioteers – although the chariots, being of wood, have decayed away.

LOOTED OR INTACT?

The terracotta army has survived for 2,000 years but it is unarmed. When they were lined up in their wooden chambers, the soldiers were richly furnished with fine weapons. But within four years, the living armies of revolt had swept through. Soldiers entered the chambers and seized the weapons to aid them in overthrowing the Qin regime of tyranny, burning the wooden chambers as they left and destroying the palaces and other buildings of the funerary complex. And what of the emperor's tomb with its fabulous treasures? Sima Qian is enigmatic on the subject – some believe he says that the army also looted the tomb, while others maintain it is still intact. Archaeologists have still to find out.

Ranks of terracotta warriors guard the emperor's tomb.

SPLENDOURS OF ANCIENT CHINESE TOMBS

Jade for eternity

Jade had a special significance for the ancient Chinese. It represented the immortal beings of the other world and was thought to have life-giving properties. Jade amulets were worn to prolong life and jade was placed with the dead to preserve their souls in eternity and to help them to overcome the grim perils of the afterlife, where demons and evil spirits abounded and the bureaucrats of the Celestial Deity waited with records of their earthly deeds and misdeeds.

Prince Liu Sheng was the son of Jingdi, one of the early emperors of the Han dynasty who had seized the imperial throne in 206 BC. Liu Sheng was appointed ruler of the kingdom of Zhongshan in northern China, one of the ancient states that now formed part of the Han Empire. He and his wife, Dou Wan, were determined that they should enjoy eternal life. They had magnificent tombs constructed at Mancheng, not in the normal style of wooden underground chambers but cut straight into the hillside 50 metres (165 feet) deep, drawing permanence for themselves from the enduring qualities of the stone.

The tombs were laid out as if they were palaces for life. On either side of the entrance were long, narrow stables and storerooms. Four magnificent chariots, complete with splendid horses, were installed in the stable block of Liu Sheng's tomb and two more placed in the passage. On the right side, a great quantity of food and wine was stored along with other domestic objects. The passage opened out into a central chamber in which stood a wooden hall with a tiled roof. Two tents were set up here in which the dead prince could hold banquets and conduct religious rites. His private apartment lay behind, built within the rock-cut cave out of closely fitting stone slabs and sealed by a white marble door. Stone figures of servants waited to do the prince's bidding.

Dou Wan's tomb was similarly laid out and furnished. The couple's private chambers were filled with their prized possessions, ready for their use. Bronze wine vessels inlaid with gold and silver were among their treasures – one in Liu Sheng's tomb bore an inscription encouraging him to eat and grow

ABOVE: These two exquisite gilded bronze leopards were used as weights to hold down the edges of the funeral pall in Liu Sheng's tomb. Lesser individuals had jade pigs as weights.

BELOW: The "Jade Princess", Dou Wan, was laid with her head resting on a beautiful pillow of gilded bronze, with ends in the form of deer's heads.

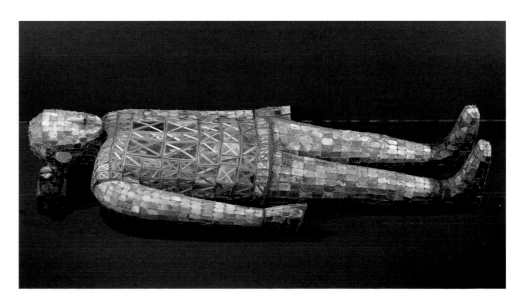

fat, that he might live long in good health. Silver and gold acupuncture needles were present, to treat any ailments. Exquisite gilded bronze ornaments included a pair of leopards in Liu Sheng's tomb.

The prince and his consort occupied the centre of these chambers, enclosed within a wooden coffin and lying on a white marble bed. Each was encased from head to foot in a suit of the preserving jade. Craftsmen had worked for as much as 10 years to produce the suits, laboriously piecing them together from more than 2,500 specially shaped plaques of jade. The plaques were fastened together with gold wire at each corner – that used in Dou Wan's suit weighed 680 grams (24 ounces) in all. The suits were constructed in pieces to make it easy to put them on when death came upon the prince (in 113 BC) and princess – feet, legs, body front and back, sleeves, gloves, helmet and face mask.

Sealed within their jade suits, Liu Sheng and Dou Wan hoped their bodies would last for ever. To make doubly sure, they also had the tombs sealed – rubble was piled against the sealed door and the openings filled with iron. But it was all in vain – in 1968, when the tombs were accidentally discovered, all that remained of the jade prince and princess themselves were a handful of dust and a broken tooth.

Lady Dai

In contrast, the body of a lady who died some 50 years earlier was miraculously preserved with much less effort. She was the wife of the Marquis of Dai, a Han nobleman in the kingdom of Changsha. Wrapped in 20 layers of brocade, her body was laid to rest inside a nest of lacquered coffins placed in a wooden chamber which was carefully sealed within layers of charcoal and clay. As

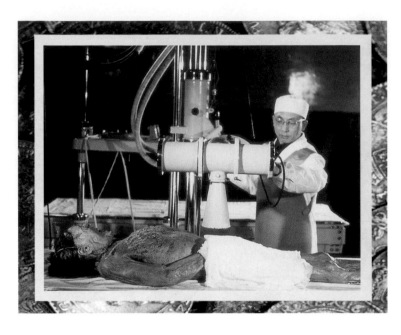

ABOVE: Radiography and other sophisticated modern scientific techniques have been used to reveal details of Lady Dai's health and diet and the cause of her death.

this arrangement meant that her tomb was airtight, her body survived so well that when she was discovered her skin was still supple, her long black hair was still carefully arranged and it proved possible to conduct an autopsy on her. The cause of her death? Lady Dai had been fond of her food and was rather overweight; she also suffered from gallstones and lumbago. Shortly after eating a musk melon she had a heart attack which carried her off at the age of about 50.

The funerary mound at Mawangdui that covers her tomb is one of many in the area, most of which have been plundered. The vast size of this mound had daunted grave robbers, however, and it was not until a hospital began to be constructed on the site that the mound was disturbed, revealing the grave shafts of three burials. When these were excavated in 1974 they proved to contain the bodies of Li Cang, Marquis of Dai, who died in 186 BC, his wife and one of their sons. The inventory of grave goods that always accompanied burials, for the use of the other world's officials, showed that the son had died in 168 BC. Lady Dai had

outlived both of them, for she was buried last.

A great household of 162 model servants accompanied Lady Dai, carved from peachwood, painted or dressed in silk. Some were attendants but others were entertainers – dancers and musicians with their instruments: pipes, zithers and mouth organs. Real instruments were also included among the grave offerings. The tomb was packed with other valuables belonging to the lady – bales of silk cloth, rich clothing, including silk slippers and colourful robes, bronze mirrors and tin bells. She was very well supplied with food of all kinds and with herbal remedies for heart disease.

A huge array of lacquerware was also stacked in several compartments of her tomb. Lacquer was extremely expensive, costing 10 times as much as bronze, so it was only wealthy and important people who took it with them into the grave. Lady Dai had containers and ladles for serving food, dishes, cups and bowls, spoons and chopsticks for eating and drinking, boxes, trays, and many other household objects of the beautiful lacquerware, finely decorated in black. Some of the bowls bear an inscription inviting the user to drink wine from them. One lacquer box contained a vanity set including combs and brushes, powder, a cosmetic mirror and a hairpiece.

Lady Dai's coffins were also of lacquered wood, some plain and some decorated. A silk banner covered the innermost coffin, its decoration depicting the lady's journey to the other world. In the bottom register her grieving family is shown offering sacrifices beside her bier, while below lurk the monsters of the underworld. In the centre of the banner she is seen supporting herself on a stick, flanked by phoenixes waiting to escort her to the celestial realms depicted in the upper register.

Lady Dai's vanity box had two compartments. The lower one contained nine small boxes with cosmetics, comb, brushes and other toilet equipment, while the upper half could hold clothing accessories such as gloves.

ROYAL TOMBS OF KOREA

The Three Kingdoms

The martial emperor Wu Di greatly expanded the Han Chinese state. Among the areas he conquered was northern Korea, where in 108 BC the Han established four provinces or commanderies. The Koreans proved troublesome subjects and only one province, the Lelang, survived for long. Chinese power in Korea finally came to an end in AD 313, a time when native tribes had begun to coalesce into three states, frequently at war with each other. Koguryo in the north was strongly influenced by China. Paekche in the southwest had links with Japan and the lands to the south. Shilla in the south-east was separated from Paekche by Kaya, an area of autonomous city states, which it gradually swallowed up by military conquest. Joining

forces with the Chinese, Shilla then defeated Paekche in AD 663 and Koguryo in 668.

All three kingdoms had a very marked social hierarchy, from poor peasants up to godlike kings. Prosperous agriculture and industries at home and profitable overseas trade brought great wealth to the kingdoms, which found expression in the lavish furnishings of the royal tombs. In Koguryo, the tombs were built of cut stones in the shape of square-based pyramids. The majority were plundered in the past but the fine paintings that decorated their walls still survive, giving a vivid picture of all aspects of life in the Koguryo state. Occasionally the looters missed a few objects, gold and gilded bronze ornaments which give a hint of the richness of the original grave offerings.

In Paekche, tomb robbers were similarly active and many burial mounds also suffered at the hands of the Chinese and Shilla conquerors in 663, who burned and looted extensively. By chance, however, the tomb of

King Munyong near the one-time Paekche capital, Kongju, survived intact and was discovered by accident when repair work was taking place on a neighbouring painted tomb. Built of grey bricks decorated with lotuses, it had an entrance tunnel leading to a barrel-vaulted chamber. A carved stone animal guarded the burials. White porcelain from Liang and other Chinese imports filled the tomb, surrounding two lacquered coffins. One contained the burial of Munyong, who died in AD 523, while the other was that of his queen, who outlived him by three years. Of the royal pair nothing survived except two teeth, but their grave goods were magnificent.

Both king and queen wore a golden crown, an upright cut-out sheet looking like a tree in flower. Holes in the 'trunk' were used to attach the crown to a cap. Wooden pillows decorated with gold were provided for their head and feet and both wore bronze shoes. The king wore a silver belt and a

sword, and the royal couple were both richly provided with jewellery, including a gold hairpin, silver bracelets, a belt with a silver pendant, gold earrings and jade beads.

Splendours of Shilla

Unlike those of their neighbours, the tombs of Shilla's royalty, built around Kyongju, were strongly protected against robbers. The remains of the royal dead were buried in a chamber cut into the ground or built of wood at ground level. The chamber was then completely covered with large cobbles set in clay and a vast earthen mound was erected over it. One of the most impressive mounds, excavated in recent years, contained two royal graves. The southern grave was that of a king, buried wearing a gilded bronze crown. A sacrificed girl had been thrown

ABOVE: At least 10 magnificent gold crowns have been found in Shilla tombs. All are variations on the same theme – a circle of gold supporting sheet gold uprights and dangling gold and jade ornaments.

LEFT: Vast earthen mounds were constructed over cairns of cobbles to protect the élite tombs around the Shilla capital at Kyongju. More than 155 are known here and many exist elsewhere in Shilla.

down beside the chamber. A separate chamber adjacent to the king's burial was filled with an enormous number of iron weapons and pots as well as four glass vessels imported from China and the West. Shilla, which

exported gold, probably traded with the west by both land and sea.

The northern chamber was much more splendidly furnished, indicating that the lady buried here had ruled in her own right alongside the king – ruling queens are known from Shilla history, although this particular queen is not mentioned. She was decked in a magnificent crown of sheet gold. This followed the usual form for Shilla gold crowns, being made of a gold band supporting uprights in the shape of stylized trees. Gold spangles and jade gokoks (comma-shaped beads) fastened with gold wire decorated it. The queen also wore a massive golden belt with dangling pendants. This too is a type of ornament found in several of the remarkable Shilla royal tombs, of which a number have now been investigated.

TANG AND MING TREASURES

Concealed in haste

The Tang dynasty, who seized the Chinese imperial throne in AD 618, was instrumental in securing Shilla's victory over its rivals in Korea in 668, but was unable to consolidate its own position there. Nevertheless, the Tang state controlled a huge empire, its influence extending to the western end of Central Asia and into southern China and Manchuria, bringing it into trading contact with the states of West Asia and South-East Asia. The empire enjoyed its greatest glory under the emperor Xuanzong, who reigned from AD 712 to 756.

Love brought about the emperor's downfall. He became enamoured of Yang Guifei, a young woman who had been the consort of one of his sons.

In his besotted state, he bestowed positions of power on her relatives. One of the emperor's generals, An-Lushan, fearing his own position threatened, rebelled in 755 and the emperor was forced to flee his capital. To his anguish and shame, he was also forced by his troops to execute his beautiful paramour.

As the court fled, many nobles and members of the imperial household must have hidden their valuables. Although the Tang dynasty was eventually restored, some members did not return to retrieve their treasures. It was probably one such abandoned hoard that was discovered in 1970 in Hejia, a suburb of the Tang capital Chang'an, in a mansion that had belonged to the family of the emperor's cousin. Two large pottery jars and a silver vessel between them contained more than 1,000 pieces of treasure.

These included a handful of foreign silver coins – Sassanian, Byzantine and Japanese – reflecting the extensive overseas contacts of the Tang. A vase of fine stone onyx was probably imported from the Sassanian Empire and many of the silver vessels, although made in China, recall Sassanian art

ABOVE: Trade along the Silk Road brought Tang China many imported luxury goods from the West. Particularly important was fine Sassanian silverware, the styles of which influenced Chinese art and craftsmanship.

RIGHT: Huge stone statues, including elephants, which played an important ceremonial role, line the Spirit Way leading to the Ming imperial cemetery.

in their decoration and form. A gold pedestalled bowl reflects the two traditions, with a background dotted with flowers and leaves in western style, combined with a lotus-flower form and animal designs which are purely Chinese. Peonies were a craze of the court at Chang'an at this time, and a number of the silver bowls bore a scroll decoration of these flowers.

Imperial cemetery

The Ming dynasty was founded in 1368 after a period of civil war in China. Continuing troubles from nomads along the northern border led the Ming emperors to strengthen and rebuild the Great Wall and the third emperor, Yongle, moved the capital to Beijing, closer to the north than the previous capital, Nanjing.

Forty-five kilometres (28 miles) from the new capital, Yongle had a vast funerary complex laid out in a carefully chosen valley. A great processional road, the Spirit Way, was constructed, lined on either side by huge stone figures of guardian warriors, mythical beasts, elephants and camels. Passing through a series of monumental gates, the Spirit Way led up to the Phoenix and Dragon Gate, set across the road to prevent malevolent spirits (which, it was believed, could fly only in straight lines) from penetrating the sacred necropolis beyond.

Thirteen emperors were laid to rest here. Each was buried within a massive tomb under a gigantic tumulus set at the end of a series of courtyards containing ceremonial buildings. The vast scale of the tombs deterred archaeologists from excavating them until the mid-twentieth century when Dingling ("tomb of Security"), the tomb of Wanli, was investigated.

Splendid mausoleum of an unworthy emperor

Wanli was just a boy when he came to the throne in 1572 and for the first 10 years of his reign China prospered under the efficient rule of his minister, Zhang Juzheng. After

the latter's death, however, the weak, extravagant, irresponsible emperor began a regime of self-indulgence and neglect of duty that undermined Ming power. The dynasty collapsed in 1644, 24 years after Wanli's death.

Wanli began construction of his tomb in 1584. Employing 600,000 men and costing 227,000 kilograms (eight million ounces) of silver, the huge walled precinct with its four courtyards, administrative buildings and pavilions was completed in 1590. Wanli gave a great banquet within the complex to celebrate.

When archaeologists decided to investigate Wanli's tomb in 1956, they were puzzled where to start. A massive wall surrounded the great tumulus – where was the entrance? Selecting a place in the wall where some of the bricks were loose, they struck lucky, for behind these lay the archway of the outer entrance. A tunnel led from here into the mound. Digging out the earth from this passage and passing through an antechamber, the excavators came to a pair of massive doors of white marble, firmly sealed. When they were closed, a mechanism caused a stone pillar to fall in place as a bar locking the doors from the inside. The archaeologists, determined not to damage the doors, discovered they could be opened by inserting a strong but flexible metal rod between them and levering the pillar out of the way.

An outer hall led them to another set of doors, which they opened in the same way. They now found themselves within the sacrificial chamber, gazing at three marble thrones, the central one belonging to the emperor and the other two to his two empresses, who died in 1611 and 1620. All were beautifully decorated, the emperor's with dragons and those of his wives with phoenixes.

At the far end, through another set of marble doors, was the burial chamber itself, in which three coffins were placed, containing the bodies of Wanli and his two empresses. All three were furnished with elaborate headdresses of gold, silver and other precious materials. That of one of the empresses,

ABOVE: A huge porcelain urn stood before each throne in Wanli's tomb. Filled with sesame oil and furnished with a wick, they were intended to light the tomb through eternity.

The Phoenix crown of Empress Xiaoqing was made of brilliant kingfisher feathers, gold, rubies, sapphires, pearls and white stones, over a lacquered bamboo framework. Gold figures of dragons and a phoenix decorate its top.

Xiaoqing, was made of brilliant blue king-fisher feathers and jewels set on a frame of lacquered bamboo and surmounted by gold figures of dragons and a phoenix. Around the coffins were heaped many fine objects of jade, gold, silver and several varieties of porcelain. Silks and brocades were also furnished in abundance. Small personal objects included chopsticks of gold and silver.

SHIPWRECKS OF THE PORCELAIN AND SPICE TRADE

Europe and China face to face

Trade between east and west, bringing silk and spices to Europe and silver to China, had during medieval times been conducted largely along the Silk Road through Central Asia. In the mid-fourteenth century, however, this trade was disrupted by major crises – the spread of bubonic plague, which decimated the population of China, Europe and the Central Asian trading cities, followed immediately by the creation of the short-lived hostile empire of Tamerlane (Timur-leng) in Iran and western Central Asia. The Ottoman conquest of the eastern Mediterranean in the fourteenth and fifteenth centuries brought to a close the flourishing trade through these regions.

The nations of Atlantic Europe began in the fifteenth century to look for other ways to gain access to the riches of the Orient, intrepidly exploring the unknown seas and lands to both their east and west. In 1497–8 the Portuguese navigator Vasco da Gama succeeded in sail-ing round the Cape of Good Hope and reaching India, and by 1555 the Portuguese had established trading stations throughout the east, on the coasts of India, southern China and the islands of the East Indies, as well as Africa. Throughout the sixteenth century they monopolized the spice trade, allowing other nationals to trade only under licence from them. By 1600, however, they were facing competition from the Dutch and English and domestic troubles led to the decline of their international importance.

The Dutch and English now battled for control of the east, the Dutch rapidly gaining dominance in the East Indies and Sri Lanka (Ceylon) while the English established the "factories" that marked the beginnings of their trading empire in India. Here they soon faced competition from the French, but France's repeated defeats in European wars prevented her consolidating her toeholds in India. Although the Dutch monopolized trade with the East Indies, England was able to use India as a base from which to trade with China, exchanging Indian silver and opium for Chinese silk, tea and porcelain and acquiring spices and cotton cloth from India itself.

BELOW: Some of the gold ingots salvaged near the wreck of the *Geldermalsen* were cast in the shape of a Chinese lady's shoe. Each weighed around 370 grams (13 ounces).

The perils of the deep

Ships plying the sea routes between Atlantic Europe and the east faced many hazards. Scurvy, caused by lack of vitamin C, decimated crews and it was not until the late eighteenth century that it could be prevented by issuing sailors with regular rations of lime juice. Other illnesses were also rife and ship-board accidents were common in bad weather. It was not unusual for a ship from the Netherlands to have lost half its crew by the time it put in at the Cape of Good Hope, the midpoint of its journey to the East Indies.

Storms and rough seas presented a constant and unpredictable risk. The determination of the ship's location was still largely dependent on dead reckoning from the position of the midday sun and bad weather could quickly put out the captain's calculations, allowing the ship to run on to known reefs and rocks. In addition, often the maritime regions through which the ships sailed were poorly known and inadequately charted. A southern continent was for centuries believed to exist, on the grounds that this gave symmetry to the world, but it was not until the early seventeenth century that Europeans first set eyes on the shores of Australia and its outline was not fully established until Cook's expeditions in the 1760s and 1770s. Even what had been discovered and charted could be distorted – captains whose ships ran aground through carelessness were not above charting dangerous shores and rocks in the wrong place, to cover up their mistakes in navigation.

And there were human dangers too. Nations at war considered it perfectly proper to seize one another's merchant ships and cargoes. The VOC (Vereenigde Oost-Indische Compagnie, or Dutch East India Company) ship *Witte Leeuw*, for example, was wrecked in a sea battle with the Portuguese off Africa (see p.21). European traders could get caught up in local

RIGHT: A Chinese junk wrecked off Vietnam around 1690 was rediscovered in the 1980s. Its cargo included a rich collection of porcelain vessels destined for the Dutch domestic market.

hostilities between native princelings and might have their ships confiscated or sunk. Pirates abounded, both European buccaneers on the high seas and native pirates in East Indian waters and the China Seas. Nevertheless, there were fortunes to be made from successful voyages and the trade generally prospered.

The *Geldermalsen*

Batavia (modern Jakarta) was the centre of Dutch trade in the east. From here, agents of the VOC shipped spices from the East Indies and porcelain from China. The spices were paid for with gold, silver and manufactured goods brought out from Europe. Gold was cheaper in China than elsewhere in the east, so ships carrying porcelain from China often also brought back gold to be used in East Indies trade.

By the eighteenth century, tea, which was in great demand in Europe, had become one of China's most valuable exports. English ships loaded tea in Chinese ports and sailed home directly, whereas Dutch shipments of tea, porcelain and gold were taken first to Batavia, where the gold was unloaded for local use. This meant that tea shipped by the English arrived sooner and was fresher. So the Dutch made a new arrangement. Instead of calling at Batavia, their ships were to take the direct route home, unloading the gold on

to waiting smaller ships when they passed through the Sunda Straits.

On December 18, 1751, the VOC ship *Geldermalsen* began her journey along this route from Guangzhou (Canton) in China, where she had been loaded with a valuable cargo of 311 tonnes (306 tons) of tea, along with 147 gold bars each worth about 365 Dutch guilders and about 235,000 pieces of porcelain, mostly mass-produced wares that were popular with the Dutch middle classes.

Various hazards lay along the route and on the sixteenth day the captain, Jan Morel,

was expecting to sight a dangerous reef. Assured by his boatswain, Christoffel Van Dijk, that they had already passed it, the captain altered his course to sail south. Van Dijk was mistaken, however, and as dusk fell, some three hours later, the ship crashed on to the reef.

All was chaos and confusion. The crew succeeded in refloating the ship but she was badly holed and as night came on she began to sink. Someone attempted to salvage the gold bars, but they were lost in the sea. Men piled into the *Geldermalsen*'s two boats but, when only 32 were aboard, the boats came adrift, leaving the remaining two-thirds of the crew to drown. The survivors reached Batavia 10 days later but the VOC did not salvage the lost ship.

The "Nanking Cargo"

For more than two centuries the *Geldermalsen* lay undisturbed. In the early 1980s a salvage diver, Mike Hatcher, was working on a Chinese junk wrecked on the Admiral Stellingwerf Reef, east of the Indonesian island of Bintan, and located a VOC wreck nearby. From 1985 Hatcher and his partner Max De Rham turned their attention to this wreck, from which they recovered a large quantity of porcelain packed in wooden crates. Most of this consisted of dinner services and tea sets, along with a number of figurines, all made to VOC specifications. In the centre of the wreck the salvors found the private baggage of the wealthy passengers and company officials, including finer pieces of porcelain that they had hoped to trade on their own account. In the last days of the salvage operation, exploration outside the wreck revealed the lost gold bars – or at least, 126 of them. Auctioned at Christie's in 1986 as the "Nanking Cargo" – for the ship's identity was not at first established – the material salvaged from the *Geldermalsen* fetched a record price. It is curious to reflect that the porcelain now so highly prized was only five per cent of the value of what the ship was carrying, while its precious cargo of tea would now be worth relatively little even if it had survived 200 years in the sea.

The Sinan wreck

For many centuries before the arrival of European traders, China had been active in overseas trade. Under the outward-looking Sung dynasty, which ruled from the eleventh to the thirteenth century, they traded with Japan, where Chinese porcelain and celadon pottery were in great demand, with Korea, itself a major producer of fine pottery, and with other lands as far away as East Africa. Between 1405 and 1433 the great Chinese admiral Zheng He sailed with a fleet of more than 200 ships throughout the eastern seas and further west, consolidating links with East Africa, Arabia and India and bringing back many exotic goods, including a giraffe, and the king of Sri Lanka.

In 1975 fishermen trawling between two islands off the south-west Korean coast discovered Chinese pottery in their nets. Some of their number, recognizing that they must have disturbed an ancient wreck, alerted the authorities, who paid the fishermen the value of their finds and mounted a major rescue operation. The location was particularly difficult to work in, owing to the swirling mud and icy waters, but the wreck proved well worth the effort. The ship, a Chinese vessel, had left its home port of Ningbo (near Shanghai) in 1323, loaded with fine green celadon and white porcelain, destined for Japan, and had called in at a Korean port where it had taken on some locally made celadon. Continuing its journey, it had met with some unknown disaster, perhaps a storm, and had sunk. The muddy seabed had soon swallowed it up, preserving its timbers. Its excavators were able to recover virtually the whole vessel intact, and it has now been reconstructed in the Korean National Maritime Museum at Mokp'o.

The cargo too was intact – 28.4 tonnes (28 tons) of Chinese copper coins and numerous other metal objects, a large quantity of sandalwood and 20,000 pieces of pottery, packed in peppercorns to cushion them, inside the wooden cases that still bear the Chinese inscription "great luck". However, it was the archaeologists, not the merchants, whose great luck it became.

ABOVE: Great care had to be taken while lifting the cases of porcelain from the *Geldermalsen*.

BELOW: Many fine celadon vessels were recovered from the Sinan wreck. This pottery was a special variety of stoneware, with an iron-oxide glaze that gave it a generally green colour.

REDISCOVERING THE WRECKS OF MODERN TREASURE SHIPS

ABOVE: The Battle of Tsushima Strait was a resounding victory for the Japanese, who captured or destroyed almost all the Russian fleet, at the cost of only three vessels of their own.

The *Admiral Nakhimov*

Ownership of wrecks can be a vexed question. Sometimes it is possible to settle it amicably. For example, in 1972 the Dutch government transferred to the Australian government its rights to VOC ships wrecked off Australia. Frequently, however, disputed ownership can bring about serious problems and even diplomatic troubles between nations. Such was the case of the *Admiral Nakhimov*.

In 1904 the Japanese took exception to Russia's activities in the Far East. These had been building up over several decades and included the construction of Russia's Pacific port of Vladivostok, the linking of this with Moscow by building the Trans-Siberian railway, Russia's treaty relations with China and finally its annexation of Manchuria in 1900. The Japanese therefore broke off diplomatic relations and on February 10 declared war. The Russian authorities were not averse to a war at this time, hoping to distract the atten-

tion of the swelling ranks of dissidents from the serious domestic problems that led ultimately to the Russian Revolution in 1917.

As an attempt to rouse patriotic feelings by winning easy glory the Russo-Japanese War was a complete failure, for the Russians were heavily defeated. After war was declared, they moved their Baltic fleet of 38 ships to Vladivostok and thence proceeded south toward Japan. Among the fleet was the cruiser *Admiral Nakhimov*, apparently carrying a cargo of $53 million in gold. Reaching Japanese territorial waters at Tsushima Island, the fleet was attacked by the Japanese and soundly beaten. In the battle the *Admiral Nakhimov* was hit by a torpedo and severely damaged. Attempts to save her failed, so her commander, Rear-Admiral Nebogatoff, ordered that her sea-valves be opened to ensure that she sank quickly.

Disputed ownership

Several attempts were made by the Japanese to salvage the great treasure between 1938 and 1954. The Shintiki Deep Diving

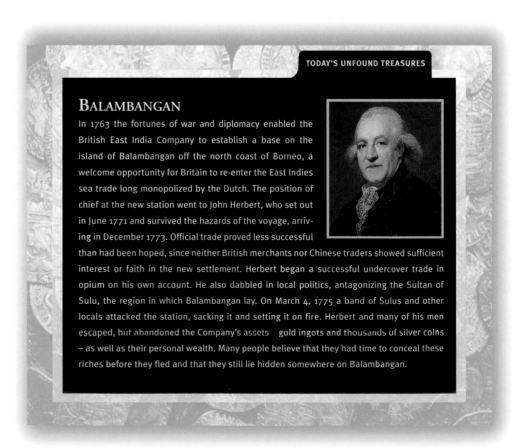

BALAMBANGAN

In 1763 the fortunes of war and diplomacy enabled the British East India Company to establish a base on the island of Balambangan off the north coast of Borneo, a welcome opportunity for Britain to re-enter the East Indies sea trade long monopolized by the Dutch. The position of chief at the new station went to John Herbert, who set out in June 1771 and survived the hazards of the voyage, arriving in December 1773. Official trade proved less successful than had been hoped, since neither British merchants nor Chinese traders showed sufficient interest or faith in the new settlement. Herbert began a successful undercover trade in opium on his own account. He also dabbled in local politics, antagonizing the Sultan of Sulu, the region in which Balambangan lay. On March 4, 1775 a band of Sulus and other locals attacked the station, sacking it and setting it on fire. Herbert and many of his men escaped, but abandoned the Company's assets – gold ingots and thousands of silver coins – as well as their personal wealth. Many people believe that they had time to conceal these riches before they fled and that they still lie hidden somewhere on Balambangan.

Research Institute dived to the wreck and cut into it using small charges of explosives. They eventually abandoned their operations for lack of funds. A new attempt was made in 1980 by the Nippon Marine Development salvage company and this time the Russians made a fuss. They filed a claim to the ownership of the wreck, which they said had been sunk by its commander, not by the enemy. The question of ownership hinges upon this point, for if the Japanese had captured or sunk the ship, international law says that it would have become a legitimate war prize and therefore Japanese property. Since it was a Japanese torpedo that caused the damage that led to the *Admiral Nakhimov*'s sinking by her commander, the issue was not clear-cut. Nevertheless, the Japanese went ahead and started salvaging the gold, raising the first ingot in September 1981.

War gold

After Germany invaded Russia in 1941, Britain and the USA agreed to supply Russia with military equipment such as tanks and aircraft. These were conveyed by sea through the Arctic Ocean, from Reykjavik in Iceland to the Russian port of Murmansk. The journey through the Arctic seas was not an easy one, but British convoys successfully supplied the Russians until early 1942. At this point the Germans, who had occupied Norway, began seriously to attack the convoys, causing considerable losses. Despite this onslaught, the vital supplies continued to be sent.

In April 1942 the cruiser HMS *Edinburgh* escorted a convoy of 33 merchant ships, minesweepers and destroyers to Murmansk. Some ships were lost or damaged en route but the majority arrived safely. On April 28 the *Edinburgh* set off on her return journey, escorting 13 merchantmen and carrying a valuable cargo – 5.1 tonnes

ABOVE: Despite the immense difficulties of the salvage, Keith Jessop and his team raised the first gold bars from the *Edinburgh* on September 21, 1981, to their great excitement and satisfaction.

(5 tons) of Russian gold then worth £45 million, which was stowed in the bomb rooms. Unfortunately, the convoy was spotted by German reconnaissance planes and on April 30 was attacked by German destroyers and submarines.

The *Edinburgh* was hit in two places by torpedoes fired by the German submarines. Although the British cruiser managed to sink one of her attackers, the destroyer *Hermann Schoemann*, she was seriously maimed and the captain, Hugh Faulkner, gave the order to abandon ship. Once aboard the minesweeper *Harrier*, he gave orders for the *Edinburgh* to be torpedoed and sunk, to prevent her cargo falling into enemy hands.

Salvage from the icy waters

The *Edinburgh* now lay in 244 metres (800 feet) of freezing Arctic water. A salvage company, Risdon-Beazley, gave serious consideration to her recovery in 1954, but the

difficulties seemed insuperable. By 1980, however, many technical advances in reconnaissance and diving technology had taken place and the salvage of the *Edinburgh* no longer seemed impossible, although it was still a daunting task. Several companies put forward bids to undertake her recovery and the contract was awarded to Jessop Marine Recoveries Ltd, who undertook to cut into the wreck – a more fitting way to deal with the ship, which had been designated an official war grave in 1957, than other proposals to use explosives to penetrate the wreck.

Negotiations between Jessop and the British and Russian governments resulted in a formal agreement that the proceeds of the recovery should be split in the proportions 45 per cent to the salvors, who undertook all the labour and expense of the recovery, two-thirds of the remaining 55 per cent to the owners of the gold, the Russians, and the rest to the British, who had undertaken the risk of carrying it in 1942.

The first task was to locate the wreck precisely. A survey ship, the *Dammator*, used sidescanning sonar to search the area in which the naval action had taken place and detected a large wreck. Was it the *Edinburgh* or the German destroyer that she had sunk? A remote-controlled robot was used to investigate the wreck, which proved to be the *Edinburgh*. Next a fully equipped salvage vessel was brought in.

The task was not an easy one. Not only were the divers working in Arctic conditions – they wore special suits heated with hot water which occasionally scalded them – but they were also attempting to salvage the gold from a room in which active bombs were also stored. Their heroic efforts resulted in the recovery of 431 gold bars, but the remaining 34 had to be abandoned when bad weather closed in.

Rapid

Zuytdorp

Batavia

Vergulde Draeck

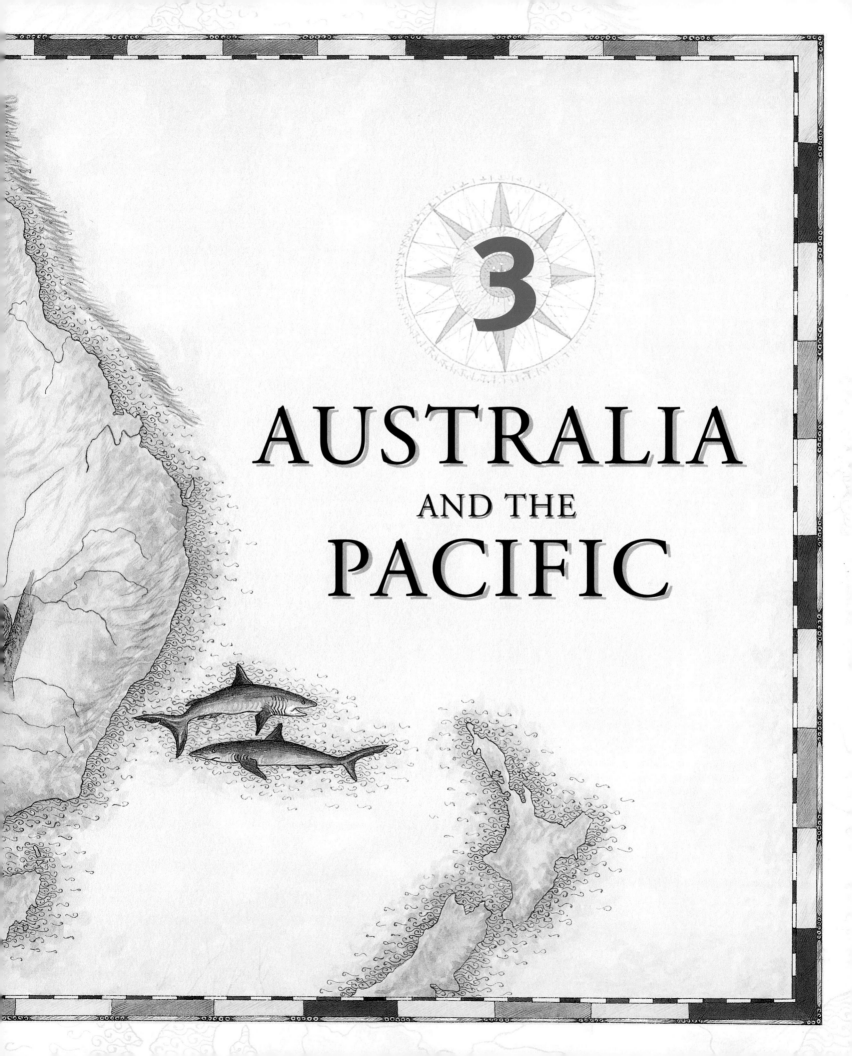

3

AUSTRALIA
AND THE
PACIFIC

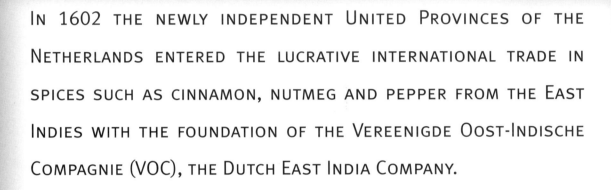

In 1602 the newly independent United Provinces of the Netherlands entered the lucrative international trade in spices such as cinnamon, nutmeg and pepper from the East Indies with the foundation of the Vereenigde Oost-Indische Compagnie (VOC), the Dutch East India Company.

THE BATAVIA

Wreck of hopes

Dutch navigational and military skill, combined with ruthlessness, soon brought the VOC marked success in the cut-throat competition with its Portuguese rivals, who had long held a virtual monopoly in this trade, and with the English, who were also newly entering the market. In 1619 the VOC established a fortified base for this trade at Batavia (modern Jakarta) on Java and, when the company launched the first of its new, larger trading ships in 1628, it named the vessel after this prospering trade "factory".

The *Batavia* set sail gloriously on October 29 in consort with seven other vessels, but already all was not well. Her captain, Adriaen Jacobsz, a coarse and violent individual though a good seaman, had quarrelled in the past with the Commander of the whole convoy, Francisco Pelsaert, and ill feeling between them flared up repeatedly. Soon a terrible storm scattered the convoy and the *Batavia* reached the Cape of Good Hope in company with only two other ships, from which further misfortunes soon separated her. Pelsaert was in poor health, keep-

ing to his cabin for much of the voyage, and discipline on the ship became lax. One of the passengers, a beautiful married lady called Lucretia van den Mylen, sailing to Batavia to join her husband, was assaulted.

The ship was following a sea route pioneered a few years earlier by Hendrik de Brouwer which ran east from the Cape of Good Hope as far as the recently discovered and little-known coast of Australia before turning to sail north to Java. Seamen were aware that treacherous rocks and coral reefs lay along the shores of this continent, but their location had barely begun to be charted. Jacobsz and his crew therefore kept a close watch out for these hazards. On the morning of June 4, 1629, however, they believed from their calculations that they were still well to the west of Australia's shores and were not troubled by what seemed to be the moon's reflection on the sea – but which was in reality surf from low breakers. Suddenly the ship shook violently and ground against some obstruction – she had struck on Morning Reef, one of the northern group of islands in the Houtman Albolhos, an archipelago so low-lying that it was virtually invisible.

ABOVE: These tastefully decorated silver vessels were among the luxury goods that the VOC hoped to sell in India to the Mogul emperor and wealthy courtiers.

It soon became clear that there was no chance of refloating the ship. In panic, the passengers fought for a place in the longboat while unruly members of the crew broke open the liquor store and got deliriously drunk. Those who could took refuge on tiny Beacon Island near the site of the wreck – an island that was to acquire the sinister nickname "*Batavia*'s Graveyard". Some food and water were salvaged from the wreck before she broke up and sank but it was obvious these would not last long. Pelsaert and Jacobsz, with about 40 others, set off in the ship's boat in search of water. Finding none on the islands to the north or on the coast of mainland Australia, they carried on, hoping desperately that they would reach the town of Batavia. On June 27 they sighted land – the island of Nusa Kambangan in Java, where to their immense relief they were

able to moisten their parched throats with fresh water. They finally reached Batavia, ill and exhausted, on July 7. On the 15th Pelsaert set out again on another VOC vessel, the *Zaandam*, to attempt to rescue the people he had left and the VOC's treasure.

Cornelisz the monster

On Beacon Island things had been going from bad to worse. The ship's supercargo, Jeronimus Cornelisz, the most senior man remaining there, seized control and set about reducing the number of survivors in order to eke out the remaining provisions. First he enlisted the support of 36 disreputable and conscienceless soldiers and members of the crew, who took an oath to obey him. He then got rid of most of the loyal soldiers by sending them off in the longboat, without their weapons and under the command of Wiebbe Hayes, to search for water. The remaining soldiers he dispatched on rafts with his own followers, who systematically drowned them. He induced 45 of the

survivors to transfer to Seal Island, an inhospitable ribbon of coral, where he left them to die of starvation. Other survivors he murdered individually, sparing some of the women to become concubines. He himself seized the hapless Lucretia van den Mylen.

Against all odds, however, Wiebbe Hayes and his men had found both food and water, on the substantial West Wallabi Island further to the west. They signalled their discovery with beacon fires – at first, to their surprise, no one came, but eventually they were joined by a handful of resourceful individuals who had managed to escape Cornelisz. Hearing the grim news of the murders, Hayes set about fortifying and defending his position. None too soon, for Cornelisz and his followers had determined to wipe them out, on the principle that dead men tell no tales. Battle was joined on July 27, Hayes and his party raining stones on their attackers. Several men were killed, Cornelisz was captured and the mutineers withdrew.

They renewed their attack on September 17 but were again beaten off. By a miraculous coincidence, the *Zaandam*, its progress having been slowed by bad weather, now appeared off West Wallabi and Hayes managed to reach the ship first, bringing news of the dreadful situation. The mutineers now also arrived, in the guise of peaceful survivors, secretly intending to seize the ship, but being forewarned, the crew of the *Zaandam* quickly overpowered them. Sailing on to Beacon Island, the ship rescued the few pitiful survivors of the mutineers' murderous activities – 125 had perished at their hands. Skilled divers from Gujarat were put to work on the wreck, from which they salvaged the bulk of the precious cargo. Pelsaert conducted an investigation, with torture, of Cornelisz and his henchmen – each blamed the others but enough evidence was gathered to convict and execute Cornelisz and six of the ringleaders. Almost all of the others were executed when the *Zaandam* returned to Batavia.

The lost wreck

Much of the *Batavia*'s valuable cargo was taken off in the first days after she struck the reef. Divers from the *Zaandam* recovered most of the rest after she sank, including three casks of cochineal, a red dye that was valued almost as highly as silver, and many of the money chests. The *Batavia* had been carrying 12 of these, containing in total 250,000 silver guilders, and 10 were recovered. One other chest lay pinned down by a cannon while the twelfth had been opened and its contents scattered by the drunken sailors shortly after the *Batavia* was wrecked. The ship had also been carrying a silver dinner service belonging to Pelsaert and this too was not recovered by the *Zaandam* divers. Pelsaert died the following year, and within a few years the VOC abandoned hope of recovering anything more from the wreck.

Knowledge of the western Australian coast and its hazards became better and more detailed as the centuries passed, but the vague grasp of its geography in earlier times had led people to believe that the *Batavia* had been wrecked on the southern group of islands in the Houtman Albrolhos archipelago, which they named the Pelsaert Group. Searches around these islands, of course, failed to reveal the wreck of the *Batavia*, although they did yield that of another VOC ship, the *Zeewiijk*, wrecked there in 1727 and largely salvaged by its survivors.

One scholar, however, the historian Henrietta Drake-Brockman, was convinced that the search was being undertaken in the wrong place. Having exhaustively studied both Pelsaert's journal and other contemporary accounts of the wreck and its aftermath, she argued that the northern group of islands had been the scene of the disaster. In 1960, however, a small investigation around the Wallabi Islands by the journalist Hugh Edwards and the underwater photographer Maurie Hammond yielded no trace of the *Batavia* and her crew, so Drake-Brockman's theory was still unproven.

In 1963 the group that had explored the *Zeewiijk* turned their attention to the northern islands, where Drake-Brockman's work had convinced them that the wreck should lie. Max Cramer, a member of the group who lived nearby in Geraldton, on the mainland, began a systematic search on the islands for traces of the survivors of the wreck. A lobster fisherman on Beacon Island, Dave Johnson, showed Cramer and his colleagues a skeleton that that been discovered locally, which they saw, with excitement, had a broken neck and a musket shot in the ribs. Was it one of Cornelisz's victims? Undoubtedly so, for as soon as Johnson learned that they were searching for traces of the *Batavia*, he was able to show them the wreck itself – he had noticed it three years earlier but hadn't realized that it was of any interest except as a source of scrap metal.

The *Batavia* yields her secrets

With considerable effort and great ingenuity, Cramer, his brother and another diver, Greg Allen, recovered a cannon from the site. The date and VOC seal engraved on it left no doubt that the *Batavia* had been found. A full-scale expedition was mounted, with army and navy support, and detailed investigation of the wreck began. More cannon were raised, along with many everyday objects such as earthenware jars that had originally held spirits. Some coins were also found. Hugh Edwards and others became involved too, exploring the islands and uncovering the remains of the camps where Wiebbe Hayes and his companions had lived and fought off the mutineers' attacks. In the wake of the great public interest generated by the discovery of the *Batavia*, in 1964 the Australian government passed a law to give protection to this and other historic wrecks. Later laws strengthened this protection. Nowadays the public are encouraged to visit and explore these wrecks but are forbidden to damage them or remove objects from them.

Who owns wrecks? In principle a ship continues to be the property of its original owners and their heirs, so the *Batavia* and other VOC ships wrecked off Australia belonged to the Netherlands. In 1972 the

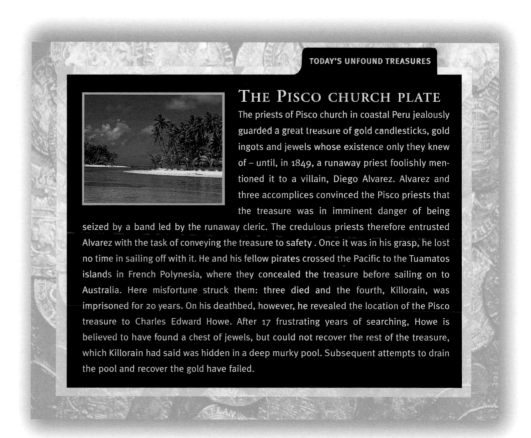

TODAY'S UNFOUND TREASURES

THE PISCO CHURCH PLATE

The priests of Pisco church in coastal Peru jealously guarded a great treasure of gold candlesticks, gold ingots and jewels whose existence only they knew of – until, in 1849, a runaway priest foolishly mentioned it to a villain, Diego Alvarez. Alvarez and three accomplices convinced the Pisco priests that the treasure was in imminent danger of being seized by a band led by the runaway cleric. The credulous priests therefore entrusted Alvarez with the task of conveying the treasure to safety . Once it was in his grasp, he lost no time in sailing off with it. He and his fellow pirates crossed the Pacific to the Tuamatos islands in French Polynesia, where they concealed the treasure before sailing on to Australia. Here misfortune struck them: three died and the fourth, Killorain, was imprisoned for 20 years. On his deathbed, however, he revealed the location of the Pisco treasure to Charles Edward Howe. After 17 frustrating years of searching, Howe is believed to have found a chest of jewels, but could not recover the rest of the treasure, which Killorain had said was hidden in a deep murky pool. Subsequent attempts to drain the pool and recover the gold have failed.

Pelsaert had hoped to trade with eastern potentates, more than 7,000 coins from the two unsalvaged chests, cannons and anchors, as well as many small personal objects such as pewter spoons.

And now the *Batavia* again sails the seas. In the early 1980s a Dutch shipwright, Willem Vos, decided to build a replica of a seventeenth-century trading ship. The idea took off and in 1985 a foundation was established, based at Lelystad in the Netherlands, to construct a replica of the *Batavia*, using traditional techniques and materials (but employing modern tools and equipment). Historical information about the constructional details of VOC ships and of European seventeenth-century vessels in general were complemented by the findings of the Australian archaeologists investigating the wreck, so that the replica could be as faithful a reconstruction of the *Batavia* as possible. In 1999, as the millennium drew to a close, the mammoth task was completed and the new *Batavia* set sail once again for Australia.

OTHER DUTCH TREASURE SHIPS WRECKED OFF AUSTRALIA

A desperate plight

Despite the hazards, most VOC ships sailing along the Brouwer route to Batavia arrived safely. The next major loss was the *Vergulde Draeck* (Golden Dragon), which set sail from Texel in the Netherlands on October 4, 1655 with a crew of 193 men under Captain Pieter Albertsz, and three women passengers. All went well at first and the ship arrived safely at the Cape of Good Hope the following March. Pursuing her journey eastwards, blown by the Roaring Forties and making good progress, she suddenly struck a submerged reef off the western Australian coast

Dutch government transferred its rights over these ships to the Australian government. Scientific documentation and excavation on the wreck and on Beacon Island have continued over the years, with the Western Australia Maritime Museum beginning a major investigation in 1973. More skeletons have been uncovered on Beacon Island, although many more still lie hidden beneath its sandy soil. Much of the *Batavia* had disintegrated during its long sojourn on the seabed but a large section of the hull survived and divers and conservators were able to lift this

in sections and reassemble it in the museum.

They also built a structure that had been planned almost 400 years earlier. The trading station at Batavia had been founded only a decade before the ship's ill-fated voyage and was still under construction. The *Batavia* was carrying the carved and dressed stones to erect a monumental portico in the "Waterpoort", the gateway to the fortified citadel of the town. These stones were recovered from the wreck undamaged and erected in the museum. Here too are others of the *Batavia*'s treasures: silver tableware that

on April 28, 1656 and at once sank.

There was no time to salvage anything from the ship and those who had the misfortune to be below decks at the time were drowned. Albertsz and 74 others struggled ashore. A few provisions were washed up from the wreck and one of the ship's boats survived. The situation was desperate and the captain decided to send the pilot and six volunteers off in the longboat to seek help. Five weeks later the seven exhausted, starving men landed in Batavia.

Despite the unfavourable season – winter with its violent storms was just beginning – two ships were dispatched to rescue the survivors and the cargo, trade goods worth around 100,000 florins and eight chests containing silver coins worth 78,600 florins. The ships were soon blown apart and neither could find any trace of the wreck, despite searching for several months; one ship lost 11 of its crew; and they abandoned the search and returned to Batavia. Two ships were then sent from the Cape of Good Hope but were also unsuccessful; and so was a final expedition in 1658. Traces of wreckage from the ship still lay on the shore, but of the ship's company there was no trace at all.

Rediscovery

In 1931 a boy discovered 40 seventeenth-century Dutch silver coins in the sand dunes of Cape Leschenault but it was not until 1963 that the wreck itself was discovered. Divers over the reef found various objects, including ballast bricks, an elephant tusk, silver coins and a cannon bearing the VOC monogram. These they presented to the Western Australia Maritime Museum, whose staff were able to identify them as coming from the *Vergulde Draeck*. Over the years, divers from the museum have worked on the wreck site, documenting and excavating the surviving remains.

This was a difficult task. On sinking, the ship had broken up very rapidly and its fragments were scattered widely over the reef. They became heavily encrusted and most remains became indistinguishable from the reef on which they had come to rest. Only the ship's

cannon and anchors could easily be made out, marking the site of the wreck. Some portions of the ship, including the captain's cabin with the treasure chests, sank into deeper water. The ravages of nature were exacerbated by the activities of treasure-hunters after the discovery was publicized in 1963 – several had used dynamite to blow up portions of the reef and wreck, in an attempt to get through the encrustation.

Despite these problems, however, the museum's divers were able to recover more than half of the coins and other items from the cargo. Eight boxes of iron bars, welded together by concretions, proved particularly difficult to excavate and raise. Among the other finds were the remains of wooden barrels, associated bones showing them originally to have contained the ship's provisions of salt beef, pork and other meat.

Lost without trace

The *Zuytdorp*, built in 1701, was one of the VOC fleet regularly sailing between the Netherlands and Batavia. On July 27, 1711

LEFT: Pottery "Beardman" jugs and silver coins were among the objects recovered from the *Vergulde Draeck*.

BELOW: Excavation of the northern part of the *Vergulde Draeck* in 1983 yielded many interesting finds, including this astrolabe.

she set sail on her third such voyage, in company with another VOC ship, the *Belvliet*. Between them they were carrying a treasure of gold and silver bars and silver coins, including all those minted in 1711 in the Middleburg Mint. Both ships spent some time in the Dutch provisioning station of Cape Town on the Cape of Good Hope, enlisting sailors to replace those lost to scurvy on the first leg of the journey – 112 of the *Zuytdorp*'s 286-strong crew had perished. The *Zuytdorp* succeeded first in making up her crew and set sail again without her sister ship on April 22, 1712, in company with the *Kockenge*, another VOC ship.

During the journey the vessels became separated. The *Kockenge* reached Batavia safely on July 4, but the *Zuytdorp* had vanished. The mystery of her disappearance endured for more than 200 years.

Tell-tale timbers

In 1927 pieces of ship's timbers and eighteenth-century coins were found washed up at the base of a cliff some 64 kilometres (40 miles) north of the Murchison River. Could these be the remains of the long-lost *Zuytdorp*? Desultory investigations over the years were transformed into serious research when in 1954 the geologist Dr Phillip Playford heard of the

TODAY'S UNFOUND TREASURES

STOLEN GOLD

Andrew Robertson was a Scottish sailor who, by 1826, had settled in Callao, Peru .The port was regularly visited by prosperous ships, including the *Peruvian*, which on one occasion was carrying two million piastres in gold. Robertson could not resist the temptation. With 12 hand-picked men, he seized the ship. Determined to share the treasure with as few people as possible, he chose two villains, Williams and George, and together they cast adrift all but four of the crew. They then anchored off Agrihan, a small Melanesian island in the Marianas group, where they are believed to have hidden the gold. Setting sail again for Hawaii, the three overpowered the remaining crew members, scuttled the *Peruvian* and went ashore pretending to have been shipwrecked. After a prudent interval, Robertson and Williams (George had "disappeared") found a skipper, Thompson, to convey them to the Marianas. On the way, Williams "accidentally" drowned. Robertson attempted to dispose of Thompson in the same way, but he was picked up by a Spanish frigate commanded by Señor Medinilla, the governor of the Marianas. Medinilla soon captured Robertson and persuaded him to lead them to the treasure. As they landed on Agrihan, Robertson fell or threw himself into the water and was drowned. The secret of the treasure's location died with him.

discoveries. From 1958, he and a few colleagues explored the area both on the shore and on the cliffs above. They found a thick, ashy deposit on the cliff top, the remains of a huge fire – probably a signal fire lit by the wretched survivors of the wreck in the forlorn hope that it would be spotted by their companion vessel, the *Kockenge*. The team also found other objects salvaged from the ship by the survivors – glass bottles, the hoops from provision barrels and broken clay pipes.

Many coins that had come to rest among the rocks at the foot of the cliff turned out to be 1711 Middleburg silver pieces – precisely the cargo known to have been travelling in the *Zuytdorp* – so there could be no doubt of the identity of the vessel that had been wrecked here. Investigating the ship and recovering her cargo, however, was a prodigious task,

for dangerous currents made diving over the wreck difficult and hazardous. A team of experts in many relevant fields became involved in salvage operations after the site became the responsibility of the Western Australia Maritime Museum in 1964. They have succeeded in recovering not only much of the silver bullion but also cannon, the ship's bell and other objects. They have also mapped the wreck, using a variety of sophisticated techniques including aerial photography. Playford continued to study the remains on land, aided by many experts.

The question that they were particularly interested in answering was: where had the survivors gone? The area lacks drinking water and is situated in inhospitable terrain, so the shipwrecked mariners could not have lasted long here alone. But there was no sign of their dead bodies. Could the local Aboriginal groups have taken pity on them and helped them to survive? Some clues suggest that they did. Dutch artefacts have been discovered in Aboriginal camps in the area. And genetic evidence of *Porphyria variegata* has turned up among the region's Aboriginal population – a disease that was established in the Cape of Good Hope, from which the *Zuytdorp* had recruited a large complement of sailors. It seems therefore that the *Zuytdorp*'s crew had inadvertently become the first European settlers on the Australian continent, intermarrying with the Aboriginals whose local knowledge and bush craft had preserved their lives.

WRECK OF THE RAPID

American traders

In the early nineteenth century Americans also began to take part in the trade with China. Given the distances involved, the vessels used had to be large to carry goods in

ABOVE: The original salvors of the *Rapid* missed thousands of silver dollars, recovered recently along with other objects like the ship's bell.

BELOW: Divers from the Western Australia Maritime Museum excavate and record details of the *Rapid*'s hull.

economic quantities and fast so as to undertake the journey in a reasonable and competitive time. The *Rapid*, built in 1807 near Boston, proved her worth on her maiden voyage in 1809. On September 28, 1810 she set out from Boston again, carrying 280,000 Spanish dollars with which to purchase the desired Chinese goods.

All went well at first. The ship called at the Cape of Good Hope and then set off across the Indian Ocean, aiming to turn north when the coast of Australia was sighted. But on the ninety-eighth day she drove on to the Point Cloates reef. Matters were made worse when a storm developed.

After some soul-searching the captain decided that there was no chance of saving the ship and gave the order to scuttle it. This would leave no trace of the ship above the water to attract the unwanted attentions of salvors; but neither would there be anything for the crew to spot again, so it was vital to memorize the spot where she went down after being set on fire by the crew. Taking to the ship's boats, the captain and crew of 22 set off on a long and difficult journey to Java. After this they sailed to Philadelphia and another ship was sent out, with orders to find the wreck and raise the gold.

Found again

In 1978 a group of people out spearfishing spotted the wreck. Archaeologists from the Western Australia Maritime Museum were alerted to the find and, between 1979 and 1982, divers from the museum worked on the wreck. They made detailed observations on the vessel itself and recorded the crew's personal possessions, abandoned when the ship went down. From these the archaeologists were able to build up a picture of the American China trade vessels and life on board them, something that had previously been known only from literature. The divers also succeeded in raising 20,000 silver dollars that had been missed when the wreck was originally salvaged.

AUSTRALIAN GOLD RUSH

GOLD FOR THE TAKING

Gold prospectors digging at Sheep Station Point on the Turon river.

In the 1840s gold was discovered in California and the excitement this event generated reached even Australia. Many abandoned their lives in Australia and took ship for the gold fields of America. One of these was Edward Hammond Hargraves, who soon returned to Australia, where he taught others the techniques used in panning gold. Now all that was needed was the gold itself. Hargraves or others with whom he was working eventually found gold at Bathurst, New South Wales, in 1851. Immediately a human tide began to flow in this direction. And the same year other sources were found at Ballarat and Bendigo in Victoria. All were easy to work, requiring only simple equipment. Tens of thousands of people poured into the gold areas, hoping to make their fortune, and many came away satisfied, with a certain amount of gold.

In March 1866 the *General Grant* was due to sail from Melbourne to Liverpool. She was carrying a regular load of wool, hides, zinc, timber and bark, as well as two sturdy chests containing about 71 kilograms (2,500 ounces) of gold. Among the 56 passengers there were quite a few who were returning home with the small fortune they had made in the gold rush, so the total quantity of gold on board was likely to have been considerable.

GONE DOWN

The captain, Henry Loughlin, set a course for Cape Horn. This route took advantage of prevailing westerly winds, which gave good speed, but it was not at that time well charted. Progress was good, and Loughlin noted that the ship had passed New Zealand and the Auckland Islands. Then the weather turned nasty. The wind dropped, slowing the ship, and fog prevented the captain from taking the daily observations necessary to chart the vessel's position. When the fog began to lift, after two days, everyone on board was horrified to see land looming up ahead of them. Worse still, the absence of any wind made it impossible to control the ship and the current pulled her mercilessly toward the rocks of what turned out to be Disappointment Island, west of the Auckland Islands.

The ship struck the rocks with great force and the rudder was smashed. Further damage rapidly took place as she was scraped along the rocks like cheese on a grater. A break opened up in the rocks – a cavern, into which the ship was pushed and jammed by the current. The pounding of the sea swell continued to batter the ship and it was clear that she would soon sink.

Three small boats were available to take the shipwrecked passengers and crew to safety – far too little space for the 80 people who had been on board the *General Grant*. The longboat was soon crowded with 40 people; the sea picked it up and capsized it, drowning all but three of those who were aboard. Many individuals clung to the gold that was to have made their fortune, and were dragged down into the depths of the sea by it. The unfortunate women were hampered by their petticoats, which quickly became waterlogged and heavy, and only one woman reached safety.

Only 15 of the 80 passengers and crew managed to leave the ship in the boats. Captain Loughlin was not among them, but went down with his ship. The 15 survivors set to, rowing back the way they had come, toward the distant shores of the Auckland Islands, a journey that took them two gruelling days and nights.

FIRE FOR LIFE

A natural leader emerged, an Irishman called James Teer. Twenty years of hard living as a gold prospector had given him many practical skills and the knowledge needed for survival in rough conditions. The priority was to light a fire to keep everyone warm and dry. Someone produced matches but they were all damp except one. Miraculously, they succeeded in lighting a fire with this and were careful to keep the fire burning throughout their sojourn on the island.

Fortunately, the island was well provided. The castaways were able to build simple shelters out of grass and woody bushes and to make themselves clothes from the skins of the seals that they caught and ate. With eggs, fresh water and pigs available, they were able to eat heartily. This was not a balanced diet, though, and after a while they began to suffer from scurvy.

After nine months on the island, four men decided to attempt to escape and get help. Stocked with provisions and fortified by the good wishes of the others, they set off in one of the boats – and were never heard of again. Another member of the group was injured and died of blood poisoning. But on November 21, 1867 a sail appeared and the survivors knew that they were going be rescued. It turned out that the approaching ship was coming to hunt seals. Refusing the captain's kind offer to take them immediately back to civilization, the indomitable party elected to stay and join in the seal hunting.

DISAPPOINTMENT ISLAND LIVES UP TO ITS NAME

James Teer was the first to go in search of the lost gold. As a survivor, he had a clear idea of the appearance of the wreck site. He chartered a steam tug and criss-crossed the area where he had last seen the ship. No luck.

In 1870 another survivor, David Ashworth, was offered the opportunity to accompany an expedition to search for the wreck. After reaching the general locality, three crew members stayed with the ship while the captain, Ashworth and six other members of the crew took a whaleboat to explore the cavern where the *General Grant* had gone down. The three waited for days but the whaleboat and her crew were never seen again.

Another survivor of the shipwreck, Cornelius Drew, made a separate attempt to locate the ship in 1876 but again without success. Further expeditions were made over the years by hopeful people but none met

David Ashworth.

with any better luck. One recent attempt was made by divers experienced in salvage work. They were able to examine the whole of the interior of the underwater cavern and could find no trace at all of the *General Grant*. They suggested that she might have stayed in one piece and floated out of the cavern after sinking, rather than immediately breaking up. If so, she may have finished up anywhere.

El Gran Grifón

Girona

Kronan

St. Ninian's Isle
Broch of Burgar

Oseberg

Gundestrup

Feje

Broighter

Cuerdale

Snettisham

Gleninsheen

Water
Newton

Mooghaun

Sutton Hoo

Hoxne

Croydon

Tournai

Amfreville

Hildesheim

Hochdorf

Agris

Vix

Erstfeld

Rogozen
Vratsa

Varna

Cerveteri

Pompeii
Herculaneum
Cosenza

Vergina

Prince de Conty

Toledo

Mycenae

Knossos
Mallia

EUROPE

FARMING COMMUNITIES SPREAD ACROSS EUROPE DURING THE SEVENTH AND SIXTH MILLENNIA BC. BY THE FIFTH MILLENNIUM THOSE IN SOUTH-EASTERN EUROPE LIVED IN SUBSTANTIAL SETTLEMENTS, OFTEN FORTIFIED WITH A PALISADE, AND TRADED EXTENSIVELY WITH THEIR NEIGHBOURS.

CHIEFTAINS' GOLD FROM THE DAWN OF EUROPE'S AGE OF BRONZE

Gold for the ancestors

Although there was undoubtedly conflict and competition between these communities, often this was expressed more through the accumulation and display of prestige materials than by military activity. The early farmers had made simple pottery; the skills involved and particularly the technology needed to fire fine pots at high temperatures developed gradually. Now these skills were to find a new outlet. The farmers had occasionally come across pure copper and gold occurring

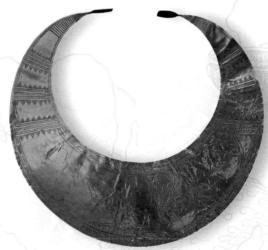

ABOVE: Magnificent gold lunulae – flat neck rings – were a distinctive product of the first metalworkers in the British Isles.

LEFT: This gilded silver vessel from the Rogozen hoard, found in Bulgaria, is of Greek manufacture and depicts an episode from the life of the hero Heracles.

TOP: One of the richly furnished burials at Varna. This individual was buried with a number of gold discs and bracelets and several massive stone axes.

naturally in the places where they sought stone for making tools and this strange type of "stone", which when hit changed shape instead of breaking, was made into small ornaments by cold hammering. But around 4500 BC it was discovered that heating metal made it possible to shape it more easily, and soon kilns were being used to smelt copper ores, and gold and copper were being melted and cast into simple shapes. Metal objects were now added to the repertoire of prestigious display goods such as dentalium and spondylus seashells, fine flint axes and blades and beautiful graphite-decorated pottery, and they were in some ways more impressive. Gold in particular is likely to have had a deep significance for these people, as for many societies throughout history.

In 1972 spectacular proof of this significance was found when a cable trench being laid alongside a lake at Varna in Bulgaria exposed part of a Copper Age cemetery. The people buried here had lived beside the lake in

ABOVE: Ireland was one of the major gold-working areas in the Bronze Age, producing masterpieces like this finely decorated collar from Shannongrove, Co. Limerick.

stone and copper tools around the "head", jewellery on the "body". In three graves clay masks lay where the face would have been, and these were decorated in gold. Three of the empty graves contained large quantities of gold objects, weighing about 1–1.5 kilograms (2¼–3¼lb) in each case. Puzzling over the meaning of these cenotaphs, some archaeologists have concluded that they were intended as the symbolic burials of long-dead ancestors. In this case the richly furnished male burial was probably a spiritual rather than a worldly leader: a priest or magician rather than a chief.

International metal traders

In Europe by 2000 BC bronze was in wide-spread use – tin was added to the copper to make it harder and therefore more suitable for making tools. As tin is a rare material, occurring only in certain area, its new importance provided a tremendous stimulus to international trade.

Tin was to be found in Cornwall along with gold, but the greatest producer of gold was Ireland, which was also rich in copper ores. Trade between the two areas is attested by the discovery in Cornwall of a number of Irish lunulae, which were traded for Cornish tin to alloy with Irish copper to produce the bronze that was now being used in substantial quantities to make axes, halberds and daggers. Lunulae were the most characteristic products of the Irish goldsmiths. These huge, crescent-shaped metal collars, generally made of gold, were popular exports to various parts of northern Europe during the Early Bronze Age. Made of gold hammered into a thin sheet, they are incised with geometric patterns of very fine lines, similar to decoration on the goldwork from the rich chieftain's burial found at the Bush Barrow in England and on the pottery beakers that were prestige drinking vessels. Sheet-gold earrings and gold discs to wear on clothing were also produced at this time

Ireland continued to be a major centre for goldwork throughout the Bronze Age. From

houses raised on piles to keep them dry. The cemetery must have been in use for a considerable period since it contained around 300 graves. Men, women and children were buried in carefully dug rectangular pits. Most of the men were laid out on their backs with their limbs extended, while women were generally laid on their right side with their knees drawn up and their heads bent forward, but there was no apparent difference in the offerings buried with them. Almost everyone was furnished with a number of pots and some tools and ornaments, of stone or sometimes copper. A number of burials, however, were more lavishly furnished.

One man, probably aged between 40 and 50, was buried with an astonishing array of gold objects in addition to offerings of pottery, shell and bone ornaments and copper tools. In his right hand he held a stone hammer-axe with a shaft of beaten gold; this was probably a badge of office like a sceptre or staff. Heavy gold rings adorned both arms and all over his body were small gold discs and beads that must originally have decorated his clothing. A large gold disc was at his waist and beneath this the excavators found a gold tube which they think was a penis sheath. Large gold discs covered each knee. In all this man had 990 gold objects, weighing more than 1.5 kilograms (3¼lb).

Curiously, there were several graves just as richly furnished which contained no bodies. About one-sixth of the graves were empty of human remains – too many to be the graves of people whose bodies were lost, so they may have some other significance. In each the grave goods were carefully arranged in the positions they would have occupied had there been a body in the grave: pots and

around 1200 BC many hoards were deposited, presumably hidden by their owners in time of danger. These included gold earrings, bracelets and necklaces of twisted gold ribbons or bars – elegant pieces known collectively as torcs. Other gold objects were decorated by punch and repoussé techniques. Of these the most splendid are the gorgets, like the one found by chance in a rock cleft at Gleninsheen, County Clare, in 1932. This is a massive collar decorated with rounded bands hammered up in relief from behind (i.e. repoussé). Between the bands are fine rope patterns. Each end of the gorget is completed by a massive gold disc decorated with repoussé dots and circles, sewn on with gold wire.

The most spectacular hoard of Irish goldwork was discovered in 1854 by men constructing the West Clare railway. A stone was untidily jutting out of the side of the railway cutting at Mooghaun North, perhaps part of a stone setting. The workmen pulled it out and were greeted by a torrent of gold objects – at least 138 in number.

The men dived on them and many were sneaked off and sold. A few were retrieved, including a spectacular gold collar, and are now to be seen in the National Museum of Ireland and the British Museum.

TREASURES OF THE MINOANS AND MYCENAEANS

Exiled from Troy

Heinrich Schliemann's fascination with the legendary world of Homeric Greece and his determination to rediscover its truth had led him in 1870 to excavate Hisarlik in Turkey and reveal its identity as Troy (see p.29). But when in 1873 he smuggled a hoard of precious Trojan goldwork out of Turkey, he made himself persona non grata with the authorities and was forced to turn his attentions elsewhere.

Where better to go than the Greek city of Mycenae, home of the high king Agamemnon, who had led the Greek heroes to Troy? Returning here in triumph, his overweening pride angering the gods, the conquering king was ingloriously struck down by his treacherous wife Clytemnestra and her lover Aegisthus, along with his unwilling mistress, the Trojan princess Cassandra, and his followers. The Greek geographer Pausanias, travelling in Greece in the second century AD, stated that Agamemnon and his family had been royally buried within the city walls, while Clytemnestra and her lover were ignominiously interred outside.

Schliemann applied for permission to dig at Mycenae and was most indignant when permission was made conditional on his resolving his dispute with Turkey. The Greek authorities had learned a lesson from this altercation: granting Schliemann his permit in 1876, they hedged it round with many strict requirements to ensure that there was no repeat of the Trojan pillage. Schliemann was to open no more than one trench at a time, his activities were to be supervised and authorized by a government representative, the experienced archaeologist Panagiotes Stamatakes, and all the finds without exception were to remain the property of Greece and in Greek hands.

Proud Mycenae

Mycenae still stood, a glorious and romantic ruin atop its steep mountain. Massive walls, traditionally built by the giant Cyclops of huge, carved-stone blocks carefully fitted together, surrounded the citadel and were pierced by the magnificent Lion Gate, with its lintel carved with two lionesses rampant flanking a pillar. Other expeditions had worked here in previous decades and the walls and gateway had been partially cleared. It was generally held that Pausanias's reference to the royal tombs located them within the outer wall of the town. Schliemann took a different

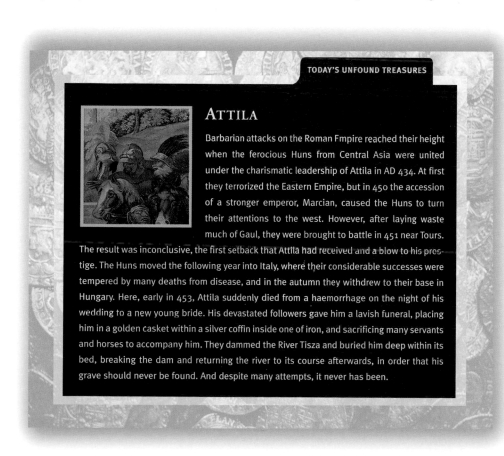

TODAY'S UNFOUND TREASURES

ATTILA

Barbarian attacks on the Roman Empire reached their height when the ferocious Huns from Central Asia were united under the charismatic leadership of Attila in AD 434. At first they terrorized the Eastern Empire, but in 450 the accession of a stronger emperor, Marcian, caused the Huns to turn their attentions to the west. However, after laying waste much of Gaul, they were brought to battle in 451 near Tours. The result was inconclusive, the first setback that Attila had received and a blow to his prestige. The Huns moved the following year into Italy, where their considerable successes were tempered by many deaths from disease, and in the autumn they withdrew to their base in Hungary. Here, early in 453, Attila suddenly died from a haemorrhage on the night of his wedding to a new young bride. His devastated followers gave him a lavish funeral, placing him in a golden casket within a silver coffin inside one of iron, and sacrificing many servants and horses to accompany him. They dammed the River Tisza and buried him deep within its bed, breaking the dam and returning the river to its course afterwards, in order that his grave should never be found. And despite many attempts, it never has been.

view, looking for them inside the citadel.

In August 1876 Schliemann and his wife began work at Mycenae. From the start they were in conflict with the unfortunate government representative, who did his best to hold them to the terms of the permit. His interference to stop several trenches being dug at once and to prevent the work going destructively fast brought down upon him the wrath and insults of both Schliemanns. However, their ill humour was dispelled by the magnificence of the finds that came to light.

Immediately inside the gate the ground opened out on the right into an esplanade.

ABOVE: The magnificent gold death mask attributed by Schliemann to Agamemnon. The five gold masks and other gold finery from the shaft graves found within Mycenae's citadel mark them out as royal graves.

Here Schliemann began excavating in October, revealing sculptured slabs that seemed likely to mark graves. Digging down deeper, in November the workmen uncovered a tomb. Lying within this were three bodies, adorned with gold diadems and other jewellery and accompanied by gold and silver vessels. Four more tombs were

uncovered nearby, each with a number of burials richly furnished with jewellery and goldwork. Among these items was a magnificent silver bull's head with gold horns and a gold floral medallion on its forehead.

The mask of Agamemnon

Five of the bodies wore magnificent death masks of gold. Made of beaten gold, they portrayed the rulers whose faces they had covered: a smiling, wide-eyed, almost imbecilic young man, a round-faced elderly man and a magnificent and noble bearded man in his prime. Looking at the latter, Schliemann had no doubt that he was gazing on the face of Agamemnon, although the storms that had greeted his enthusiastic identification of the Trojan remains with their heroes made him reluctant to say so publicly.

Along with the bodies Schliemann had uncovered a quite staggering amount of treasure. "Agamemnon" and several of the other men were wearing gold breastplates. Hundreds of gold leaves were scattered in the tombs, some forming part of diadems attached to gold bands around the forehead. A golden helmet in the shape of a lion's head, innumerable golden discs, massive gold cups, miniature battleaxes of gold, fine gold bracelets and other jewellery – the finds far outstripped the treasures Schliemann had carried off from Troy. Among the most beautiful objects after the mask of Agamemnon was a pair of engraved gold signet rings, one showing a chariot drawn by two mettlesome horses, the other a battle between four warriors; they were works of extraordinary craftsmanship. Similarly impressive in their workmanship and beauty were two daggers of bronze decorated in gold and silver on a black metallic background. One showed leopards hunting wild ducks along a river, the other a battle between lions and men carrying huge shields.

Schliemann had achieved another coup.

Some might still doubt that Hisarlik was really Troy, but Mycenae's identity was never in dispute. Why doubt, then, that these magnificently furnished graves were those of Agamemnon and his royal line? Schliemann was exceedingly annoyed that he did not manage to keep any of the splendid objects he had uncovered, but the glory and fame that he craved were now his. Although we now know that the occupants of these shaft graves died at least 300 years before the time of the Homeric heroes, Schliemann's achievement is in no way reduced. He had again revealed a new chapter of the Greek pre-Classical heroic past – the stuff of legend, but real.

Land of the Minotaur

His dispute with the Turkish authorities resolved, Schliemann returned to dig at Troy, but he also excavated at two more Greek sites, Orchomenos and Tiryns, at the second of which he uncovered the remains of a palace whose walls were adorned with magnificent frescoes. He now yearned to add Crete to his investigations. He therefore

BELOW: A pair of magnificent gold cups of Minoan workmanship from a tholos (beehive-shaped) tomb at Vapheio near Sparta show scenes depicting the capture of wild bulls with ropes and nets.

began negotiations to dig at Knossos, where previous work by local investigators had already revealed substantial buildings. But he ran into difficulties. The owner of the fields in which Knossos lay knew something of Schliemann's wealth and demanded the exorbitant price of 100,000 francs for the land. Schliemann beat him down to 40,000 francs, but withdrew his offer when he found that the land was not as valuable as it had been represented to be: there were only 889 olive trees instead of the stated 2,500. His business sense and hatred of being cheated triumphed over his antiquarian interests. Perhaps he would have renewed his attempt had not Troy engrossed him and death overtaken him in 1890. It was left to an Englishman, Arthur Evans, to follow the story into Crete. Four years after Schliemann's death, he purchased the disputed olive grove and soon began excavations at Knossos.

A greater contrast with Schliemann is perhaps not possible. Arthur Evans came from a wealthy family and a long scholarly tradition and held the post of Keeper of the Ashmolean Museum in Oxford. His excavations at Knossos were orderly investigations, but, like Schliemann, he was impatient to obtain results and, like the German, he uncovered a new and unexpected chapter of the past: the world of the legendary king Minos.

Bronze Age civilizations

On the evidence of the frescoes that Evans uncovered here, this world was one in which young men and women performed unbelievable feats of daring acrobatics on the horns and backs of massive bulls, watched by ranks of politely interested noble spectators. Massive plaster double axes crowned the walls and a stately staircase led up to the private apartments where the queen took her bath in a beautifully ornamented terracotta tub. Below ground was a maze of rooms and passages, an actual counterpart to the Labyrinth of legend in which the Athenian Theseus was supposed to have slain the

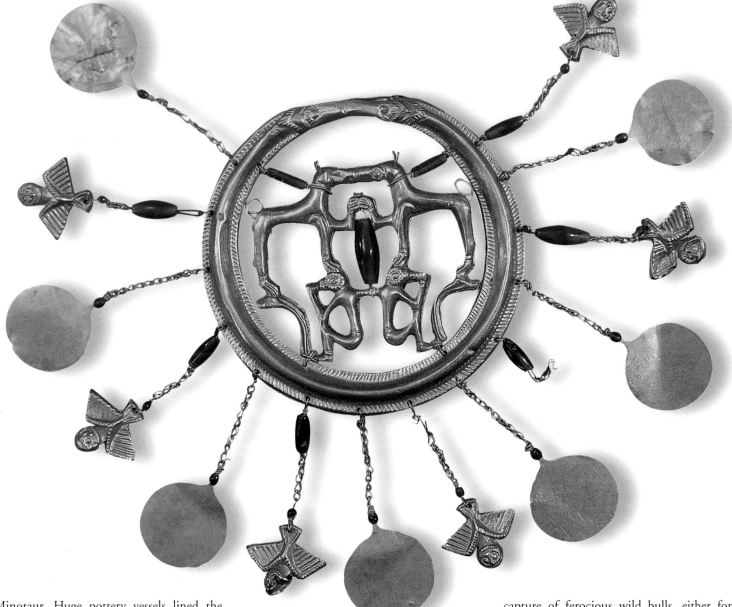

ABOVE: This elaborate Minoan earring of gold and carnelian was reputedly found by sponge divers off the island of Aegina, but was probably plundered from the royal burials at Mallia on Crete.

Minotaur. Huge pottery vessels lined the storerooms, filled originally with the agricultural riches of the island: grain, olive oil and wine. The Minoans had been a race of seafarers as well, their pottery covered with images of the sea, particularly octopuses. Theirs had been the first civilization to emerge in the Aegean, still flourishing at the time of Mycenae's warrior kings, but by 1450 BC in decline, no match for the later Mycenaeans who came from the mainland citadels to take control of Crete. In the centuries before the Trojan War, which occurred around 1200 BC, the Mycenaeans traded widely throughout the eastern Mediterranean, Odysseus's terrifying adventures with Scylla

and Charybdis coming straight out of Mycenaean experience of the perilous Strait of Messina.

These civilized Aegean palace dwellers were masters of craftsmanship. Many of their masterpieces have been turned up in the years since Evans and Schliemann. At Vapheio, near Sparta, a tomb yielded two fabulous gold cups, their sides depicting the

capture of ferocious wild bulls, either for sacrifice or for the sport of bull-leaping. Huge nets are stretched in which a bull has become entangled. A tame cow lures another bull, who is swiftly secured. But it is a risky business: one man has been tossed and trampled, while another is being gored.

The workmanship in some pieces is breathtaking. The Aegean craftsmen had mastered the difficult art of granulation, building up decoration from tiny beads of gold. One such piece is a pendant formed of two wasps holding a honeycomb, crowned with a cage containing a gold bead. This was found in French excavations at Mallia, an early palace on the north Cretan coast.

GOLDEN OFFERINGS FROM THE TOMB OF PHILIP OF MACEDON

End of a glorious era

Philip II of Macedon (382–336 BC) tends to be overshadowed by his famous son, Alexander the Great, whose achievement in conquering most of the world known in his day still seems more the stuff of legend than sober truth. But Philip himself was a remarkable man who brought his backward, barbarian kingdom on the edge of the civilized Greek world to the position of master of Greece.

When the tiny Greek city states drove back the might of the vast Persian Empire in 490 and 480 BC, there began a period of tremendous confidence and self-esteem in the Greek world and particularly in the city of Athens, which had been sacked by the Persians. Under Pericles, Athens had rebuilt its shattered monuments in great splendour, creating masterpieces of architecture and sculpture of which the Parthenon is justly the most famous. The other arts, such as music, drama and poetry, similarly flowered, and this was a time when the finest minds of the age were bent on the understanding of everything in the world around them. Philosophy, medicine, natural science, mathematics and political science were all endlessly and earnestly discussed in the streets and groves of Athens.

This glorious world did not endure for long. Athens and Sparta, which could both claim to have led the Greeks to victory in the Persian Wars, soon came to blows in a power struggle that was perhaps inevitable. Athens turned the Delian League, which it led, into an Athenian Empire, and the Spartans felt the threat to their own power, an unease exacerbated by their suspicion of Athenian democracy, the antithesis of their own oligarchical tradition. In the wars that followed, both cities were badly mauled. Plague eventually brought Athens to its knees, but victorious Sparta had had its wings severely clipped. Thebes, hitherto a minor player on the Greek stage, stepped into the partial power vacuum and in the early fourth century BC these three city states began to tear each other and their neighbours to shreds, with Persia dipping its fingers into the muddied waters from time to time. Things came to a head with the battle of Mantinea in 362 BC, which left all the participants severely weakened.

Warrior king

Enter Philip II. Youngest son of the king of Macedon, an ancient kingdom in the north which was almost outside the Greek world, he had been sent in his youth to Thebes as a hostage. Here Philip encountered the charismatic Epaminondas, Thebes's principal general, a brilliant soldier and strategist, and learned much from him. In 359 BC his brother was killed in battle and Philip, aged 23, became king of Macedon. Swiftly crushing both his rivals for the throne and the hostile tribes on his borders, he set about turning his little kingdom into a state capable of playing its part in the contemporary world.

In the second year of his reign Philip led his superbly trained army against the city of Amphipolis, an Athenian colony that controlled gold and silver mines in Thrace. Taking the city by the siegecraft for which he was later to be renowned, Philip now gained a huge guaranteed annual income with which to fund his wars. The Athenians were not amused: they had lost control of the city some years before and had been making efforts to regain it. They failed to take effective action against Philip, but instead harboured a permanent grudge against him.

Mopping up Greece

Philip now began to take an active interest in the continuing Greek conflicts. By 349 BC he was master of Thessaly and Thrace and

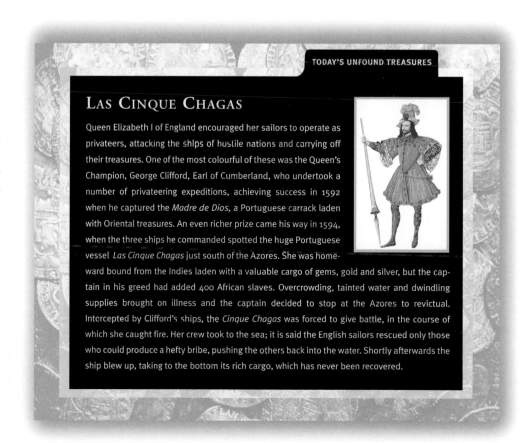

TODAY'S UNFOUND TREASURES

LAS CINQUE CHAGAS

Queen Elizabeth I of England encouraged her sailors to operate as privateers, attacking the ships of hostile nations and carrying off their treasures. One of the most colourful of these was the Queen's Champion, George Clifford, Earl of Cumberland, who undertook a number of privateering expeditions, achieving success in 1592 when he captured the *Madre de Dios*, a Portuguese carrack laden with Oriental treasures. An even richer prize came his way in 1594, when the three ships he commanded spotted the huge Portuguese vessel *Las Cinque Chagas* just south of the Azores. She was homeward bound from the Indies laden with a valuable cargo of gems, gold and silver, but the captain in his greed had added 400 African slaves. Overcrowding, tainted water and dwindling supplies brought on illness and the captain decided to stop at the Azores to revictual. Intercepted by Clifford's ships, the *Cinque Chagas* was forced to give battle, in the course of which she caught fire. Her crew took to the sea; it is said the English sailors rescued only those who could produce a hefty bribe, pushing the others back into the water. Shortly afterwards the ship blew up, taking to the bottom its rich cargo, which has never been recovered.

The tradition of golden death masks among the Bronze Age kings at Mycenae found echoes a thousand years later in a delicate gold mask from the Archaic burial ground at Sindos in Macedonia, found with a bronze helmet.

completed his control of the north in 347 by taking over the Chalcidice peninsula. Its chief city, Olynthus, had appealed to Athens for help, but Philip was a diplomatist as well as a warrior. He bribed a number of Athenians to act on his behalf, and moves in the Athenian assembly to declare war on him were repeatedly voted down by his adherents. Events in the next few years galvanized Athens into open war against Philip, and Thebes also turned hostile. But at the battle of Chaeronea, in 338, he decisively defeated both of them, becoming effectively master of Greece.

Next Philip turned his attentions to the Persian Empire, whose sack of Athens in 480 was still an unavenged wound. His preparations for war against the Persians were well advanced when, in 336, domestic problems caught up with him, and it was left to his son Alexander to conquer Persia.

Domestic troubles

In 357 BC Philip had married Olympias, a princess from the neighbouring kingdom of Epirus, who became his principal queen. Two important consequences came of this marriage – it secured Philip important allies and it brought Alexander into the world – but at a personal level it was not a success. A classic domestic tragedy developed, Olympias using Alexander and his sister in her battle against her husband and ruining their relationship with their father. Despite their antipathy, however, Alexander and Philip fought side by side for Macedon and Alexander was his father's acknowledged heir.

Things took a desperate turn for the worse when, in 337, Philip married a seventh wife, a young woman called Cleopatra, the only one of his wives who was a member of the native Macedonian aristocracy. At the marriage feast Alexander, who felt his position as heir was threatened, quarrelled violently with his father and he and his mother withdrew to her native Epirus. Although Philip later became reconciled with Alexander, his marriage to Olympias had entirely broken down and young Cleopatra became his new principal

queen. The following year she bore him a child, underlining the precariousness of Alexander's position. Philip tried to ease the situation by marrying his daughter to her uncle, Olympias's brother, who was king of Epirus, but at the wedding a disaffected Macedonian nobleman assassinated Philip. Although this nobleman held the dagger, the mind and will behind it could well have been that of Olympias. Alexander ascended the throne and Philip was cremated and entombed with all pomp and honour.

Searching for the royal tombs

The kings of Macedon had recently moved to a new capital at Pella, but the old capital, Aigae, continued to be the royal burial ground and a major centre. In 274 BC it was captured by Pyrrhus, King of Epirus, and was left under the guard of a band of Gaulish mercenaries who took the opportunity to pillage the royal tombs. The destruction they left was later tidied and a huge mound erected to cover the royal graves. In the centuries that followed, Macedon lost its elevated place on the stage of history and the location of Aigae was forgotten.

In 1952 Professor Manolis Andronikos of Thessaloniki University began investigating the town of Vergina as the possible location of Aigae. A huge mound dominated the site, and when Andronikos in his 1976 excavations found many traces of destruction in the surrounding cemetery, he dared to believe that the mound was the Great Tumulus. In 1977 things began to move fast. Beneath the southern portion of the mound he came upon the façade of a massive subterranean chamber tomb. The professor's team began to clear this, expecting to find a

ABOVE: The golden larnax containing the cremated remains of a member of the Macedonian royal family, probably King Philip II, is elaborately decorated with floral designs and the royal sunburst motif.

hole showing that robbers had broken in. But to his amazement, as they cleared the massive doors he realized that these were still intact: the tomb had not been pillaged. He now had to revise his plans. Instead of using a robber's entrance hole, he had to imitate their methods and make one himself, by removing the keystone of the arch at the back of the 10-metre (33-feet) long tomb.

Andronikos found it hard to contain his excitement as he peered into the tomb through the hole left by the removed keystone. What would he see? One of the younger members of the team climbed down a rope into the tomb and positioned a ladder for the professor and the others. To their surprise the interior walls of the tomb were quite plain. But the finds were extraordinary. With all speed, but taking the utmost care, Andronikos and his team recorded, photographed, lifted and packed the material from the tomb and transported it back to Thessaloniki. It was only then that they could relax and begin to appreciate the splendour of the things they had found.

Royal gold

They did not yet know to whom the tomb had belonged, though it was evidently a Macedonian royal grave. Clearly the occupant had been a warrior, for it contained many pieces of armour and weapons: an iron helmet, three pairs of bronze greaves (leg guards), a sword with gold and ivory on its handle, an iron breastplate and the remains of a leather shield, both decorated with gold plaques, and many spears. There were also vessels of fine pottery and of silver, with small heads of gods and heroes placed to hide the

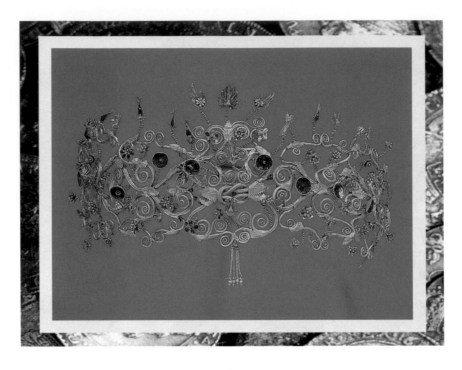

ABOVE: A beautiful golden diadem was found beside the gold and purple cloth within the smaller larnax. The floral design combines plant stalks, leaves and flowers in an intricate pattern.

ABOVE: Delicately made wreaths of oak and myrtle leaves, flowers and berries modelled in gold were worn by the two individuals buried in the royal tomb at Vergina. One was slightly damaged by the cremation pyre.

join between handle and body. And a decorated circle of gold found near the helmet must have been a royal diadem or crown.

Five tiny ivory portrait heads were also found, and of these two could be instantly recognized as Philip and Alexander, known from other representations. The others were

presumably other members of the family – among them Olympias perhaps.

Pride of place within the tomb went to a sarcophagus of fine marble in which Andronikos expected to find a funerary urn of fine pottery or bronze. Instead it contained an amazing collection of funerary materials. First came a magnificent box (a larnax) made of more than 10 kilograms (22lb) of gold. In the centre of its lid was the starburst symbol of the Macedonian royal house. Inside the larnax the excavators found a magnificent gold wreath of oak leaves and acorns. Under this the bones of the king were carefully arranged – charred from the funerary pyre but still intact, and washed clean of ash – wrapped in what had been a purple cloth but was now a mere coloured stain.

Other occupants

Between the tomb chamber and the façade was an antechamber, which Andronikos and his team got into by removing a block from the party wall. Within this chamber there was another marble sarcophagus, inside which was another golden larnax – smaller than the first but with the same starburst on the lid. And inside the larnax was a similar bundle of bones to that in the first, but this time the gold and purple cloth in which they were wrapped had survived. Beside it was a headdress of gold flowers.

Pieces of gold, ivory and glass were the only surviving remains of gilded furniture. A golden wreath of myrtle leaves had fallen beside the sarcophagus. One of the most magnificent objects in this chamber was the golden cover from a quiver and bow case decorated with scenes from the fall of Troy. A pair of gilded greaves stood beside it.

Whose tomb?

The finds from the tomb showed clearly that one of its occupants was a king of Macedon and a warrior. Could it be Philip II? The material in the tomb that could be dated belonged to the appropriate period: the late fourth century BC. The ivory portrait heads were also a clue in this direction. Andronikos believed the tomb was Philip's, but could this be proved?

Physical details of the bones seem now to have clinched this identification. Those in the tomb chamber belonged to a man aged between 35 and 55, narrowing the identification down to two candidates: Philip II, who was 46 when he was murdered, or his son Philip Arrhidaeus, who was murdered in 317, aged about 40. Alexander was only 33 when he died, and he was buried in a splendid tomb in Egypt, as yet undiscovered. All other male members of the royal family in the appropriate period died much younger.

The skull was studied by a team at Manchester University who specialize in reconstructing faces from skeletal remains. They were able to establish that the individual had suffered an eye wound inflicted from above – exactly matching the ancient information that Philip had lost his right eye from an arrow fired at the siege of Methone. A slight asymmetry of this individual's jaw also matched one of the portraits thought to be of Philip. Although there are still sceptics, most people now believe that this tomb houses the remains of Philip II of Macedon.

SPLENDOURS OF THE BARBARIAN WORLD

Idle warriors

When the Greeks began to establish colonies on the northern shores of the Black Sea in the seventh century BC, they encountered barbarian societies of Scythians and Thracians among whom the élite were horse-riding warriors. These, the Greek ethnographer Herodotus claims, regarded idleness as noble and agricultural work as dishonourable. Warfare and plundering were the most noble way to live. Nevertheless, there was a substantial lower class of cultivators, whose produce the Greeks were keen to acquire in exchange for luxuries such as wine and the

BELOW: This gold rhyton in the form of a deer's head was one of four drinking vesels from the Thracian hoard found at Pangyurishte in Bulgaria – the others represent a goat, a bull and a ram.

gold and silver vessels to drink it from. We may imagine that the peasants did the work while the élite drank the wine. The Greeks also sought slaves, a common by-product of warfare.

The Persians also encouraged the Thracian taste for wine and luxury tableware at much the same time, employing Thracian mercenaries in their war against the Scythians in the sixth century BC. The Thracians began making their own metal wares, using silver from the local deposits. The Macedonians, neighbours to the south of the Thracians, eventually seized control of both the mines and the region and both Philip and Alexander employed Thracian mercenaries in their armies. After Alexander's death in 323 BC, foreign involvement in Thrace grew less but a love of wine and fine silver and gold vessels was firmly established.

Noble burials

Most dead Thracians were cremated and their ashes buried in flat grave cemeteries, but the small number of aristocrats were accorded a more lavish burial in substantial barrows. About 20,000 of these still dominate the

ABOVE: Many of the silver vessels from the hoard found at Rogozen are either of Classical workmanship or inspired by Classical themes and designs, like this large gilded dish.

RIGHT: A single silver greave decorated in gold was found in the chieftain's tomb at Vratsa. The gold stripes on the face are tattoos, which Thracian noblemen wore to indicate their rank.

FAR RIGHT: A silver-gilt plaque from a hoard found at Lenitsa in Bulgaria. It depicts a Thracian warrior clad in full body armour. Mounted warriors were the elite of Thracian society.

landscape in Thrace, but the vast majority have been opened and plundered in the past, though nowadays they are protected by law.

There are a few exceptions. The Mogilanska grave mound at Vratsa in Bulgaria was found to contain three undisturbed tombs. The principal one consisted of two chambers. Within this were buried the prized possessions of a Thracian chief: his chariot and the two horses that drew it, and his riding horse, splendidly equipped with a silver bit and 200 silver harness decorations. A young female attendant had been sacrificed with the horses, a spear through her ribs.

In the main chamber lay the nobleman himself, a man of about 30. He was accompanied by his weapons and armour: an iron sword, a quiver filled with bronze arrows and several daggers, a helmet and, curiously, a single greave. The latter was an extraordinary object. It was made of silver with a design inlaid in gold, in the form of a face striped with tattoos.

A young woman of about 18 was buried with the man. She also was arrayed in her finery, gold earrings and a beautiful wreath of gold laurel leaves very similar to those buried with Philip II of Macedon. A knife driven through her chest showed that she too had been sacrificed. Herodotus reported that when a Thracian nobleman was buried his many wives would compete to be selected as his favourite by friends of the deceased. The fortunate winner would then be sacrificed to accompany her lord, while the others would retire in shame.

Troubled times

Herodotus claimed that the Thracians would have been a great and dominant nation if they had not always been fighting one another. When not at war among themselves they were often subject to invasions by others: not only their Macedonian neighbours but also bands of Celts who passed through the regions in the fourth century BC before settling in Anatolia. In the face of these conflicts and troubles, many wealthy

individuals hid their valuables in the ground – and not all returned to find them again.

A puzzling hoard was discovered in 1986 at Rogozen in Bulgaria. It consisted of 165 silver vessels, some gilded. Probably contained in two sacks when they were hidden, they together weigh exactly 3,600 Persian sigloi (just under 20 kilograms/44lb). Why had this weight been assembled and why had it been hidden? We shall never know. Suggestions include its collection to pay tribute (but why was it never delivered?) and its concealment to avoid Celtic raiders (but why the measured amount?). The pieces in the hoard were a great mixture. Some were Greek imports, such as a bowl decorated with a scene from the adventures of Hercules. Others were locally made pieces but showed considerable Greek influences in both style and subject matter. Others again showed more distant influences, from as far

afield as India (as a result of Alexander's expedition in which Thracian mercenaries participated) and Celtic western Europe. The distance goods and ideas could travel is clearly shown by the Gundestrup cauldron (scc p.106), found in Scandinavia; this is decorated with Celtic motifs, among others, but is of Thracian workmanship.

CELTIC TREASURES

Local lords made good

Around 600 BC the Greeks founded a colony at Massilia (Marseilles) in Mediterranean France and this soon became the major base for Greek trade into central Europe. The Greeks were after raw materials such as metal

ores, timber and furs. In exchange they were offering a whole new way of life: the civilizing influence of wine-drinking. In order to facilitate this trade they gave lavish gifts to Celtic chiefs in areas that were strategically placed on the trade routes that led up the valley of the River Rhône into central France and from there along the rivers Seine and Saône, and Rhine, to the Atlantic coast and central Germany. These gifts were often purpose-made to suit barbarian taste, like the gigantic bronze krater (wine-mixing vessel) given to the potentate who ruled the hillfort of Mont Lassois, situated at the crucial transshipment point where the trade route left the Rhône to branch out westwards along the Seine. The krater, 1.64 metres high (5 feet 5 inches), was buried in the grave of a woman known since her discovery as the "Vix princess", along with a quantity of other valuable grave goods, including a

This bronze and iron helmet plated with gold and inlaid with red glass was found in the Seine at Amfreville in France. Fine armour like this was designed for display on ceremonial occasions rather than protection in battle.

massive gold torc at her neck.

A number of rich burial mounds have been excavated in the vicinity of several German hillforts. In these were placed many, imported treasures, such as fine Greek pottery, as well as locally made luxuries, Etruscan bronze jugs and even Chinese silk, finally deposited here after who knows what adventures. Many of the mounds have been looted, sometimes not long after the burial; one at Magdalenenberg in southern Germany was robbed within 50 years of its construction. In 1977, however, ploughing revealed a stone kerb round a low mound at Hochdorf, near the hillfort of Hohenasperg, and excavation of the mound uncovered a completely intact royal burial within a substantial wooden chamber (now decayed away). A huge bronze cauldron decorated with figures of lions and filled with locally made mead was the main imported Greek luxury within the chamber. A wooden cart encased in decorative ironwork bore a large collection of bronze vessels. The prince himself lay on an elaborate bronze couch amid a blaze of gold: gold-coated slippers on his feet, a belt decorated with gold around his waist, with a gold-hilted dagger in a golden sheath, enormous gold bracelets on one arm, elaborate gold pins fastening his clothing and a gold ring about his neck.

Celtic adventurers and goldworkers

By the fifth century BC the scene had changed. The Greeks were no longer trading through Massilia but through ports on the northern Adriatic coast, via the Etruscans, who controlled much of northern Italy. Celts from various parts of central and western Europe were now on the move, raiding adjacent lands or leaving home to seek their fortune as mercenaries. Many of these returned eventually with Mediterranean goods acquired as plunder or as wages, while others settled in the lands they visited, particularly northern Italy. Celtic traders also travelled widely, and it was presumably a Celt who deposited four magnificent gold

torcs and three gold armbands under a stone at Erstfeld on a route leading through the Alps via the St Gotthard pass. We can only speculate what trouble caused him to hide his stock-in-trade – the work of a single goldsmith (perhaps himself) – and what misfortune befell him to prevent his return.

Gilded warriors

Classical writers describe the Celts as a warrior society, and this view finds confirmation in their own oral traditions and in their rare burials, where weapons and armour feature prominently. Severed heads were stuck on posts at the entrance to their hillforts and displayed in special stone racks in sacred places such as the shrine at Roquepertuse in southern France. Although they went into battle with shields of wood and leather, and helmets of bronze or iron, and some ferocious bands fought naked, the élite warriors also possessed elaborate parade armour of bronze decorated with enamel and sometimes gold. Chance has preserved a few such

BELOW: This selection of gold torcs were found at Snettisham in Norfolk, Ipswich in Suffolk and Needwood Forest in Staffordshire.

objects, masterpieces of Celtic craftsmanship. Among these are the magnificent gold-plated iron helmet discovered in pieces in the 1980s in a cave at Agris in France and the similar helmet of bronze and iron, covered by a repoussé gold band and inlaid with red enamel, which was found in 1861 in an old channel of the Seine at Amfreville.

Élite Celtic men and women also wore magnificent jewellery, particularly torcs of twisted bronze or gold with huge elaborate terminals. A collection of fabulous gold torcs was discovered by chance at Snettisham in Norfolk, England, in 1948, when a field was deep-ploughed. There were three hoards, each containing several torcs, and in one there was also a hollow gold collar. The most impressive item was a torc made of electrum – in this case two parts silver to three parts gold. Each of the eight strands of which it was twisted was made up of eight wires twisted together clockwise. The ends were soldered into massive, ring-shaped terminals with a decoration of swirling patterns and blocks of fine cross-hatching.

Two further torc hoards were found at the site in 1950 and in 1990 a bronze vessel was discovered containing nearly 600 pieces of

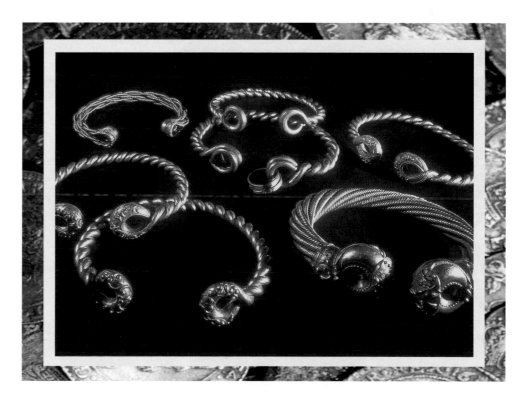

metalwork, including more than 50 torcs. At this point the British Museum decided to investigate the field in detail and its excavations revealed another five hoards. A total of 12 hoards, including nearly 200 torcs, of silver, electrum, bronze and especially gold, were uncovered, along with bracelets and coins, placed mainly as small hoards of a few items each, packed tightly in pits. Opinions are divided on the significance of these hoards. One suggestion is that this was a tribal "bank", a place of safe storage for valuables. More probably the hoards were votive offerings, deposited in a sacred spot. Hoards elsewhere in Europe placed in similar unmarked locations contain the same limited range of objects – torcs, armrings and coins – which may have had a particular ritual significance.

The Broighter hoard

In 1896 ploughing near the shores of Lough Foyle in County Derry uncovered what proved to be Ireland's richest Iron Age gold hoard. As well as two necklaces of loose chains and two torcs of twisted wire, the hoard contained a gold basin and a much more massive hollow torc decorated all over with repoussé designs. The centrepiece was an exquisitely made golden boat, complete with mast, steering oar, rowers' benches and oars. A major dispute arose over the nature of this hoard. Was it composed of personal valuables buried with the intention of recovery? Or was it a votive offering thrown into the waters of Lough Foyle, which had formerly covered the spot? The difference was crucial: if it was an offering, then the finder could proceed with the hoard's planned sale to the British Museum, but if the original owner had intended to recover it, then it was "treasure trove" and thus became the property of the Crown (all Ireland at that time being under British rule). In the end it was decided that the latter was the case and King Edward VII gave it to the Royal Irish Academy, which placed it in the National Museum of Ireland, thus ending the British Museum's hopes of acquiring it.

Cast upon the waters

Rivers, springs, bogs and lakes, among them Lough Foyle, had a special sacred significance for the Celts and their Germanic neighbours in central and northern Europe. Precious offerings were ritually deposited in them on many occasions – as thank-offerings for military victories, for example, or as part of fertility rites. Llyn Cerrig Bach, a former lake on Anglesey, the island stronghold of the British Druids, received a quantity of such offerings, including a slave chain (there was a flourishing trade in slaves, generally war captives, for whom there was a ready market in the Roman world), weapons, horse trappings, and part of a war trumpet. Beautifully decorated parade armour and weapons were thrown into rivers such as the Thames, including the magnificent Battersea Shield, a decorative bronze facing from a wooden shield, with superb bronze enamelled bosses.

One of the most magnificent offerings to the watery gods was a huge silver cauldron, found at Gundestrup in Denmark. This was probably made for a Celtic patron by a Thracian silversmith in the second century

ABOVE: This young girl was sacrificed and buried in the bog at Windeby in Schleswig, Germany.

BELOW: Panels on the outside of the silver Gundestrup bowl depict gods between whose raised arms mortals perform ritual activities, while whole ritual scenes run around the inside of the bowl.

The Broighter gold boat formed part of a hoard of superb Celtic goldwork. This model is one of the earliest pieces of evidence for sailing ships in northern Europe, although clearly it could also be propelled by rowers.

BC. Many different cultural influences can be seen in its designs. But the greater part of the subject matter of the decorative panels that run around this splendid object is Celtic. Here we see a line of Celtic warriors with shields and spears accompanied by three who blow carnyxes: the long, animal-headed war trumpets that were supposed to have struck terror into the hearts of their enemies. A cross-legged figure in knee-length trousers sports horns on his head: probably the Celtic god Cernunnos. Another god is seen in the act of drowning a victim in a bucket, symbolizing the human sacrifices that were performed in these watery places.

Quite a few such sacrificial victims have been discovered in bogs, particularly in Scandinavia. Although these were both men and women and included young and older individuals, they all had certain features in common. One was that they appeared, from the fine state of their hands and nails, to have done little manual work, implying that they were chosen for sacrifice well in advance of the occasion and led a specially privileged life of ease from their selection until their death. Another common feature was their last meal (known to archaeologists from their well-preserved stomach contents), which seems to have been a ritual concoction containing a wide variety of plants, perhaps chosen to symbolize spring. Bog sacrifices were usually committed naked to their watery grave. And

in almost every case these victims were killed in several ways: knocked on the head, the neck broken, strangled, the throat cut, stabbed in the chest, beheaded; most had suffered two or three of these fates, for what ritual reason we can only guess.

TREASURES FROM ETRUSCAN TOMBS

Etruscan cities of the dead

The Etruscans of central Italy were keen importers of fine Greek pottery. Etruscan tombs began to be discovered in the sixteenth century and soon they were being regularly looted for the fine pottery and metalwork that they contained, which were avidly collected by the wealthy to adorn their mansions. Tomb robbers are still active in the region, some of them exceptionally skilful in locating and entering tombs.

Official investigations of these tombs were greatly encouraged by the work of

Carlo Lerici in the 1940s. He looked into tombs using a periscope with a camera attached to photograph their contents and the wonderful paintings that occasionally decked their walls.

The Etruscan cities were at their height between 700 and 500 BC. Like Greece, Etruria consisted of a series of city states, culturally but not politically united. From their homeland in central Italy the Etruscans expanded southward into Campania and north into the Po plain, and for a while controlled Rome. During the fifth century BC, however, their lands were progressively lost to Gauls in the north, Greeks in the south and the growing power of the Romans. Control of the rich iron-ore sources on the island of Elba gave the Etruscans considerable wealth in this newly iron-using age, and they were great sea traders. Their rich arable lands provided abundant agricultural wealth and they were highly skilled engineers, building fine roads, ambitious bridges and monumental gateways and city walls.

But the Etruscans are best known for their tombs. They constructed great cities of the dead: rock-cut chambers in hillsides, such as those at Norchia, free-standing stone edifices often enclosed in massive tumuli and underground rooms, often mirroring the houses of the living in detail. The façades of these tombs were often carved to look like house doorways opening off carefully laid-out streets. Frequently the tombs contained furniture carved in stone, particularly couches on which the dead were laid, as if attending banquets in the underworld. A small proportion of the tombs are decorated with vibrant paintings that give a wonderful glimpse of the lives of the Etruscans, who scandalized their Greek neighbours by their style of living and feasting, men and women mixing freely.

Golden offerings

One tomb was decorated with plaster replicas of many of the possessions of the deceased. More often the tombs contain the actual

TOP LEFT: Paintings in the "Tomb of the Leopards" depict a funeral banquet. Men and women recline on couches, eating and drinking. One holds up an egg, Etruscan symbol of fertility.

LEFT: These elaborate Etruscan earrings incorporate portrait busts in their pendant attachments – perhaps depicting their owner.

treasures of the departed: in many cases high-quality Greek pottery was included, but also many objects of superb native workmanship. Particularly fine are the bronze mirrors, inscribed with fine lines representing scenes from Etruscan and Greek mythology. Etruscan goldwork reached a pinnacle of skill, and even today it is not known how they achieved the finest granulation, forming a surface that looks powdered, as a background for exquisite figured decoration.

One of the most richly furnished tombs of the Etruscans was opened up in 1836 by Archpriest Regolini and General Galassi in the Banditaccia cemetery at Cerveteri, one of the largest and most splendid Etruscan necropolises. The tomb lay within an enormous tumulus. In the main burial chamber an Etruscan lady was laid out on a stone couch and covered by a golden shroud, while a man lay on a bronze couch in the antechamber, along with the remains of a wagon finely decorated in bronze. The offerings placed with them included Greek vases, a number of gilded silver bowls and a quantity of gold jewellery.

SUDDEN DESTRUCTION: THE ERUPTION OF VESUVIUS

Fire from the Underworld

The Bay of Naples was a popular Roman resort and retirement home on account of its mild winters and balmy summers. Many

villas were dotted around it and there were several flourishing towns; Misenum at the head of the bay, the major port and market centre at Pompeii and the quiet resort of Herculaneum with its fishermen and elderly refugees from the bustle of Rome. On the island of Capri across the bay the emperor Tiberius had built a series of splendid palaces as a place of retreat from the cares of government. The long-inactive volcano Vesuvius, which overlooked these towns, had in the past deposited volcanic ash, producing exceptionally fertile soil on which grew luscious grapes that made excellent wine.

The occasional incident disturbed the peaceful lives of the bay's inhabitants. In AD 59 a brawl in the amphitheatre had led the senate to close it for a decade; three years later an earth tremor had rocked Pompeii, causing considerable damage. But in August of 79 most citizens had put these unpleasant matters behind them: the buildings damaged in the earthquake were being repaired and people were looking forward to the Festival of the Divine Augustus towards the end of the month.

Some people were a little unsettled by a series of minor rumblings that occurred as the month went on. They packed their possessions and left, but most people were untroubled and stayed on. Then the animals began behaving curiously – the birds fell silent, all the cats left town and the dogs barked without reason – and several sources of water dried up. On August 20 an earth tremor shook Pompeii, with a sound like distant thunder, but the next day things seemed to be back to normal. People had just settled down again when catastrophe struck.

Around lunchtime on August 24, a public holiday, a sudden almighty explosion was heard and the ground shook violently. Over at Misenum, well out of range, the writer Pliny and his uncle, an admiral, observed broad sheets of fire rising from Vesuvius and a mushroom cloud of soil, ash, pumice and other debris hanging over it.

Perilous love of possessions

Wide-awake citizens of Pompeii dropped everything and fled at once. The vast majority got out of the city, though many died in the countryside as they struggled to put distance between them and disaster. Quite a few people, however, fatally delayed: they searched for members of their family off celebrating in other parts of town; they went home and packed up everything they could carry; they set off but turned back to collect something they had forgotten. Some thought they would be safe in their basements, out of the full force of the blast.

Disaster rapidly overtook them: a blanket of stifling ashes and a hail of stones fell on those in the open, while poisonous gases overcame those who remained under cover. Soon all were dead. The horrified citizens of neighbouring Herculaneum watched the terrible eruption and thanked the gods that they had been spared all but a scattering of ash and pumice. Not for long, however. Around midnight a tide of volcanic mud burst from Vesuvius and poured down on Herculaneum, engulfing it completely. More than 150 people had gone down to the town's boatsheds and were trying to escape by sea, but the eruption had churned up the water and any boats that put out capsized. The horrified crowd was overwhelmed by the gases, mud and ash that poured down on them. One richly dressed woman fell dead beneath an archway, to be rediscovered in recent times along with her golden rings, bracelets and earrings.

Rediscovery

The earthquake of AD 62 and the eruption of 79 so soon after made it seem inadvisable to return to the area, and the emperor sanctioned a massive resettlement programme, housing refugees in nearby towns such as Neapolis (Naples). Many people returned once the eruption had passed, to salvage what they could of their possessions. Pompeians managed to dig many things out of the wreck of their homes but

ABOVE: Bejewelled gold rings deck the fingers of this unfortunate victim of the mudslide that engulfed the town of Herculaneum on the night of August 24th, AD 79.

LEFT: A painting by the 19th century artist Karl Pavlovic Bryullov imaginatively reconstructs the scene of terror and despair as Vesuvius erupts and destroys the Roman town of Pompeii.

The vast house of Quintus Poppaeus and his family was more like a country villa than a town mansion. A wooden box in its storeroom was packed with treasures of silverwork, including this beautiful mirror.

ABOVE: A number of elaborate silver dishes with raised decoration were among the treasures packed together in the villa at Boscoreale. One shows a woman personifying Africa, another this elderly man.

Herculaneum was completely inaccessible beneath its solidifying blanket of volcanic mud and ash. Gradually the deserted towns passed into history and then were forgotten.

In 1709 a peasant digging a well at Resina, the new town built over Herculaneum, found a quantity of carved stone. An Austrian, Prince d'Elboeuf, bought some of the land and began tunnelling into the ruins, bringing out many beautifully preserved Roman remains. The King of Naples came to hear of the site and he too began investigations: still by tunnelling, though rather more systematically. Within a decade he also initiated work at Pompeii. Eighteenth-century travellers on the Grand Tour visited the excavations and rambled through the tunnels, observing the labourers mining the rooms for objects. Beautiful vases decorated with relief mouldings and fine marble statues were not only appreciated by the sponsors of the excavations but found a ready market when offered for sale among the avid collectors of the time. Many a noble home in Britain, Italy and France was adorned with objects mined from these and other sites.

In the mid-nineteenth century Giuseppe Fiorelli was appointed to excavate Pompeii and began the systematic uncovering of the buildings, carefully recording his finds. At Pompeii he invented a technique to recover the form of the long-decayed bodies of the inhabitants. At the time of the eruption Pompeians who died were encased in the falling ash, which gradually hardened. Although their bodies had decayed away, leaving nothing but their bones, a void was left in the solidified ash and this acted as a mould into which Fiorelli poured plaster, recovering the form of the body, complete with clothing.

Treasures re-emerge

As the years have passed, excavation techniques have improved, and work at Pompeii and adjacent sites has reaped the benefit. Nevertheless, the sheer scale of the preserved remains has made the task of excavation a daunting one, fraught with problems. Herculaneum, situated as it is beneath a modern town, has been particularly hard to investigate, the immensely hard tufa in which it is encased presenting a major challenge.

Many of the inhabitants of Pompeii, Herculaneum and the surrounding villas were wealthy people, their houses resplendent with vessels of silver and fine mosaics. Some people escaped with their personal finery as well as their lives and others returned to retrieve their treasured possessions; but many failed and their treasures lie where they were left. The priests of the temple of Isis prayed to the goddess before packing up a sack of money, statuettes and sacred vessels. They entrusted this to one of the priests and he set off, but before he got far he was overwhelmed by a hail of volcanic rocks. Many others died in this way in the streets, burdened with treasures that could now do them no good.

In some houses families had got as far as gathering their finest possessions before they too were overcome by the fumes. Others packed their treasures and left them in hopeful safety as they abandoned their houses. In the huge dwelling of Quintus Poppaeus (now known as the House of Menander) at Pompeii a wooden box had been used to hold 118 pieces of household treasure. These included silver mirrors, the front plain and highly polished, the back tastefully decorated – one bears a fine portrait of a lady. There was also tableware,

ROMAN SILVER HOARDS

Hidden from danger

The eruptions at Pompeii and Herculaneum were a stupendous catastrophe in which nature rather than people buried an unusually rich selection of Roman treasures. But there were also many occasions when individuals felt the need to bury their valuables until a safer time and never succeeded in retrieving them.

One such hoard was probably concealed by a wealthy officer on campaign in Germany at the time of Augustus in the early first century AD. Engaged against the untamed Germanic tribes beyond the imperial borders, he had with him a silver folding table and more than 60 pieces of silver tableware: goblets with chunky relief decoration, larger cups – each with a gilded medallion in their centre, to be glimpsed and gradually revealed by the drinker – silver dishes, including one with hollowed scoops to hold 12 eggs, a large krater in which the rich wine was mixed with water and a ladle with which to serve it. This hoard was discovered in 1868 during construction work at Hildesheim, near Hanover.

Pepper pots and coins

A far more recent find comes from Hoxne in Suffolk, England. On November 16, 1992 Eric Lawes was looking for a lost hammer when he discovered a hoard of Roman material. He reported it immediately and the next day a team of archaeologists excavated and removed the hoard, recovering a great deal of fragile and elusive evidence that would have been lost by casual removal of the material from the ground. As the objects were of gold and silver and had been buried with the intention of recovery, the Hoxne hoard counted as treasure trove. This meant that they belonged to the Crown but that their

including silver eggcups and dishes, and a number of pieces of gold and silver jewellery. In the villa at Boscoreale, outside Pompeii, a slave was sent to conceal a sack of family silver and gold. Making her way into the industrial quarters of the estate, where wine and olive oil were pressed, she dumped her burden in a well but was not quick enough to make her own escape. When rediscovered in 1895, the hoard was found to include 1,000 gold coins, gold and silver jewellery and a number of silver dishes. One dish had a solid bust of a man in its centre – perhaps the owner of the house.

Tables had been laid in many houses in preparation for the midday meal. In the house now known as the House of the Philosopher, guests were expected and fine silver cups had been set out on the table – but no one ever came to eat.

ABOVE: Two very small silver vases with intricate decoration in the form of foliage were found in the Hoxne hoard, along with five bowls and many spoons and ladles.

full market value, nearly £2 million, was paid to the finder as a reward.

The original owner, a Roman who perhaps lived in the small settlement at Scole, some 3 kilometres (2 miles) from the find spot, had buried the treasure carefully, clearly expecting to retrieve it. Everything had been stacked within a wooden box with iron fittings. Hay had been used to separate some pieces and textiles had been wrapped round others. A number had been placed within smaller inner caskets of wood or ivory, several with silver padlocks.

More than 14,000 coins of gold and silver formed part of the hoard, along with 24 of bronze. These were very useful for dating: they all belonged to the fourth and early fifth centuries, the latest being coins of Constantine III (AD 407–11). This suggests the hoard was buried around or shortly after the time when the last Roman legions were withdrawn from Britain, in AD 410. On the other hand, many of the silver coins had been clipped: some of the edge had been removed, reducing their size. This was

probably done because people in Britain no longer had access to silver for manufacturing new coins, so they took silver from existing coins and used it to make forgeries of existing issues. At least 178 of the silver coins in the Hoxne hoard are such forgeries. So the hoard belongs sometime during the period between 410 and 450, when coinage ceased to be used in Britain.

The hoard also contained 29 beautiful pieces of gold jewellery: bracelets in the form of thick bands decorated with attractive scenes, others made in a lacy punched openwork style. One bore the name of its owner, Juliana. There were also rings that had once held jewels – the latter had been removed before the hoard was buried – necklaces and an elaborate chain. This had been worn looped over the shoulders and under the arms, fastened by a large central brooch on the back and chest.

Most of the remaining items were silver tableware, much of it gilded: ladles, spoons, a splendid striped tigress which had once been the handle of a large jug. But the most unusual and interesting pieces were four gilded silver pepper pots. Pepper was an extremely valuable commodity at the time, imported from India in exchange for gold from the first century AD onwards. Two of the pepper pots were of sheet silver, in the form of an ibex and a dog chasing a

ABOVE: This exquisite silver pepperpot has many of its details delicately picked out in gold. It may represent the empress Helena, mother of Constantine, or it may be a generic portrait of an empress.

LEFT: These are two of the 14,865 gold, silver and bronze coins found in the Hoxne treasure. The lower one was issued by the imperial usurper Eugenius (392–394).

TOP: This prancing tigress was originally one of a pair of handles from a silver vase. The silver figure has inlaid stripes made of niello (black silver sulphide).

THE *EGYPT*

In May 1922 the P&O liner the *Egypt* was travelling through the English Channel, carrying passengers to Bombay but also loaded with more than 1,000 gold bars, a similar number of silver bars and 37 boxes of gold coins, all securely packed into the strongroom on one of the lower decks. As they passed Ushant, thick fog descended and they began sounding the foghorn at frequent intervals. Despite this precaution, a little farther south the ship collided with another vessel, the French steamer the *Seine*, and everyone was forced to abandon ship. The ship sank in very deep water, so Lloyd's, her insurers, decided she could not be salvaged. It was not long, however, before they were approached by hopeful salvors, the Swedish engineer Peter Sandberg, his colleague James Swinburne and the Italian company Sorima, who managed to locate the wreck. To get into the strongroom, the salvors adopted the drastic expedient of controlled explosions, directed by an underwater observer. A special grab carried away blasted debris and eventually raised the gold and silver from the strongroom. The salvors called a halt when they had recovered most of the treasure. They left behind scattered gold and silver valued in 1922 at £52,000 – several million pounds at today's prices.

hare. A third showed Hercules fighting a giant, while the fourth is the bust of an empress, perhaps St Helena, mother of the emperor Constantine the Great (reigned AD 307–337). Constantine gave official acceptance to Christianity, and his mother was a devout Christian. This and a number of other pieces in the Hoxne hoard show the owners had been Christians, as many Romans were by the fifth century AD.

Avoiding persecution

In contrast, the owners of the Water Newton treasure were among the secret followers of Christianity in the days when it was forbidden by Roman law. Although the Romans were generally tolerant of other religions and themselves embraced imported religions on the principle of hedging their bets, they were firmly opposed to any monotheistic sect that

refused to pay lip service to the cult of the divine emperor, as did the Christians and the Jews. Some emperors actively persecuted Christians, others were more lenient. But it was safer to practise the Christian rites strictly under cover, worshipping in the private houses of the secret congregation. Participants in these ceremonies used sacred objects that could be disguised as domestic utensils, and communicated with secret signs, such as alpha and omega (the first and last letters of the Greek alphabet, symbolizing God, the Beginning and the End) or the Chi-Rho, a sign combining the Greek letters CH and R, the beginning of Christ's name.

A set of silver church plate used in such secret worship was found at Water Newton in Cambridgeshire in 1975. This small town, near modern Peterborough, was a centre of Britain's pottery-making industry

in Roman times, with strings of potteries along the banks of the River Nene, an important waterway which brought in raw materials and took away the finished goods. The Water Newton hoard was deposited around AD 350. It contains 28 pieces: a jug, bowls, cups, a wine strainer, a gold coin and a number of triangular silver plaques bearing the Chi-Rho symbol. Such plaques were common votive offerings among many religions of the time, promised to the gods in exchange for divine favours, and these Christian examples adapted the pagan tradition to their own ends.

Pagans in revolt

The periods of political trouble within the Roman empire frequently induced wealthy people to hide their belongings for safe keeping. The Iceni, a Celtic people who had settled in East Anglia on the eastern side of England, had started their involvement with the Empire as its allies, a client kingdom in the newly conquered province of Britain. Appalling mismanagement within the province and particularly inept and high-handed treatment of the Iceni brought about the great revolt led by the newly widowed queen of the Iceni, Boudicca (Boadicea), in AD 60. The army of liberation swept all before it, but by 61 the tide had turned as the Roman army's superior training told against the mass of the undisciplined Iceni. One member of the native force who did not return home was the wealthy individual who had concealed his treasure of 860 Iceni silver coins in a pot in the Fens near modern March. It was rediscovered in 1982.

RIGHT: The grave of Clovis' daughter-in-law, Arnegunde, was discovered in 1958 in the church of St. Denis in Paris. She was buried with gold and garnet jewellery and was identified by this signet ring.

THE PAGAN HORDES

BARBARIAN INVADERS

In the bitter winter of AD 406 the Rhine froze over near the Roman city of Moguntiacum (modern Mainz), and the Germanic barbarians who dwelt on the river's eastern bank poured across it into the Roman Empire, raping, pillaging, murdering and plundering. Hordes of Vandals and other tribes continued their ferocious progress through the lands of the decaying western empire, settling in Gaul, Spain and eventually North Africa.

Troubles with their warlike and uncivilized neighbours were nothing new for the Romans, but initially the undisciplined though courageous barbarian warriors had been no match for the tight and efficient organization of the Roman legions. However, by the third century many barbarians were becoming united in huge confederacies, overwhelming Roman forces by their sheer numbers. The Romans swelled the ranks of their army by employing many barbarians in their auxiliary forces, and in parts of the empire where populations were declining – for example, border regions such as the Balkans and Belgium – they encouraged tribal groups to settle, creating Romanized barbarian buffer zones.

ALARIC THE GOTH

While these tribes learned to appreciate the benefits of civilization and kept their hostile cousins at bay, they were also something of a liability. Discontented groups could suddenly turn on their Roman masters and wreak havoc. During power struggles between rival emperors in the 390s, Visigoths under their king, Alaric, were entrusted with the defence of the north-western Balkans. As troubles piled up elsewhere in the empire, Alaric went on the rampage in Italy, demanding vast sums to call off his troops, and in 410 he sacked Rome. Marching on through southern Italy, aiming for the rich grainlands of North Africa, the king suddenly died of an illness, to the Romans' relief.

Alaric was given a magnificent send-off by his people. Captives were forced to divert a river, the Busentinus, that flowed around the city of Consentia (modern Cosenza) and he was laid to rest in its bed, surrounded by the magnificent spoils taken in the sack of Rome. The captives returned the river to its bed, hiding the king's tomb, and were all slaughtered to guard the secret of its location. To this day no one has succeeded in locating Alaric's tomb with its fabulous treasures.

Childeric the Frank

Several royal barbarian burials have reappeared in other lands, however. In 1653 a richly furnished grave was discovered by chance in a Roman cemetery at Tournai in France. Warrior trappings played a prominent part in the grave furnishings, including an iron throwing axe, a horse and a sword. The sword's hilt and scabbard were magnificently decorated and there were also many pieces of jewellery, all formed of gold cells enclosing pieces of garnet. Hundreds of coins were among the other grave goods. A fur cape had also been included, ornamented with 300 gold bees. A gold signet ring gave the clue to the identity of the deceased: it read "Childerici

Regis" – "of king Childeric". Childeric, who died in AD 481, was the father of King Clovis (reigned 481–511). Clovis was a convert to Christianity and founded the Frankish kingdom around 500, expelling the Romans from Gaul and driving away other barbarian groups. His deeds were recorded by Bishop Gregory of Tours, who contrasted his godliness (however bloodthirsty) with the debauched lifestyle of his father.

Childeric had been the ruler of a much smaller state, centred on Tournai. The remarkable find of his burial was published with admirable rapidity in 1655. In 1831, however, the majority of these treasures were stolen and probably destroyed, leaving only casts from which we can still get some impression of their magnificence.

The Visigoths

One of the groups evicted from Gaul by Clovis were the Visigoths. After Alaric's death in 410, they left Italy and by 418 had established themselves in Aquitaine in south-west France, where they settled. Gradually they absorbed much of the civilized way of life of the Roman inhabitants of the area. By the 470s the Visigoths had conquered much neighbouring territory and controlled a kingdom that embraced both south-west France and the greater part of Spain. When Clovis drove them from France they consolidated their hold on Spain. The Roman Empire, now reduced to its eastern half centred on Constantinople, wrested the Mediterranean regions from them in the mid-sixth century but the Visigothic kingdom otherwise prospered until it fell to the Arabs in the early eighth century. Among its kings was Recceswith (reigned 653–672), whose magnificent votive crown of gold inlaid with jewels was among the treasures concealed near Toledo, probably during the Arab invasion. The hoard was rediscovered in 1859. The crown, which was a religious offering, is decorated with suspended jewelled letters that spell out the king's name.

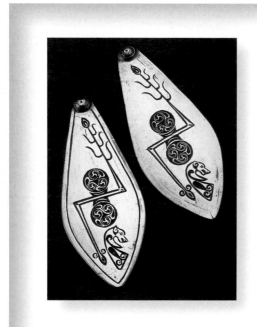

ABOVE: A hoard of silver concealed in the 7th century at Norrie's Law in Fife included this fine pair of unusual silver plaques incised with traditional Pictish symbols filled in with red enamel.

RIGHT: Iron rivets and a crust in the sand where the timbers had decayed were the only surviving remains of the Sutton Hoo burial ship, skilfully traced and exposed by the excavators.

Dark Ages

Many of the barbarian tribes who entered the Roman Empire had been driven south and west by movements of other groups from the steppe regions and from Scandinavia. By 400 the lands of the north were suffering significantly from increased rainfall, which flooded and reduced cultivable land. As well as moving across the continent into the lands of the crumbling western Roman Empire, the inhabitants of Scandinavia and north Germany, Angles, Saxons, Jutes and Frisians, took to the seas, raiding Britain, one region of the western empire that was still enjoying considerable prosperity, where they met fierce resistance. In the south and east of England they

gradually carved out kingdoms for themselves, the eventual prosperity of which can be gauged by the splendour of the burial of one of their kings at Sutton Hoo.

SUTTON HOO

The curious mounds

Mrs Edith Pretty had an interest in archaeology dating back to her youthful travels in Egypt and her father's excavations on their family estate in Suffolk. Left a widow in 1935, she decided after a time to investigate the enigmatic mounds that lay near her house at Sutton Hoo, a quiet spot on the River Deben. After consulting Guy Maynard

of the local museum, she engaged the services of an experienced and conscientious local amateur archaeologist, Basil Brown. Assisted by two of Mrs Pretty's estate workers, Brown set about investigating the largest mound, denoted mound 1, in June 1938. However, after a short while he persuaded Mrs Pretty that they would do better to look into one of the smaller mounds, and so they turned their attentions to mound 3. This, it turned out, had already been opened by treasure hunters, as had mound 2, which Brown tackled next. Here, however, he began to find ship rivets and believed he could make out the outline of a ship. Material missed by the grave robbers proved that the burial in mound 2 had been Anglo-Saxon in date.

Mound 4 proved likewise to have been robbed, but still contained the remains of a cremation in a bronze bowl.

The following year, 1939, Basil Brown yielded to Mrs Pretty's desire to excavate mound 1 and began work on this substantial task. It was not long before he began to find ship rivets. These were clearly still *in situ*, although the timbers that they had once held together had long since decayed away, leaving only a hard discoloration. Brown decided that he should trace the timbers from the inside, following the rivets, a task which he performed admirably. Maynard, who had been keeping an eye on progress, began discreetly to enquire about other ship burials, rare finds then as now, to provide

them with comparative information. Soon rumours began to circulate in the archaeological world that a new ship burial had been discovered, and Charles Phillips from Cambridge University came to take a look.

He was bowled over by what he saw and at once started the process that was to bring in professional archaeologists. This took a month to achieve, however, as Europe was poised on the brink of war. Meanwhile Basil Brown continued his painstaking work, uncovering the ghostly timbers of the enormous vessel, some 27.5 metres (90 feet) long. He came upon the burial chamber and covered it up for later study.

The professionals step in

On July 8 Phillips returned to the site to direct a team of assorted archaeologists who had been roped in and who were to become some of the most distinguished names in archaeology: Stuart Piggott and his wife (later Margaret Guido), Crawford, Grimes, assisted on some days by Grahame Clark, John Ward-Perkins and John Brailsford. They began systematically to excavate the interior of the ship and on July 21 the first jewelled object appeared, a beautiful, pyramid-shaped strap mount of gold set with pieces of garnet in a geometric design. The excavators were filled with excitement. The next day more goldwork began to appear, coming thick and fast: a set of decorative plaques of gold, garnet and glass from a purse still surrounding a heap of coins, several gold and garnet mounts from a sword belt and a superb gold buckle decorated all over with interlaced sinuous designs of stylized and elongated animals. More treasures appeared in the following days and were carefully recorded, lifted and packed. By July 30 the excavation was complete.

A team from the Science Museum in London now stepped in to survey and record the ghostly fabric of the ship, making plans and taking photographs (which, unfortunately, were destroyed the following year in the Blitz). On August 14 a coroner's inquest

ABOVE: Like many of the panels on the helmet, the massive gold belt buckle from the Sutton Hoo burial is decorated with sinuous patterns of interlaced animals and birds.

LEFT: The decorative plaques on this replica of the Sutton Hoo helmet show two scenes, repeated several times: a pair of warriors dancing in one and in the other a mounted warrior riding over a fallen enemy who stabs up at him.

was held and the material was deemed not to be treasure trove as there had been no intention of recovering it. It was therefore the property of Mrs Pretty, who, with exceptional generosity, donated it to the nation, to be housed in the British Museum, where it is still one of the main attractions.

Analysing the finds

On September 3, 1939 war was declared and archaeology had to take a back seat for six years. The Sutton Hoo finds were stored in a

disused part of the London Underground, returning to the light in 1945, when they were made the responsibility of a young assistant keeper, Rupert Bruce-Mitford, aided by a team of assistants. Their study was to become his life's work. Many of the pieces were damaged as the wooden burial chamber had collapsed on them in antiquity. Others were of materials such as iron that required skilful conservation to reveal their original appearance. Many objects had partly decayed away, leaving only the arrangement of their non-perishable portion as clues to their original form – for example, the drinking vessels and bottles of horn and wood, of which only the decorations at the mouth survived. Several objects, such as the helmet, were at first wrongly reconstructed, but were redone when clues from contemporary material made the correct form clear.

One of the most vexed questions was the apparent absence of a body in the grave. Had this been a cenotaph, erected for a king who had died far from home? Opinions varied and speculation was rife. Only in recent years has the answer been given. New excavations at Sutton Hoo were undertaken between 1986 and 1992, uncovering many simple flat graves. These contained "sand bodies" – discoloured and hardened soil replacing the decayed bodies of the dead. Advanced analytic techniques now make it possible to identify where human remains have once been from the chemicals they leave behind. These tests made it possible to establish that the ship burial had originally contained a body.

Royally furnished

The person buried in mound 1 at Sutton Hoo was clearly a person of considerable importance, presumably a king. In order to send him off fittingly to the other world, his followers had dragged a huge ship from the River Deben to the burial ground, already designated as an élite cemetery and containing other splendidly furnished graves, including mound 2, in which the burial chamber was covered by a ship. Once the great ship was in place a funerary chamber was constructed within it and offerings hung on the walls. On the east wall was a huge cauldron with a long chain by which to suspend it, two smaller cauldrons and a tub. Against the west wall were placed a great shield, decorated with gilded fittings in the form of dragons and a bird of prey, a stone sceptre surmounted by a bronze ring bearing the figure of a stag, and an iron standard. A bronze hanging bowl and a wooden lyre in a beaver-skin bag were hung on the south wall, against which leaned five spears, three angons (pikes) and a fine bronze Coptic bowl from North Africa or the eastern Mediterranean.

A large wooden coffin was then placed in the chamber and the king's body laid within it. Around him were heaped some of his personal possessions, including a down pillow, shoes and other clothing, a coat of mail, a silver bowl, combs, wooden bottles and many other objects. The coffin was closed with a substantial lid and further offerings placed on top of it. At one end was a heap of silver bowls and two silver spoons. Elsewhere

along the top of the coffin were arranged a set of gaming pieces, a huge silver dish that had come from Constantinople, a set of wooden bottles, two massive drinking vessels made from the horns of the huge and ferocious aurochs (European wild cattle) and a quantity of parade armour. This included two spears, a belt with massive golden fittings, from which was suspended the gold and garnet purse, and another belt from which hung his sword, decorated with several gold and garnet mounts. There was also a fabulous helmet, made of iron decorated with bronze plates on which two scenes from Anglo-Saxon legends were shown. Gilded bronze covered the nose and ended in a moustache, making up the body and tail of a bird whose wings were formed by the gilded eyebrows. Between them was the bird's head, with tiny garnets for eyes, and a beast with a similar head came down to meet

it, head to head, from the crest of helmet.

Who was he?

Various clues in the grave may make it possible to identify the king who was buried here. For a start the burial presented an interesting mixture of Christian and pagan symbolism. The two silver spoons bore the names "Saul" and "Paul" and could have been a christening gift. Some other objects, such as the imported silver bowls, might also have a Christian significance. On the other hand, ship burials were a traditional pagan rite for dead kings, who were sometimes cast adrift on the sea in a ship that had been set on fire.

Another useful clue is the date of the grave goods. The 37 coins found in the purse are Frankish tremisses, all minted between AD 575 and 625. They were accompanied by three gold coin blanks, and it has been suggested that together these made up 40 gold pieces to pay 40 imaginary rowers to row the deceased to the afterlife.

Taken together, we have a picture of a king who had toyed with Christianity but was a pagan at heart and who lived and died around AD 625. These considerations make it likely that the body in mound 1 is that of Raedwald, King of East Anglia, a Christian convert who rapidly slipped back into paganism and who died in 625.

VIKING TREASURES

Barbarians in Britain

Ferocious Anglo-Saxon raiders and settlers had troubled the shores of Britain since late Roman times, the Romans organizing an efficient coastal defence system against them. Even after the Romans officially withdrew in 410, the Britons continued their fight against barbarian raiders, particularly concentrating in the west, establishing strongholds in

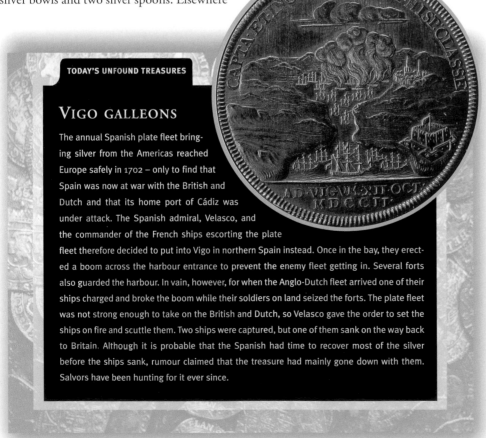

TODAY'S UNFOUND TREASURES

VIGO GALLEONS

The annual Spanish plate fleet bringing silver from the Americas reached Europe safely in 1702 – only to find that Spain was now at war with the British and Dutch and that its home port of Cádiz was under attack. The Spanish admiral, Velasco, and the commander of the French ships escorting the plate fleet therefore decided to put into Vigo in northern Spain instead. Once in the bay, they erected a boom across the harbour entrance to prevent the enemy fleet getting in. Several forts also guarded the harbour. In vain, however, for when the Anglo-Dutch fleet arrived one of their ships charged and broke the boom while their soldiers on land seized the forts. The plate fleet was not strong enough to take on the British and Dutch, so Velasco gave the order to set the ships on fire and scuttle them. Two ships were captured, but one of them sank on the way back to Britain. Although it is probable that the Spanish had time to recover most of the silver before the ships sank, rumour claimed that the treasure had mainly gone down with them. Salvors have been hunting for it ever since.

The enormous hoard of silver concealed by Vikings at Cuerdale beside the river Ribble in Lancashire in 905 is made up of a great variety of silver jewellery and dress ornaments as well as hundreds of coins.

hillforts first defended by ramparts in the pre-Roman Iron Age and now refurbished. The Britons were also beset from the north by tribes who had never been conquered by the Romans, among them the Picts from central Scotland and the Dalriada from Ireland, who had settled in south-west Scotland.

By the ninth century many kingdoms were established in Britain, including the Picts, the Saxon kingdoms of eastern England and British realms like Rheged in the west. Christianity was widely practised. Now a new threat began to emerge: in 793 a large band of Vikings from Scandinavia descended upon the monastery of Lindisfarne off the Northumbrian coast and sacked it. This was the first recorded raid on England by bands of warrior seafarers who were beginning to ravage the lands bordering the North Sea. Political turmoil on the European mainland had left these sea lanes virtually empty, encouraging movements by Scandinavian groups who had profited by trade in earlier centuries and who now began to employ the more direct method of helping themselves to the riches of the settled world, particularly those that were beginning to accumulate in Christian

RIGHT AND BELOW: These silver coins depicting Viking longships were minted in the important trading town of Hedeby in Denmark but were found in Birka, another major trading centre in Sweden.

holy places such as churches and monasteries. The Swedes continued their lucrative trade through eastern Europe with the Byzantine Empire and the Mediterranean, but the Danes and Norwegians raided and later settled in parts of Scotland, Ireland and northern England, as well as Normandy, whence they came in 1066 to conquer England.

Many hoards deposited in the ninth to the eleventh centuries bear witness to these Viking incursions. Several examples have been discovered in Pictish lands. In the 1840s eight large silver bowls were found, thrust into one of the cells between the two layers of wall in the Broch of Burgar, a much earlier fortified structure. Within the bowls were found silver chains, combs and pins and many amber beads. More recently, in 1958, a hoard was found on St. Ninian's Isle in Shetland concealed from Viking raiders beneath a slab in what would have been a church at that time (now incorporated in a later church). It consisted of 28 pieces of silver: hanging bowls, spoons, pins, various mounts for sword and scabbard and 12 beautiful brooches.

Left behind

Viking raiders on the rampage also deposited hoards, storing them while continuing their attacks, and occasionally did not return. One such hoard was deposited at Croydon, just south of London, during the winter of 872, when a Viking army wintered here. This consisted of 250 coins of very diverse origins, not only from the Saxon kingdoms of Wessex, Mercia and East Anglia but also from Carolingian Europe and even from the Arab world. The hoard also contained three silver ingots and some scrap silver (known as hack silver) in a cloth bag.

The most impressive Viking hoard was discovered in 1840 in a lead-lined chest at Cuerdale in Lancashire, England. Dating from around 905, it seems to have been assembled from many Viking sources to finance an expedition against Dublin, from which the Vikings had been evicted in 902.

Some of the silver in the hoard had been brought from Ireland, but it also contained numerous coins that had been minted specially in York, another Viking town of the time. The Cuerdale silver hoard weighed about 40 kilograms (88lb) and contained 1,000 pieces of hack silver: armrings, brooches, ingots and fragments of broken silverware. Some of the ingots had been repeatedly cut when suspicious Vikings decided to check that they were genuinely silver all through. Seven thousand five hundred coins were also included.

Plenty of treasures were nevertheless carried home to Denmark and Norway. There they might have suffered a similar fate, being deposited in the ground for safe keeping and never retrieved. This happened to a beautiful deep silver bowl decorated with birds which had been made in the Carolingian Empire in France or Germany during the eighth century and which was buried, along with

ABOVE: When the English were successful in defending themselves against Viking raids, the Vikings would turn their attentions on Francia (France), from which one raiding party carried home this fine silver bowl.

five smaller silver cups, in a field at Fejø in Jutland, Denmark. Another hoard concealed a century later at Hon in Norway comprised a wealth of beautiful gold jewellery, bead necklaces, silver and coins from Britain, France, Byzantium and the Arab world.

Prevented from resting in peace

Not all the surviving Vikings treasures derive from hoards. An exciting find made in 1904 was a royal burial at Oseberg in Norway. A queen had been laid to rest here in 834 in a trench lined with blue clay; this sealed in moisture, with the result that organic materials survived. A small ship was buried in the trench and behind its mast the burial

chamber was constructed. For additional transport, the queen was provided with a wagon, ornately carved with sinuous patterns, 12 horses and four sledges. Four beds were included, one with down- and feather-filled bedding on which lay the queen. A great selection of domestic objects were also present, such as wooden buckets, a woollen tapestry and farming tools as well as an ox and a bucket of apples. The queen was also accompanied by another woman, probably her servant or slave.

Of the valuable jewellery that she had undoubtedly been furnished with there remained not a scrap. Her grave had been robbed in antiquity, probably shortly after her death. The robbers took the treasures, however, almost as an afterthought: their real aim seems to have been to disturb the queen's burial and destroy her body, preventing her powerful spirit from continuing to exercise authority beyond the grave.

WRECKS OF THE SPANISH ARMADA

Spain against England

Elizabeth I of England (reigned 1558–1603) was an extremely shrewd politician and spent the first 30 or so years of her reign skilfully playing off Spain against France. Nevertheless, by 1584 England's relations with Spain were seriously strained. The Netherlands, fighting for independence from Spain, received a measure of support from England; Spain supported the cause of Mary Queen of Scots, who laid claim to the English throne; and English sailors, particularly Sir Francis Drake, were attacking Spanish shipping and Spanish American colonies, unofficially but with Elizabeth's private backing and approval. The situation came to a head in 1587 when Elizabeth was at last compelled to execute Mary Queen of Scots for treason. Mary named Philip as her heir to the English throne.

Philip now began to prepare for war, counting (wrongly) on the support of a large number of English Catholics. He planned to ship a large army into England, drawn mainly from his troops fighting in the Netherlands under the Duke of Parma, one of the finest soldiers of the time, while the fleet that had carried them swept the English Channel. Spanish preparations were set back when Drake "singed the King of Spain's beard" by raiding Cádiz, capturing a great ship loaded with treasure and destroying the barrels needed to carry supplies for the Armada (Spanish fleet). Elizabeth took advantage of the delay, raising militia, erecting a string of beacons around the English coast as an early-warning system and ordering coastal towns to provide ships for their defence. England already had a fine navy, organized and constructed under the direction of Sir John Hawkins: 25 first-class galleons, small but extremely manoeuvrable and armed with long-range guns. Many private merchant ships provided a naval reserve, ready to defend home waters and often involved in the overseas privateering ventures.

The Armada sails

On May 28, 1588 the great Spanish Armada of 130 ships set sail from Lisbon, but suffered from storms and was forced to put in at Corunna to refit. It set sail again on July 21 and on the 29th was sighted off Devon, south-west England. The Spanish admiral, Medina Sidonia, followed orders to make straight for a rendezvous with the Duke of Parma. The English fleet of 80 ships, commanded by Lord Howard of Effingham, with Drake, Hawkins and Martin Frobisher under him, snapped at the Spaniards' heels but there was no general engagement. Nevertheless, the Spaniards were already demoralized by these encounters: their huge galleons were difficult to manoeuvre and their tactics of naval warfare were to close with enemy ships, bombard them with heavy fire, grapple on to them and engage in hand-to-hand fighting, where their superior numbers of men would give them the advantage. It was already clear that these tactics were of little use against the swift English galleons.

The Armada anchored off Calais. The English fleet anchored nearby and was joined by more ships, bringing its total to around 140. Medina Sidonia now received a major setback: the Duke of Parma sent a message saying that the Spanish troops required a further fortnight to prepare before they would be ready to embark for England. The following night the English attacked the Spaniards with fireships: empty vessels filled with tar, set on fire and designed to explode when left to drift among the enemy. In their haste to escape from these, many Spanish vessels cut their cables instead of weighing anchor and so were unable to anchor again. By the following morning there was a confused mass of tangled ships, only a small proportion of them safely at anchor off Calais, while many were being blown away along the Flanders coast.

Disaster

Battle was now joined off Gravelines. Many of the scattered Spanish ships succeeded in rejoining the flagship, but the Spanish fleet

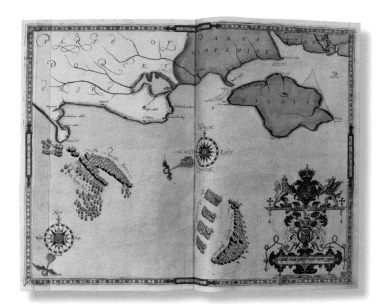

was dangerously near the shallow waters and sandbanks of the Flanders shore and at a great disadvantage against the swift English ships. Sadly mauled, short of supplies, with the winds against them, the officers of the Armada decided on August 9 to return to Spain by sailing round Scotland. The English fleet pursued them for a while but turned south on August 13 on reaching the Firth of Forth. By now there was no longer an Armada, but only a collection of ships,

each operating independently. Rumours flew in Europe, the Spanish proclaiming a great victory; these were gradually overtaken by true reports of their disastrous defeat.

Seven ships of the Spanish fleet had been lost during the fighting and many more were badly mauled. Three more disappeared eastward and a squall drove *El Gran Grifón* ashore in the Shetland Islands. At least eight more Spanish ships are known to have been wrecked on Ireland, and in several instances their men were robbed of everything by the peasants and put to the sword by the English garrison. At least 19 ships were lost on their way round the British coast, the last, *San Pedro Mayor*, as it thankfully re-entered the Channel, believing its troubles over. A further 35 ships of the Armada are unaccounted for, bringing the total of ships lost to 63. Only 67 managed to return to Spain. One ship, *La Urca Doncella*, was wrecked as it reached the Spanish port of Santander, as it had no anchor and could not stop.

On the trail of Spanish treasure

The ship carrying the Armada's paymaster-general, the *San Salvador*, had been damaged early in the fighting and had been captured by the English. Nevertheless, many of the other vessels could be expected to have had considerable treasures aboard, including the personal property of the Spanish grandees who took part in the expedition. One ship captured by Drake, the *Rosario*, yielded 55,000 gold ducats. Many were plundered by the inhabitants of the shores on which they were wrecked, but others sank before they could be looted. Numerous attempts have been made over the centuries to locate the missing ships and to recover their treasures. Of those not stripped at the time, five have been investigated and the location of at least four others is known.

El Gran Grifón

On September 27, 1588 *El Gran Grifón*, flagship of the Armada's supply squadron, badly damaged in the battles with the English fleet and further savaged by the sea, ran aground on the Shetland island of Fair Isle. Most of the crew were able to escape to land and by December succeeded in hiring a Scottish ship and making their way to Leith, the port of Edinburgh. From here, along with other survivors, they eventually sailed for Spain under safe conduct from Elizabeth but were intercepted by a Dutch fleet and most perished.

The wreck of *El Gran Grifón* remained on the rocks of Stroms Helier at Fair Isle. Much of her valuables were taken off at the time of the wreck and other material salvaged by the locals. Eventually she sank. In 1720 Captain Jacob Rowe patented a new diving device, a brass horn like an enormous diving suit from which the diver's arms protruded. It was enormously uncomfortable but proved effective for depths down to about 32 metres (108 feet). Rowe and a partner, William Evans, decided to work on the Fair Isle wreck, believing it to be a much more valuable ship, but after raising a couple of cannon they realized the difficulty of the task and abandoned it for the better chance of treasure on the wreck of the *Adelaar* (see p.131).

No further attempt was made to investigate *El Gran Grifón* until 1970, when a team of archaeological divers began work here. They found that nothing remained of the fabric of the ship, but guns and lead ingots still marked its location. Further work in 1977 uncovered a quantity of iron shot used as ammunition on the guns. The violence of the sea in this inlet had destroyed and dispersed virtually every other trace of the ship. Of any treasure that the crew may have left, only one silver coin was recovered.

The San Juan de Sicilia

In late September 1588 the badly damaged *San Juan de Sicilia* limped into Tobermory Bay on Mull in the inner Hebrides. Its

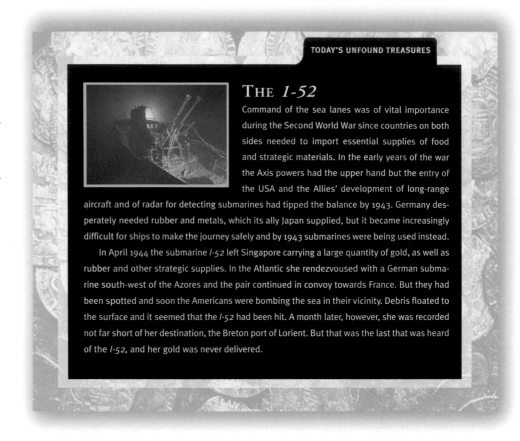

THE *I-52*

Command of the sea lanes was of vital importance during the Second World War since countries on both sides needed to import essential supplies of food and strategic materials. In the early years of the war the Axis powers had the upper hand but the entry of the USA and the Allies' development of long-range aircraft and of radar for detecting submarines had tipped the balance by 1943. Germany desperately needed rubber and metals, which its ally Japan supplied, but it became increasingly difficult for ships to make the journey safely and by 1943 submarines were being used instead.

In April 1944 the submarine *I-52* left Singapore carrying a large quantity of gold, as well as rubber and other strategic supplies. In the Atlantic she rendezvoused with a German submarine south-west of the Azores and the pair continued in convoy towards France. But they had been spotted and soon the Americans were bombing the sea in their vicinity. Debris floated to the surface and it seemed that the *I-52* had been hit. A month later, however, she was recorded not far short of her destination, the Breton port of Lorient. But that was the last that was heard of the *I-52*, and her gold was never delivered.

officers negotiated with the local laird, Lachlan Maclean, for food and water, which he gave them – in return for the loan of 100 men and weapons to help him against his old enemy, Macdonald of Mingary. Maclean spent the next few months terrorizing neighbouring islands. In November an agent of Sir Francis Walsingham (Elizabeth's secretary of state, who ran a superbly efficient secret service) got aboard the ship and blew it up.

The Earls of Argyll, Admirals of the Western Isles, had salvage rights to all shipwrecks in the area, though these were disputed by successive monarchs when the earls' loyalty was suspect or their behaviour treasonable. Rumours of wealth aboard the sunken ship began to grow and several attempts to investigate the wreck were made, using the newly developed but still primitive diving bells, and succeeded in raising a number of guns. In 1677 the job was put in the hands of the distinguished Swedish salvage engineer Hans Alricht van Treilaben, who produced a description of

the wreck and raised more guns, despite being shot at during the operations by discontented Macleans.

New technology giving hope of salvaging more came with Rowe's invention of the diving engine. Rowe, substantially in debt after the *Gran Grifón* and *Adelaar* ventures, offered his services to the 2nd Duke of Argyll, who happily raised the money to salvage the Spanish ship, and work started in 1729. As the ship had previously shown itself to be difficult to get into, Rowe and his associates spent several months systematically blowing it up. Little was now left but the hull, and what treasure there was should by now have been exposed. However, Rowe found nothing but ballast and iron shot, and the project was abandoned in 1731.

There now remained almost nothing of the ship and the absence of treasure in what had been basically a troop transporter should by now have been clear. But because no treasure had been recovered people went on hoping. Many more expeditions were mounted to investigate the wreck, the latest in 1982, and huge sums were spent, though all in vain.

The *Girona*

Better luck attended the search for the treasure of the *Girona*. Don Alonso de Leiva, the Armada's second in command, was aboard the *Rata Coronada*, which ran aground at Erris, on the north-west coast of Ireland. Unable to refloat her, the Spaniards stripped and burned her and transferred to the *Duquesa Santa Ana*. Heading for neutral Scotland, this ship was wrecked in Glennagiveny Bay, but all her crew of 600 survived. Helped by the local chieftain, they were able to join the crew of the *Girona*, damaged and undergoing repairs at nearby Killybegs, on Donegal Bay. The *Girona* was one of the largest ships of the Armada, with a complement of 1,000 men. Leaving their guns and some of the men, but loaded with 1,300 people, including a number of grandees with their valuable luggage, the *Girona* set sail on October 26, heading again for Scotland. The repairs had not been adequate: they got no further than Lacada

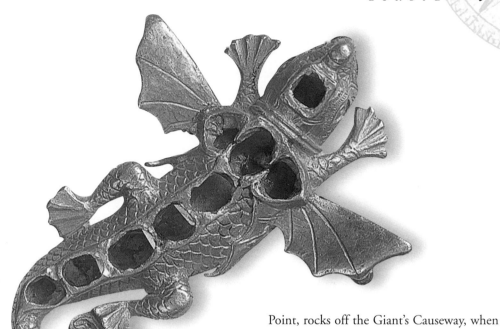

ABOVE: An engaging gold and ruby pendant in the form of a salamander was among the objects recovered from the wreck of the *Girona*. The ship was carrying many nobles and their personal treasures.

BELOW: Poor conditions made work hard for the divers investigating the wreck of the *Girona*.

Point, rocks off the Giant's Causeway, when the rudder came adrift and the ship struck with the loss of all but five of those on board.

The site of the wreck acquired the name of Port Na Spaniagh, but the reason was forgotten and it was not until 1967 that it was investigated. Robert Stenuit, after years of research, came to the conclusion that this was the probable wreck site of the *Girona* and with a colleague began diving here in June 1967, continuing work for two years in the extremely difficult circumstances of the area, with its strong currents, dissected seabed and heavy cover of seaweed and algae. They succeeded in recovering many valuables, most of them the personal possessions of the grandees aboard the *Girona*. These included a gold cross of a Knight of Santiago, a high honour, that belonged to de Leiva himself, nearly 50 pieces of gold jewellery such as an exquisite ruby-inlaid golden pendant in the shape of a salamander, a ring inscribed "I have nothing more to give thee", perhaps a parting love gift, as well as 405 gold coins, more than 750 silver coins and several gold chains. These are now displayed in a special room in the Northern Ireland National Museum and the wreck has been designated a protected monument, as have three other Armada wrecks, the *Juliana*, *Lavia* and *Santa Maria de Visón*, found off Streedagh Strand on the north-west coast of Ireland.

THE SEARCH FOR CHARLES I'S SILVER

THE KING'S RETURN

When James VI of Scotland became James I of England on the death of Queen Elizabeth I in 1603, he took his family south to England and never revisited his native land. In 1625 James died and his son Charles, who had been little more than a baby when they left Scotland, became king of both realms. Charles I was crowned with great pomp in London, but the Scots required that he be separately crowned king of Scotland as the two countries were not united (and were not to be so for nearly a century). For eight years this remained a bone of contention: Charles was willing to be crowned Scotland's king in England, but the Scots quite reasonably maintained that the ceremony should take place in Edinburgh. At last, in 1633, Charles made preparations to visit his northern kingdom and receive its crown.

King Charles I.

In May the king set forth from London accompanied by 150 lords and a huge baggage train. Determined to make an impressive show with his Scottish subjects, Charles took with him many of the royal valuables, including a huge silver dinner service, gold and jewels, tapestries to hang on the walls, church vessels and magnificent robes and garments for the many entertainments that were to take place. Many of the lords in his train were also lavishly equipped, the English determined to impress the Scots with their splendour.

The Scots were not to be outdone. Feverish activity had been taking place in Edinburgh for the past year: old buildings were refurbished and new ones constructed, and preparations were made for lavish entertainments such as masques, processions, banquets and displays. The coronation took place in St Giles Cathedral and was followed by great celebrations. Over the following weeks Charles made a royal progress through the Scottish lowlands, being loyally received with lavish gifts by many of his towns and noble subjects. The baggage train, already huge, swelled enormously.

THE BLESSING OF BURNTISLAND?

At the end of the tour, the king came to Burntisland at the mouth of the River Forth, from which he was to take a ferry across to Leith and thence to set off on his homeward journey. The king and his courtiers were to make the crossing in a fine warship, the *Dreadnought*, while the baggage and the rest of his entourage were to be carried in a large ferry boat, the *Blessing of Burntisland*. Shortly after they began the crossing a sudden storm unexpectedly got up. The *Dreadnought* experienced some difficulties but arrived safely in Leith. The *Blessing of Burntisland*, however, was seriously overloaded. A poorly secured cart broke loose and smashed into another, which caused the ferry to become unbalanced, and within minutes it had sunk. All but two of the 30 or more on board were drowned and the king's huge treasure disappeared into 37 metres (120 feet) of water.

A red-headed woman was said to have been heard on the shore just before the fateful voyage, cursing the ferry. Was she a witch? Had she called up the storm? The idea took root and the following spring 19 people were executed as witches for allegedly causing the storm to occur.

For centuries the ferry and its treasures lay irretrievably lost, 1.6 kilometres (1 mile) offshore in the cold, murky silts of the Forth. Modern technology, however, has at last made it possible to investigate such difficult locations and in 1997 the Burntisland Heritage Trust and the Royal Navy teamed up to search for the wreck using side-scan sonar equipment. The following year they located the wreck of a wooden vessel that they believe could be the *Blessing*, interestingly located at the spot where a dowser, Ian Longton, had predicted that it would lie. Sophisticated equipment designed by Dr Colin Stone gave the Trust an enhanced image of the wreck site, a series of bumps on the muddy bed of the Forth, and produced a sub-bottom picture confirming that a wooden wreck lay within the mud. Later divers saw and touched a timber protruding from the mud at the wreck site.

When the discovery was officially announced in January 1999, the site was designated as a protected wreck on which only licensed investigation is permitted; illicit activity carries the penalty of an unlimited fine. By now the team was confident that they were on to the wreck. Even if it proves not to be the wreck of the *Blessing of Burntisland* itself, then at least it is certainly the wreck of a wooden vessel. Such wrecks are rare off Scotland and whatever vessel it proves to be it will be interesting. The vessel carrying the dowry of Ann of Denmark, wife of James VI and I, also foundered in the Forth and has never been found. Only time will tell as the divers pursue their investigations.

WRECKED OFF EUROPE

The *Adelaar*

Early on the morning of March 25, 1728 the inhabitants of the tiny hamlet of Greian on the Hebridean island of Barra flocked to the shore to see if the previous night's storm had brought ashore any interesting flotsam. What they found far outstripped their expectations: a mass of dead bodies littered among pieces of wreckage and smashed casks. The islanders began the salvage at once. It was no time before their chief, Roderick MacNeil, materialized and took over the organization of the salvage, closing the island's shipping so that the word would not leak out. Despite his precautions,

however, Macdonald of Boisdale, the local representative of Alexander Mackenzie, the Admiral of the Western Isles, came to hear of the wreck and brought in the forces of authority. He hotfooted it to Barra, where he was told that if he wanted the treasure he could take away the corpses too. He then reached an accommodation with MacNeil that gave him possession of a proportion of what had been recovered.

Mackenzie now sent his brother-in-law, Eugene Fotheringham, to supervise activities on Barra. Fotheringham was obstructed but managed to lay hand on papers that revealed the ship's identity – she was the *Adelaar*, a VOC (Vereenigde Oost-Indische Compagnie, or Dutch East India Company) ship outward bound from Middleburg to Batavia in Indonesia, via the north coast of Scotland – and these documents gave him an idea of the

ship's contents. These included a quantity of coin and general trade goods such as textiles with which to pay the local potentates in Indonesia and China for spices, porcelain and tea.

The law regarding shipwrecks was not entirely clear-cut. Did the *Adelaar*'s contents still belong to the VOC? Lawyers consulted on the matter decided hesitantly against the VOC. Could the admiral's rights be maintained by force? Probably. Mackenzie set off for Barra, backed by a troop supplied by Macdonald of Boisdale, in theory just lightly armed for their own defence on the road. With him were Jacob Rowe, the inventor of the diving engine, and his partner William Evans, frustrated by their lack of success in salvaging *El Gran Grifón* and happy to take a new commission that promised rich rewards.

The sea's strong currents made work on

the wreck dangerous and had driven material from the ship into deep gullies that were hard to penetrate. Despite these extreme difficulties, however, Rowe and Evans succeeded in raising most of the treasure: 17 chests containing silver and copper coins and gold bars. It was safely conveyed to Edinburgh, where it was deposited in the Bank of Scotland.

The salvors were not to enjoy their prize, however, for now the VOC stepped in. The Dutch company claimed the salvaged treasure and, contrary to expectation, its claim was upheld in court. Mackenzie was allowed nothing but his expenses and a salvage award, the size of which provoked further dispute, and he ended the proceedings considerably out of pocket.

In 1972 a team of Scottish divers, including Colin Martin of St Andrews University, returned to the wreck and surveyed it, undertaking limited excavation two years later. Nothing was left of the ship by now but they recovered some cannon and a few small personal effects such as pieces of jewellery, as well as a great deal of valuable archaeological evidence.

The *Prince de Conty*

France, Britain and the Netherlands were competing in the eighteenth century for control of trade with the valuable lands of the east, the source of silks and other fine textiles, spices and tea as well as porcelain. Britain's East India Company was founded in 1600 and the Dutch VOC in 1602. The French were slower

to become involved, and eventually other nations, such as Sweden and Denmark, also attempted to secure a share of the trade.

In 1746 one of the French East India Company's ships, the *Prince de Conty*, was on its homeward journey from a voyage to China, Indonesia and Brazil, and was only a few kilometres short of the Company's base at Lorient in Brittany when it struck the southern headland of the small island of Belle Isle. The Company was able to salvage some of the goods aboard, using a diving bell and assisted by English prisoners. The tea had not only been ruined but had also been dispersed, as had the porcelain, but the heavier guns and the ballast were still in place where they had sunk. In 1985 archaeologists relocated the wreck and began painstaking excavations. These recovered a quantity of Chinese Qian period porcelain, a finer grade of pottery than had hitherto been found, as well as a few fragments of the chests that had once held the tea, and a number of small gold ingots of the types recovered from the VOC's *Geldermalsen* in the 1980s.

The *Kronan*

King Karl XI of Sweden commissioned an English shipwright, Francis Sheldon, to construct his flagship, the *Kronan*. Work began in 1665 and the ship was launched in 1668 but not completely finished until 1672. She was a mighty 60 metres (197 feet) in length and with a displacement of more than 2,134 tonnes (2,100 tons) was one of the largest ships of her time, carrying around 128 guns. In 1676 she was the vessel of Baron Lorentz Creutz, the Commander-in-Chief of the fleet defending Sweden against a combined Dutch and Danish fleet, and she carried a crew of 550 along with 300 soldiers. In a battle between the forces in late May, she managed seriously to damage the Dutch flagship. On the morning of June 1 she prepared to engage in battle again. Her gun ports were open, ready to fire on the enemy, when suddenly a freak squall caught her and she heeled over. Water poured in through the open gun ports

ABOVE: Clay helped preserve the scarlet jacket worn by one of the seamen who died beside a gun on the lower deck when the *Kronan* blew up.

BELOW: Small ingots of Chinese gold, weighing around 370 grams each, were among the cargo salvaged from the *Prince de Conty* in 1985.

Franzen had to search the area near the long stretch of shore where the bodies of the victims had been washed up. It was not even certain that the remains would be in one place, as the explosion could have scattered them widely. Initially Franzen and his colleagues used side-scan sonar to search for the ship, but abrupt temperature changes at different depths made it impossible for this to give effective results. Then they tried a magnetometer. In 1979 they explored 34 square kilometres (13 square miles) without discovering anything, but the following season their patience was at last rewarded. The magnetometer showed up a massive anomaly which proved to be the *Kronan*.

Work on the remains of the ship has yielded fascinating details of life in the seventeenth century, from that of the humble sailors to Creutz himself, an adviser to the king. Creutz's cabin was comfortably furnished, with a leather chair embossed with the initials of himself and his wife. Among his possessions were found 105 gold coins, and a further 150 were discovered elsewhere in the ship. The ship's doctor's medical supplies were also found, along with a golden breastplate that Creutz had worn on ceremonial occasions. Other finds included a number of personal treasures: the gold ring of Creutz's wife, who had died the previous year, altered to fit the finger of her devoted husband, a book of psalms, a pair of leather mitts, a ribbon with a flower. A great selection of guns from many different sources was also recovered, painting a picture of Sweden's military successes over the previous half century. Not all the ship's guns were present: despite the difficulties, some 60 had been salvaged soon after the disaster, by a team using the diving bell invented by Hans Alricht van Treilaben.

and at the same moment there was a massive explosion in her magazine. She sank immediately, taking almost all with her. There was 42 survivors: one, Anders Sparrfelt, was blown some 50 metres (164 feet) into the air by the explosion, flew over the ships of the enemy and landed in the sail of a Swedish ship. The bodies of Creutz and many others were washed ashore over the following days. It was a disaster for Sweden.

Anders Franzen is an experienced and dedicated marine engineer. He was responsible for locating and raising another Swedish warship, the *Vasa*, which went down in 1628 and which is now one of Sweden's main tourist attractions. Once work on the *Vasa* was complete, his interests turned to locating the *Kronan*. As the exact spot where the ship went down was not clearly known,

ABOVE: A diver works on one of the bronze guns found on the *Kronan*. Conditions on the wreck site limit each diver to around 50 minutes underwater per day.

TOP: A metre-high mound of 35,000 silver coins marked the area off the Scilly Isles where the Dutch vessel *Hollandia* went down after being blown off course in 1743.

NAZI GOLD AND LOOTED TREASURES

War plunder

September 1939. Europe was at war. Hitler and the Nazis inexorably moved forward, occupying Denmark, Norway, Poland, the Netherlands, Belgium, Luxemburg and France, Yugoslavia and Greece. The advancing military machine was accompanied by a Nazi cultural organization of equal efficiency, the ERR, performing the age-old practice of plundering the defeated but executing it with unprecedented thoroughness. Initially restricted to the property of Jews, Freemasons and other groups persecuted by the Nazis, the looting had, by 1940, been officially extended to embrace everyone's valuables. Tens of thousands of paintings, tapestries, manuscripts and other art and cultural treasures, recent and ancient, were seized, taken into "safe keeping" and transported to Berlin. Detailed catalogues of the looted treasures were prepared, running to hundreds of volumes.

In June 1941 the Nazis began to advance on the Soviet Union, their one-time ally. One of their aims, in a campaign of extreme ruthlessness and barbarity, was to wipe St Petersburg (Leningrad) from the face of the earth. Where convenient, works of art and other cultural valuables were to be confiscated but otherwise everything was to be destroyed. In September the official looters reached Peterhof, the magnificent complex of palaces and parks founded by Peter the Great outside St Petersburg, where they found thousands of books and works of art ready crated for them to take: the Russian

BELOW: The works of many famous artists, such as this french Impressionist painting by Edouard Manet, entitled "Wintergarden" were hidden by the Nazis and rediscovered by American soldiers in the Merkers saltmine.

authorities had ordered these to be packed but had failed to take them to safety. Although some of the exquisite furnishings of the palaces were also removed, a great deal was wantonly and deliberately destroyed, as was the case with other palaces around St Petersburg. One of the few survivors was the Amber Room in the Catherine Palace at Tsarskoe Selo (modern Pushkin), regarded as one of the wonders of the modern world.

The tide turns

By November 1942, despite the huge numbers of Russians who had been killed and the immense suffering of the beleaguered people of Stalingrad, dogged Soviet resistance to the Nazis was beginning to take effect. Gradually the Nazis were driven back and the Soviets advanced towards the German border. The tide was also turning in other arenas: by the middle of 1943 the Allies were in control of North Africa and in the autumn began to advance through Italy. When they landed in Normandy in June 1944 they started slowly to beat back the Nazis from the west.

The Nazis began to be concerned for the safety of their own possessions as well as that of the foreign treasures they had looted. It was time to hide away the spoils and put their valuables beyond the enemy's reach. The paintings and furniture in particular posed a problem as it was necessary to store them in a suitable atmosphere. The salt mines, cold and with a constant humidity, were an ideal choice of hiding place and many paintings were transferred to them. So was a huge quantity of gold.

The Reichsbank in Berlin suffered a direct hit by a bomb on February 3, 1945. Although this left the safes intact, it was felt that such a narrow escape was not worth risking again and that the huge reserves of gold bullion, much of it stolen from occupied nations, should be taken somewhere less vulnerable and less accessible. Among the valuables in the bank were the effects of the Jews and other people murdered in the

A watercolour gives some impression of the former splendour of the Amber Room set up in the Catherine Palace at St Petersburg.

REFLECTED SPLENDOUR

TRAVELS OF THE AMBER ROOM

The Amber Room had already had a curious wandering history. Andreas Schlüter, court architect to the kings of Prussia, first proposed the idea of a room decorated with amber to his patron, King Frederick I. Gottfried Wolfram, amber master to the Danish king, was invited to Prussia and in 1701 began work on an Amber Room in which windows would be separated by amber panels. The project had its ups and downs and Schlüter and Wolfram were both separately dismissed. The king transferred the idea to his castle at Charlottenburg, Berlin, in 1707 and in five years the room was ready. However, Frederick died the following year and his successor, Frederick William I, had the Amber Room dismantled.

The Tsar of Russia, Peter the Great, had heard of the celebrated room and when he visited Prussia in 1716 he expressed an interest in it. Frederick William presented it to him as a diplomatic gift. The following year it was transferred to St Petersburg in eight carts, packed in 18 boxes, under the supervision of Count Alexei Golovin, one of Peter's courtiers. The room proved difficult to reassemble and so the pieces were taken to the city's Summer Palace and virtually forgotten. When Peter's daughter, Elizabeth, became empress she decided to reinstate the Amber Room. There were not enough pieces for the chosen room, so she had her court architect, Bartolomeo Francesco Rastrelli, construct further mirrored pilasters to go between the amber panels. For a while the Amber Room was used for receptions.

ON THE MOVE AGAIN

In 1755 Elizabeth began work on expanding and improving the Catherine Palace and decided to install the Amber Room there. So it was again dismantled and Rastrelli supervised its installation in its new setting. This was a larger room, so again Rastrelli added new pieces: gilded sculptures, mirrors, pilasters – and canvas panels painted to look like amber. Later Catherine the Great replaced these fake panels with ones of real amber, work that was completed in 1770. The Amber Room was now in its final, glorious form. Three walls of the room were covered in amber panels arranged in three tiers. The eight large central panels included four decorated with Florentine mosaics made in tiny pieces of precious stone, depicting scenes inspired by the five senses. The whole room sparkled as the panels were reflected in the mirrors on the walls and pillars.

As the Nazis approached St Petersburg in 1941 it was decided that the Amber Room's panels were too fragile to be moved, so they were carefully covered in paper and cloth. However, the Amber Room's fame made it an obvious target for the official Nazi art collectors. A group from the ERR supervised the packing up of the panels, a task which took several days, and these were shipped in 28 crates to Königsberg near the Polish border, the regional headquarters of the SS. Here they were displayed in the Königsberg Palace as German treasures finally restored to their homeland and here they remained until 1944, when they were packed up – and vanished.

This is the last that was heard of the panels from the Amber Room, despite many attempts to trace them. Since 1983 the Russians have been constructing replacements within the Catherine Palace. Many other plundered art treasures have also never been recovered: undoubtedly some were destroyed during the frenzied days of liberation, while others must have found their way into private collections. Occasionally some of these surface, as did five paintings that had belonged to an Italian Jewish family. These were found in 1999 in the possession of a New Zealand art gallery, legitimately acquired from a family who had purchased them in 1946 in an Italian market, where presumably they were being offered for sale by looters.

concentration camps: not only their jewellery but even the gold fillings from their teeth. It was decided that the gold and dollar reserves should be hidden in the huge Kaiseroda potassium mine at Merkers in Thuringia. The task was successfully completed by February 18.

Rediscovered treasures

But already the Allied troops had advanced well into Germany and it was not long before the Nazi authorities decided they had made a mistake. They began to transfer the more portable paper currency from the mine back to Berlin and had succeeded in moving about half when the Allies reached a point too close for comfort. Abandoning the rest of the hoard, the bank officials fled. Merkers fell on April 4 to the Americans, who had responsibility for liberating and occupying this portion of the Nazi domains. At first the goods concealed in the mine went unsuspected, but it was not long before a chance remark let slip the secret.

Immediately steps were taken to guard the mine. Going in on April 7, the Americans found themselves face to face with the remaining sacks of paper currency, placed ready to move in the main passageway but abandoned in the haste of withdrawal. After blasting away a heavy steel door that had been placed to close the passage, they found themselves in a room full of sacks of gold bars, worth more than $315,000. In addition they found 400 tons of paintings and other works of art, including works by Titian, Rembrandt and Raphael and the famous bust of Nefertiti, wife of the heretical Egyptian pharaoh Akhenaten, created more than 3,000 years earlier.

Lost gold

The Nazis still had substantial gold reserves. To safeguard these and keep them from the Allies, it was proposed that they be hidden in the National Redoubt, an area of some 52,000 square kilometres (20,000 square miles) in the Alps of southern Germany and

ABOVE: Italian 16th century jewellery of diamonds, emeralds and rubies looted from Paris was recovered by the Americans from an Austrian castle.

adjacent Italy and Austria, the area where Germany Hitler had his mountain retreat known as the Berghof. With considerable difficulty, the gold and currency were transported by road and rail to the village of Mittenwald in the National Redoubt, where they were handed over to Colonel Franz Wilhelm Pfeiffer, head of the local Alpine mountain troops. He and his men concealed the gold in carefully dug pits in the wooded mountain slopes near Lake Walchen, north of Innsbruck. Several times part of the treasure was lifted and hidden in new holes. There was a certain amount of confusion about the quantities that had been concealed and about which consignments had been placed where. In all the anxiety and haste of the time, it would have been easy for those involved in the transport and concealment of the treasure to remove a certain amount

to line their own pockets, and there seems no doubt that some did, although the majority were worthy of their trust – and were made to suffer for it.

Rumours and incomplete tales led the Americans inexorably towards the hidden gold. Finally on June 7, led by a Nazi officer who had cracked, they were taken to the site of a series of holes from which they recovered 728 bars of gold weighing a total of 9.1 tonnes (9 tons). The delighted American soldiers posed for a group photograph, gold bars prominently displayed. Then they handed the gold over to their officers, who in great secrecy took them to the Reichsbank in Frankfurt, where they were safely stored.

Another cache of 25 boxes containing 100 gold bars was recovered from a bunker on another part of the mountain, as the result of a tip-off. The sergeant in charge of the recovery handed over the boxes, which were loaded on to trucks. These were driven off by two supposed American intelligence officers with two guards – and were never seen again.

Bighorn

Santa Maria

Tenochtitlán

Monte Albán

Chichén Itzá

Titanic

SS Republic

Central America

5

NORTH AMERICA

THE OAXACA VALLEY IN HIGHLAND MEXICO, HOME OF THE ZAPOTEC PEOPLE, WAS ONE OF THE EARLY CENTRES OF CIVILIZATION IN THE AMERICAS. AROUND 500 BC THE ZAPOTECS CONSTRUCTED A MASSIVE HILLTOP CAPITAL AT MONTE ALBÁN, WITH TEMPLES AND PALACES. ON ITS SLOPES THEY BUILT HOUSES AND EXCAVATED TOMBS IN WHICH THEY BURIED THEIR DEAD WITH BEAUTIFUL POTTERY. BUT, BY AD 750, THE GLORY OF THEIR CIVILIZATION WAS PASSED AND THE ZAPOTECS MOVED AWAY.

GOLD FROM MONTE ALBÁN

ABOVE: Temple pyramids dominate the hilltop Zapotec centre of Monte Albán. On the west lies the Palace of the Danzantes in which were found slabs depicting the contorted bodies of sacrificed enemies.

LEFT: Delicate gold filigree frames a medallion of the Virgin Mary, the treasured possession of one of the hapless Spaniards whose dream of settling in the New World ended in shipwreck in 1724.

Oaxaca's glory

By 1350 the Oaxaca Valley had been infiltrated by the Mixtecs, people from small kingdoms to the west. The Mixtecs were exceptional craftsmen, who made very attractive pottery in many colours, jewellery of many different materials, elaborate and beautiful mosaics of turquoise, and superb goldwork. Metallurgy had come late to Mesoamerica: around AD 800 the techniques for working gold, silver and copper had been introduced to the region from South America, where they had a long and distinguished history. The Mixtecs were among the finest workers in these materials and their products were eagerly sought by their neighbours, including, eventually, the Aztecs.

An amazing tomb

In the 1930s the Mexican archaeologist Alfonso Caso decided to investigate the site of Monte Albán. He suspected that various objects of jade and gold acquired by museums had come from looted tombs in this ancient city, and he wanted to find out more about them and their makers. In 1932, therefore, with his wife, several assistants and a team of workmen, he began to uncover the

magnificent architecture of Monte Albán's hilltop centre, long hidden by earth and vegetation. Working beyond the citadel, he and his team also found the remains of nine tombs, six of them unlooted. Tomb 7 proved extremely exciting.

A shell trumpet and some jewellery of jade placed on the roof of the tomb alerted the team to its presence. They made a small hole in the roof and carefully climbed in. Immediately before them they found a skull, with a beautiful goblet of rock crystal: a work of extraordinary virtuosity in this exceptionally hard material. Working their way around projecting blocks in the walls of the tomb, so as not to disturb the buried remains, they glimpsed an amazing array of offerings laid out in several chambers, alongside piles of bones. The whole floor was covered with small pieces of turquoise that had once formed part of elaborate mosaic masks, as well as the scattered beads from necklaces of pearls and gold. The archaeologists carefully measured the extent of the tomb, to allow them to locate the outer door from the ground outside.

Returning to the outer world, they uncovered the doorway, buried to its lintel in soil. It was now six o'clock in the evening, but knowing what was in the tomb they felt they could not stop. It was three a.m. before they had cleared the door and could open the tomb. One of the first sights that greeted them was a superb golden diadem with a golden plume. On this first night the excavators found no fewer than 36 pieces of goldwork, including a great breastplate in the form of a human head and shoulders, surmounted by a magnificent helmet, made in one piece by the sophisticated lost-wax casting process. When morning dawned on the exhausted but exhilarated team, Caso took the valuable finds and drove them to Oaxaca City for safe keeping, while the others guarded the tomb.

For a whole week the team slaved away for 14 hours a day to uncover the riches of this amazing tomb. They found that it had originally been carved by the ancient Zapotecs. On coming to Monte Albán the Mixtecs cleared out the tomb, leaving behind only a few pots, and reused it for the elaborate burial of one of their nobility. Nine people were interred there, eight of them servants to accompany their lordly master – or mistress, for it proved impossible to say with certainty whether the tomb's owner was a man or a woman. The bodies were wrapped in cloth and placed in the tomb in a seated position. When the cloth rotted, the bundles disintegrated, scattering the bones and the finery with which they were adorned: necklaces, earrings, bracelets and other jewellery of every precious material known to the Mixtecs: gold, silver, jade, rock crystal, turquoise, coral and jet. With them were vessels also made of

LEFT: The glowing reputation of the Mixtec goldsmiths is borne out by this magnificent gold breastplate depicting a skeletal deity crowned by a serpent headdress.

BELOW: Many attempts have been made to explore the murky waters of the Cenote of Sacrifice at Chichén Itzá, where for centuries the Maya offered precious objects.

fine materials, including beautiful onyx vases. The most exciting finds were a series of jaguar bones, carved with wonderful Mixtec depictions of gods and people.

THE MAYA SACRED WELL OF CHICHÉN ITZÁ

Well of sacrifice

Edward Herbert Thompson was fascinated by the ancient Maya, whose traditions had been recorded by the Spanish missionary Diego de Landa in the sixteenth century and whose ruins in the Yucatán (Mesoamerica) had been explored and beautifully described by the explorers John Lloyd Stephens and Frederick Catherwood in the early nineteenth century. So he was thrilled when he secured a consular post in the region. In 1885 he first set foot in the city of Chichén Itzá and walked along the remains of the

Maya ceremonial road to its sacred well, the Cenote of Sacrifice.

In this region the Maya relied for their water mainly on sinkholes in the limestone (in Spanish, *cenotes*), which gave access to underground water. A particularly massive example, 62 metres (200 feet) in diameter, its sheer cliffs rising far above the water level, must have first attracted settlers to Chichén Itzá. This cenote was considered a sacred place as early as the fifth century AD, when people began to throw offerings into it. It became particularly important when the Toltec from highland Mexico took over at Chichén Itzá, and was still a holy place, attracting pilgrims from far and near, well after the Spanish conquest of the region. Diego de Landa recorded that human victims were hurled into its waters, along with all the objects that pilgrims held most precious.

Penetrating the waters

Intrigued by this account and those of other Spanish observers, Thompson wanted to investigate the well. But how? He spent years making preparations and plans, including buying the land and learning how to dive. In 1904 he returned to the cenote to begin his investigations. For three years he and his men operated a winch which he had devised; this scooped up material from beneath the waters, lifted it to the top of the well and deposited it on a platform that they had constructed. At first their finds were disappointing: lots of mud, rocks, dead vegetation, fallen wood and sometimes whole trees, and the occasional bones of an unfortunate animal that had fallen in. Was this to be all? Thompson began to suffer sleepless nights from worry, for many of his friends had invested in his enterprise.

But one day things began to change. The dredge brought up some lumps of a curious substance that turned out to be copal incense, used by the Maya. Then artefacts began to come up: knives of obsidian (volcanic glass), pottery and jewellery. But these finds were still very few and the bulk of the material that emerged was still stones and vegetation. Thompson decided that he would have to adopt more direct methods.

In 1909 he engaged the services of a Greek sponge diver and together they entered the well. Each was kitted out in diving gear, including a huge copper helmet, a heavy lead necklace, waterproof canvas suit

TOP RIGHT: The powerful airlift directed by the *National Geographic*'s divers sucked up water mixed with sediments and poured it out on to a gigantic sieve where objects could be spotted and recovered.

RIGHT: The intrepid divers were lowered into the cenote in a canvas bucket suspended from a crane high above on the mouth of the well, using a block and tackle.

BELOW: Jade was used by the Maya to create a great variety of ornaments, like this pendant found in the sacred cenote.

and iron-soled shoes. An airhose led up to the surface, where a team of workmen operated pumps to keep Thompson and his assistant supplied with air. The two divers took a lamp to help them in their search, but this proved useless because waterweed and mud made the water in the well so murky that the beam could not penetrate it. Therefore they resigned themselves to working by feel.

They had an exciting time. Every so often pieces of rock would become detached from the wall of the cenote high above their heads and come crashing down through the water – fortunately creating waves that pushed the two men to one side. They also began bringing up magnificent objects: copper bells, jade carvings and gold discs decorated with scenes, probably from Maya and Toltec history. Human bones were also recovered, demonstrating the truth of de Landa's stories. Often the objects had been deliberately broken, presumably for ritual reasons, before being thrown into the well.

Renewed investigations

When Thompson decided to call it a day, he reckoned that he had left about nine-tenths of the well unexplored. Others took up the challenge as time went on. A group of aqualung divers tried in 1954 but were put off by the poor visibility. In 1960 *National Geographic* magazine and a team of Mexican investigators began a more systematic exploration of this difficult site. They worked with an airlift, a tool often employed by underwater archaeologists, but this proved less than perfect in the conditions of the cenote. Objects from the sediments tended to get sucked up and broken, and the sediments themselves could not be excavated in a controlled manner that would have given some idea of the cenote's stratigraphy.

A more ambitious attempt was made in 1967, when water was removed to a depth of 4 metres (13 feet). This made it possible to excavate a part of the sediments as if they

RIGHT: In this scene depicted in the *Lienzo de Tlaxcala* manuscript, the Spaniards and their Tlaxcalan allies are killing nobles of the western Mesoamerican state of Michoacan for refusing to yield their treasures.

BELOW: This turquoise and shell mosaic mask representing the god Quetzalcoatl was one of the few Aztec treasures that reached Europe as the result of Cortés's expedition.

were exposed on dry land, a method calculated to retrieve the maximum amount of information about the order in which objects had been dropped into the well. It turned out that there had been two main periods when the cenote received many offerings. The earlier period included many gold and jade objects brought from far and near, along with household pottery and other domestic objects. The second period took place after Chichén Itzá had ceased to be the dominant city of the region. In this poorer period, it seems, the people who made offerings here looted earlier tombs to provide splendid objects of jade to add to their humbler offerings of wooden figurines, copper bells and pottery.

SPANIARDS IN THE AMERICAS

Unknown riches

The Italian explorer Christopher Columbus (1451–1506) had discovered the New World for the Spanish crown in 1492 and there was no lack of young Spaniards ready to seek their fortunes in this land of unknown riches. None was more ambitious than Hernán Cortés, a nobleman from Estremadura in Spain, who went out to the island of Hispaniola in the West Indies in 1504. Here he eventually rose to command an expedition sent in February 1519 by Diego Velázquez, the governor of Cuba, to explore the Mesoamerican mainland.

The country in which Cortés's expedition landed was part of the vast dominions of the Aztecs. News of the strange white-skinned Spaniards in their curious ships had been brought to the Aztec ruler, Montezuma

(Motecuhzoma II), in the previous year when a previous expedition had explored the Veracruz region. Learning of the arrival of Cortés in his empire, Montezuma sent gifts to honour this emissary of a foreign power: a gold dish and one of silver; four ritual outfits, including jewellery of turquoise, jade and gold; and a quantity of food.

Soon Velázquez sent a message recalling Cortés to Cuba. Cortés, however, had his own ideas. His appetite whetted by the richness of the diplomatic gifts, he decided to march inland with his small force of 400–500 men. Having dispatched his largest ship to bear gifts to the Spanish king, Charles V, in order to validate his authority, he burned his other ships and set off for the fabulous city of Tenochtitlán.

The Aztec Empire included many disaffected conquered areas that groaned under the burden of taxation. Other regions enclosed by the empire remained independent but with the status of official enemies. With them the Aztecs engaged in their ritual "Flowery Wars", set-piece battles in which the object was to seize captives for the frequent human sacrifices required by the Aztecs' religion. Foremost among these peoples were the Tlaxcalans. The Spaniards at first made war on the Tlaxcalans, but it was not long before the two sides joined forces against the Aztecs.

Tenochtitlán

On November 8 the army came in sight of the great Aztec city of Tenochtitlán. Constructed on an island in Lake Texcoco in the Valley of Mexico, the city was linked to the lake shores by three causeways, while surrounding the dry land of its centre were vast suburbs of *chinampas*, floating gardens with houses built within them. Cortés and his men entered the city and were met by a royal procession carrying a palanquin in which rode Montezuma. They were greeted hospitably and lodged in one of the emperor's palaces. Here by chance they discovered a door into his treasure chamber, which con-

tained riches beyond their wildest dreams.

The Spaniards resolved to lay hands on the hoard; but how? Cortés decided that the way to secure their safety and freedom of action was to control the emperor, and he soon managed to trap Montezuma, who now became a Spanish prisoner. Dividing the treasure, Cortés allocated shares to Charles V and Governor Velázquez as well as to himself. He issued one-fifth of the treasure to be divided among his army and locked up the rest securely.

At this juncture Cortés received news that Velázquez had sent another expedition, under Panfilo de Narváez, to bring him to heel. Leaving Pedro de Alvarado to guard Montezuma, he set off post-haste to the coast to deal with this new problem.

Disaster

Cortés had been moving with circumspection and diplomatic skill but Alvarado was a man of a very different character. During Cortés's absence an important Aztec feast

TODAY'S UNFOUND TREASURES

COLUMBUS'S SHIPS

In 1492 Columbus sailed across the Atlantic Ocean from southern Spain via the Canary Islands and "discovered" America. Three tiny ships made up his fleet, the *Santa Maria*, the *Pinta* and the *Niña*. On reaching Cuba, the *Pinta* parted company from the others. On Christmas Eve the *Santa Maria* ran aground off Hispaniola. Attempts to refloat her failed and eventually Columbus sailed back to Spain in the *Niña*, leaving 40 of his men behind. They built a tiny settlement, called Navidad, from timbers salvaged from the wreck. It was two years before Columbus could return – to find that the inhabitants of Navidad had been massacred by hostile natives.

In recent years work has begun to find and excavate Navidad and to locate the wreck of the *Santa Maria*. In 1976 a sixteenth-century ship was discovered on the Molasses Reef off the Turks and Caicos Islands in the Caribbean. Could this be the *Pinta*? The salvage company that was formed thought so. The governor of the islands was unconvinced and called in archaeologists to investigate – unfortunately, not before much damage had been done by treasure-seekers who had dynamited the wreck. The wreck turned out to be an unknown ship, providing a fascinating glimpse of sixteenth-century life at sea. But the *Pinta* still remains to be found.

was held and Alvarado seized this opportunity to massacre some 600 Aztecs, most of them important nobles. When Cortés returned in June 1520, having defeated Narváez, he found the city in uproar and Alvarado under siege. Soon Montezuma was dead, apparently the victim of a stone thrown by one of his subjects, and the Spanish found themselves in a desperate situation. Seizing what gold and treasures they could carry, they attempted to flee the city by night. The Aztecs had cut the causeways, and now attacked the Spaniards from canoes. Many Spaniards were killed or drowned and almost all the treasure was lost in the lake as men struggled to cross the damaged causeways.

Spanish fortunes were now at their lowest ebb, but, amazingly, Cortés managed to retrieve the situation. He and his allies defeated a vastly superior Aztec army at Otumba in July and by the spring of 1521 they and their allies were strong enough to besiege Tenochtitlán.

Piece by piece the city fell and on August

ABOVE: Spain soon exploited the New World's riches. This silver coin was among the first struck in Mexico, in 1556.

BELOW: In 1540 Francisco Vásquez de Coronado led an expedition into New Mexico and Texas in search of the fabled Seven Cities of Cibolla. They discovered plenty about the region but found no gold.

13 the new Aztec emperor was captured. The Spaniards' native allies sacked the city with unspeakable ferocity, and the Spaniards began the attempt to retrieve the lost treasure from the lake around the causeways. They dived in the area, searching the bottom with their feet, but there was little to be found. In the months since they had lost it the Aztec gold had been located and spirited away by its owners.

About one twenty-fifth of the treasure was retrieved. Cortés packed this on to a ship and dispatched it to Charles V. But the ship was intercepted on its way by a French privateer and all its treasure was seized.

Still hunting

The Spanish had been seeking gold in the New World and they had found it, although they had lost it again. They were convinced that there was more to be seized if they knew where to look. Some went south and found it, destroying the empire of the Incas and hounding the peoples of the neighbouring gold-rich lands. Others turned their eyes to the north. An expedition under Narváez was sent from Spain to conquer Florida but was shipwrecked on the coast in 1528. Alvar Núñez Cabeza de Vaca and three companions survived. For eight years they wandered across this unknown terrain, helped by some native groups, enslaved by others. Their travels took them almost to the west coast, from which they managed to make their way south to Mexico City, the new Spanish foundation built on top of Tenochtitlán. They brought back rumours of the supposedly fabulously wealthy Seven Cities of Cibolla, said to lie some distance to the north of the areas through which they had travelled. Many explorers set out in hope of locating these mythical cities, but they were doomed to failure. The cities of which they had heard were probably the prosperous settlements of the Pueblo people in the American Southwest — but of gold they had none.

SPANISH GOLD ARGOSIES

Spanish gold

Old coins occasionally turned up on Florida's beaches and in 1949 Kip Wagner joined a group diving in search of their source: a site offshore where one of the group thought he had located a shipwreck. By the end of that summer they were $12,000 out of pocket and had found nothing. Disillusioned, the group split up, but Wagner was smitten with the treasure-hunting bug and knew that he couldn't stop until he had located the elusive wreck.

His interest was reinforced when he took a walk along the beach after a hurricane and found a silver coin. He was sure that it must have been washed out from a sunken ship somewhere in the neighbourhood, but he realized he needed to know more. What ships were known to have gone down in the area and where exactly? Did any of them tie in with his coin, which was dated 1714? Wagner and his friend Doc Kelso began to scour the records in libraries near and far, looking for ships that had sunk around that time. Gradually they built up a picture of the possibilities.

One seemed too good to be true. After their conquest of Mexico and Peru, the Spanish began to exploit the rich deposits of gold and silver of these lands, annually sending the treasure back to Spain in a fleet of strongly armed galleons and merchant ships. In 1715 this fleet had the misfortune to be caught by a hurricane and all its ten ships, carrying a fabulous quantity of gold and silver, had been wrecked somewhere off Florida. But where? Some authorities thought they had gone down off the Florida Keys, others suggested Cape Canaveral. Then Doc Kelso had a stroke of luck: he found a book written only 60 years after the fleet sank. Not only did this state that the fleet had been lost off the Sebastian River, not far from the homes of Wagner and Kelso, but it also had a map marking the shipwreck site.

The clues accumulate

The next breakthrough came when Wagner and Kelso obtained a microfilm of Spanish archive material on the disaster. Written in archaic Spanish, the documents took them more than a year to decipher. They gave details of each ship's cargo and of the salvage operations at the time, in which less than half the treasure was recovered. The salvage had taken four years, during which the Spanish authorities and the divers they employed had repeatedly been forced to fend off attacks by pirates and English privateers. The expedition team constructed a fortified camp on the shore to protect themselves and the treasure during the operation.

If Wagner and Kelso could locate the camp, they realized, they would have a good fix on the precise location of the wrecks. So Wagner took to walking the beaches, armed with a metal detector. For ages he searched without success, but one day he stumbled upon it, on a sandy bluff above the beach. Wagner began to make trips into the sea, swimming out from the area overlooked by the camp. At last he spotted a promising sight: a heap of cannon lying on the seabed alongside an anchor. He heard of another wreck some way to the south and retrieved a few silver coins from it. But he realized that the investigation of these wrecks required more sophisticated equipment than he was able to muster, and the project was put on hold. Wagner was sure that one day he would be able to investigate them properly, so he obtained a lease from the Florida state

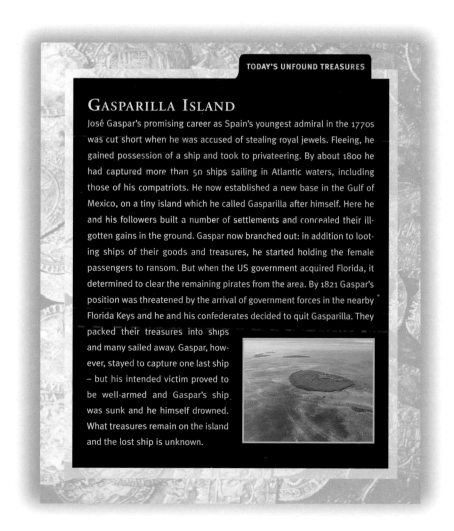

TODAY'S UNFOUND TREASURES

GASPARILLA ISLAND

José Gaspar's promising career as Spain's youngest admiral in the 1770s was cut short when he was accused of stealing royal jewels. Fleeing, he gained possession of a ship and took to privateering. By about 1800 he had captured more than 50 ships sailing in Atlantic waters, including those of his compatriots. He now established a new base in the Gulf of Mexico, on a tiny island which he called Gasparilla after himself. Here he and his followers built a number of settlements and concealed their ill-gotten gains in the ground. Gaspar now branched out: in addition to looting ships of their goods and treasures, he started holding the female passengers to ransom. But when the US government acquired Florida, it determined to clear the remaining pirates from the area. By 1821 Gaspar's position was threatened by the arrival of government forces in the nearby Florida Keys and he and his confederates decided to quit Gasparilla. They packed their treasures into ships and many sailed away. Gaspar, however, stayed to capture one last ship – but his intended victim proved to be well-armed and Gaspar's ship was sunk and he himself drowned. What treasures remain on the island and the lost ship is unknown.

A heap of silver coins, concreted with shell during their centuries underwater, lies beneath a beautiful gold rosary, the property of one of the ill-fated passengers of the 1622 Spanish treasure fleet.

authorities giving him the right to salvage material from wrecks along an 80-kilometre (50 miles) stretch of coast and exclusive rights to salvage the two wrecks he had located.

Real Eight

Wagner and Kelso got to know other people who shared their interests and by 1960 they had formed a team which included experienced divers. They bought a boat and started diving on one of the wrecks. It was hard work: the site was covered with heavy ballast which had to be shifted before the wreck could be further explored. But eventually their patience was rewarded when they found a number of silver bars, part of the cargo that the Spaniards had failed to salvage.

Now that they had begun to succeed, they decided to put the whole project on a firm legal footing. They formed a company which they called the Real Eight Corporation, from the name of the Spanish coins, *reales*, that the fleet had carried. And they began investigating the second wreck. On their first day out over it, they found a mass of coins fused together: a promising beginning which led to the discovery of a fortune in gold coins. But although this wreck was in some ways easier to investigate, they were frequently hampered by bad weather, sharks and the seabed deposits, which kept moving, sometimes exposing remains and at other times burying them deeply.

In 1963 Real Eight joined forces with Mel Fisher, another experienced diver and treasure-hunter, and his colleagues of Treasure Salvors Inc. They had their difficulties, including legal battles with unauthorized divers on the wrecks on which they held leases, and periods when they worked hard but found nothing or their equipment broke down. But they had many triumphant

ABOVE: The Spanish treasure fleet of 1622, made up of ships bearing goods from various ports in Central and South America, came together in the summer at Havana before setting sail for Spain.

Havana. The sinking of the treasure ships was a major loss and salvage attempts were put in train at once. The *Rosario* was discovered aground on the Dry Tortugas; her crew was rescued and most of her treasure recovered. The *Atocha* was also found in deep water off the Marquesas Keys, but divers could not get into her to recover anything. Of the *Santa Margarita* there was no trace. A further salvage expedition was mounted in 1626, using a special diving bell invented by the head of the expedition, Francisco Núñez Melián. By this time the remains of the *Atocha* had disappeared. The *Santa Margarita* was at last located and a considerable amount of silver from her cargo was salvaged. However, much still remained, inaccessible to the Spanish salvors.

Fisher and his associates employed every means at their disposal: searching the Florida Keys with a range of reconnaissance devices and scouring the archives for clues. The latter enabled them to narrow the area of their search to the Marquesas Keys and in 1971 they met success, discovering a wreck.

The public scramble for underwater treasure that had followed Real Eight's discovery of the 1715 wrecks had led the Florida state authorities to introduce legislation designed to give some protection to historic wrecks. Salvage permits now involved a partitioning of the finds between the state and the salvors and attention had to be paid to recovering historical information as well as treasure. An archaeologist, Duncan Mathewson, formed part of Fisher's team, recording the remains found on this new site.

One of Mathewson's tasks was to identify the ship they had found. At first it proved difficult. The official cargo of gold and silver carried by the Spanish plate fleet was marked with official stamps and attracted a 20 per cent tax. There were harsh penalties for carrying contraband treasure in order to evade this tax. But the opportunity was too tempting and most ships carried a huge illegal cargo belonging to the

moments, like the day when one of their number found an exquisite gold pendant on the beach; shaped like a dragon, it incorporated a whistle, a toothpick and an ear-cleaning spoon.

The fleet of 1622

In 1966 Mel Fisher's team decided to move elsewhere, beginning a five-year search for an earlier Spanish treasure fleet. Just like the doomed Spanish fleet of 1715, the ships

that sailed for Spain in 1622 were seriously delayed, departing in September way behind schedule and well into the dangerous hurricane season. One day out from Havana, they ran into a force-10 gale and eight of the 28 ships went down over an 80-kilometre (50 miles) stretch off the Florida Keys, including three heavily laden with treasure, the *Nuestra Señora de Atocha*, *Nuestra Señora de Rosario* and *Santa Margarita*. Others succeeded in returning to

passengers and crew. This ship was no exception and the first finds from it included unmarked gold bars which gave no clues to the ship's identity. As more objects were salvaged, however, some silver ingots marked with an official number were found and their details matched those given in the official manifest of the cargo of the *Atocha*.

The wreck, then, was the fabulous Spanish treasure ship, the *Atocha*. Fisher's luck was now in and in 1980 he struck lucky again, discovering the *Santa Margarita* nearby. Although the ship had broken up after striking the reef, the salvage team discovered a substantial chunk of her timbers preserved on the seabed. This was excavated and raised. Like the *Atocha*, the *Santa Margarita* contained a large quantity of contraband material. Much of this was carried as gold chains, which could easily have been broken up and sold once the owner reached home – though of course these unfortunates never did: about 550 people lost their lives when the eight ships sank in 1622.

Florida Keys again

A similar disaster took place in 1733. Yet again a Spanish plate fleet was the victim of a hurricane: all her 22 ships were damaged and most sank or broke up on the reefs, only one managing to return to Havana. Here a rescue and salvage team was quickly assembled, bringing immediate assistance to the survivors and over the following years recovering a great deal of the cargo from the wrecked vessels. More, in fact, than the ships were officially recorded as carrying, though by no means all that had been lost was recovered, for, like other fleets, these ships had been loaded with contraband as well as officially recorded goods.

One of the wrecked ships, the flagship *El Rubi Segundo*, was rediscovered in 1930 by a fisherman, and in the years since then many treasure-seekers have investigated the area, locating nine more wrecks. Because of the efficient original salvage operation, little treasure was still left in these wreck sites, but the surviving remains from them are of great historical value. Some treasure-hunters in

ABOVE: A diver triumphantly surfaces with one of the silver bars found in the wreck of the Spanish treasure ship *Atocha*, discovered by Mel Fisher and his team.

LEFT: The wrecks of the 1622 treasure fleet yielded a number of superb gold chains, smuggled by their owners to avoid the crippling import duties levied by the Spanish authorities.

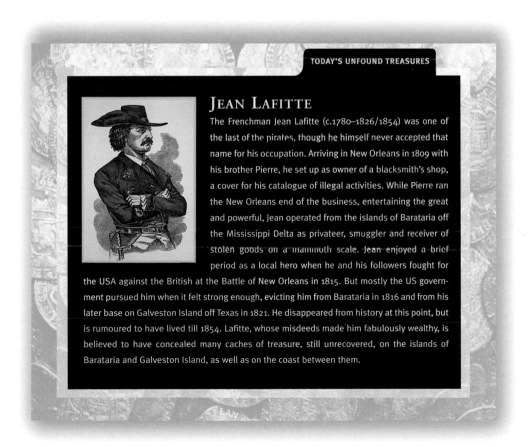

TODAY'S UNFOUND TREASURES

JEAN LAFITTE

The Frenchman Jean Lafitte (c.1780–1826/1854) was one of the last of the pirates, though he himself never accepted that name for his occupation. Arriving in New Orleans in 1809 with his brother Pierre, he set up as owner of a blacksmith's shop, a cover for his catalogue of illegal activities. While Pierre ran the New Orleans end of the business, entertaining the great and powerful, Jean operated from the islands of Barataria off the Mississippi Delta as privateer, smuggler and receiver of stolen goods on a mammoth scale. Jean enjoyed a brief period as a local hero when he and his followers fought for the USA against the British at the Battle of New Orleans in 1815. But mostly the US government pursued him when it felt strong enough, evicting him from Barataria in 1816 and from his later base on Galveston Island off Texas in 1821. He disappeared from history at this point, but is rumoured to have lived till 1854. Lafitte, whose misdeeds made him fabulously wealthy, is believed to have concealed many caches of treasure, still unrecovered, on the islands of Barataria and Galveston Island, as well as on the coast between them.

The inscription "Mater Salvatoris" – Mother of the Saviour – identifies the figure on this medallion from the doomed 1724 treasure fleet as the Virgin Mary, whose protection the wearer had sought against the perils of the sea.

the area have adopted a responsible attitude, recording their finds, but many, unfortunately, have virtually destroyed the wrecks they investigated. One wreck, the *San Pedro*, was officially designated an Underwater Archaeological Preserve, to protect it.

Mercury

The ships in which the Spanish treasure fleet brought home the gold and silver of the Americas fulfilled an equally vital role on their journey out. For the colonists who had settled in Spain's American possessions, they brought a whole range of luxury objects from home, and for the mining companies they brought vital supplies of mercury, essential for processing ore to extract silver. Adventurous people who intended to settle in New Spain also took passage on the ships of the outward-bound plate fleet.

But many of those who embarked on the journey to the New World in 1724 were destined never to arrive. Packed on board two ships, the *Nuestra Señora de Guadalupe* and the *Conde de Tolosa*, were some 1,200 people. They crossed the Atlantic safely, touching at Puerto Rico to take on supplies, but as they sailed on they ran into a hurricane off Samana Bay on Hispaniola. The *Guadalupe* ran aground on a sandbank but did not immediately sink, and most of her passengers made it ashore. The *Tolosa* initially seemed better off, managing to anchor at the mouth of the bay; but the storm tore her adrift and drove her in, smashing her against rocks within the bay. Of the 600 aboard her, fewer than 40 survived. Seven did so by a miracle: they climbed the ship's mainmast and spent more than a month clinging to life in the maintops, sustained by food and water from the wrecked ship and menaced by sharks which prevented them swimming ashore.

The survivors from the *Guadalupe* were 320 kilometres (200 miles) from Santo Domingo, the nearest Spanish settlement. On the gruelling overland journey many died. When the rest reached the settlement,

boats were sent to rescue anyone still alive at the wreck site, and to attempt, without success, to salvage the valuable cargo of mercury from the ships.

In 1976 another attempt was made. A company called Caribe Salvage contracted with the Dominican government to look for the wrecks of these two vessels, the proceeds to be divided equally between the state and the salvage company. Although they did not recover the mercury, the salvors found many beautiful objects. The Spanish authorities prohibited the carriage of non-Spanish goods, but there were plenty aboard. These included a fine brass clock made in London; the excavators had only to clean it and replace a few steel parts for it to run again perfectly, despite its centuries under the sea. There were also exquisite goblets and decanters of engraved glass, and beautiful pieces of gold jewellery of exceptional workmanship. Many of these pieces told a personal story, such as the gold cross of a Knight of Santiago or the bracelet inscribed with the name of Doña Antonia Franco, both the property of passengers on the ship. We can begin to glimpse their lives by piecing together such evidence from the wrecks.

ABOVE: Figures stamped on these gold bars recovered from the *Santa Margarita* in the Marquesas Keys were part of the official recording system introduced by the Spanish government in the 17th century to prevent smuggling.

THE "MONEY PIT"

MYSTERIOUS PIT

In 1795 Daniel McGinnis was exploring Oak Island, just across the bay from Chester, Nova Scotia, when he spotted a tree with rope marks – from a pulley? – over a shallow hollow in the ground. He immediately thought of buried treasure. The next day he returned with some friends and started digging. It turned out to be a tremendously deep pit. As they went down they uncovered a number of platforms of oak logs, some sealed with ship's putty. Discouraged, they abandoned their investigation – but returned in 1804 and dug down to 30 metres (100 feet). Probing through the next layer of putty and wood, they thought they could feel treasure chests packed with coins. But by the next day the shaft had filled with water and only the top 10 metres (33 feet) remained clear. The supposed treasure chests seemed also to have fallen from their platform, washed by the water to the depths below. The lads could do no more.

The Restall family, two of whom died on Oak Island.

But the pit was not forgotten. Over the two centuries that have elapsed since then many further attempts have been made to penetrate the mysteries of the shaft, which quickly acquired the name the "Money Pit". No one could tell if there was treasure below but the pit seemed too elaborate not to be concealing something extremely valuable.

As investigations multiplied, the area became completely churned up, with shafts sunk alongside the Money Pit in an attempt to reach its lower levels. These have revealed details of its elaborate construction. The shaft, which is at least 65 metres (212 feet) deep, drops down into a large cavern. The skilful engineers who constructed it dammed the sea from entering the area while they were working. They dug several tunnels into the shaft from the sea, and placed a number of platforms in the shaft. When they had completed their work, they released the sea from its dam. The platforms were arranged so that as soon as certain of them were removed, the sea water would be sucked into the tunnels and fill the shaft – an excellent booby trap. In order to penetrate the depths, where the supposed treasure might lie, the sea would have to be dammed again: a task requiring both skill and knowledge of the tunnels' layout.

Vast sums, totalling millions of pounds, have been spent on investigating the Money Pit, and six people have lost their lives. But with modern technology it has proved possible to penetrate some of its mysteries. A stone bearing the date 1704 has been found nearby, though whether this relates to the Money Pit is uncertain. The cavern at the base of the shaft was photographed in 1971, using a video camera, and this seemed to show three chests, along with a well-preserved severed hand. Divers were lowered 72 metres (235 feet) into the cave but did not report anything.

WHOSE TREASURE?

If the pit does conceal treasure, what is it? A number of people have suggested that Captain Kidd's mysterious island (see p. 38) bears an uncanny resemblance to Oak Island, although the name "China Sea" on the chart seems to go against this theory. "Blackbeard" (Edward Teach), who died in 1718, also claimed to have left vast treasures and he is another who is tentatively linked with the Money Pit.

The people of Chester claimed to have seen mysterious lights and fires on Oak Island in 1763. Could these have been lit by the builders of the gigantic booby trap? Another suggestion links the Money Pit with a party of Royal Engineers operating during the American War of Independence, hiding threatened supplies of British government money. Or could it have been the men of a disabled Spanish galleon who had concealed their treasure there rather than risk sailing the ocean with it? If the supposed treasure is ever recovered, its date and nature should provide some of the answers. Until then we can only speculate. It seems unlikely that the end-result will justify the expense of the investigations that have taken place nor the devastation that these have wrought on this part of the island, but the attempts have at least satisfied a great craving for adventure.

THE GOLD RUSH AND THE *CENTRAL AMERICA*

Gold Rush

When James Marshall spotted gold at Sutter's Mill, California, in January 1848, he set in train the great Gold Rush. Within a year more than 100,000 people had poured into the state: prospectors seeking their fortune and sometimes succeeding overnight, along with shopkeepers, hoteliers, bar-keepers, bankers and prostitutes to provide the services the prospectors might want. Some people came to the gold fields overland, joining wagon trains along the pioneer trails from the east. Those who could afford it preferred to make the journey by sea, braving the elements rather than the hostile Indians.

The United States Mail Steamship Company operated a fleet of steamers that linked New York and eastern ports with Aspinwall in Panama. From here a railway carried passengers to and from the west coast, while other steamers regularly plied the sea lanes to San Francisco. The *Central America* operated on the Atlantic route, and in August 1857 the paddle steamer set out from Aspinwall with passengers and mail, and a load of gold from the Californian fields. More passengers joined the ship in Havana, bringing the total number aboard to 575 and the value of gold being carried to $2,189,000.

Although at first the journey was pleasant, on September 10 a storm began to brew up, developing into a hurricane that swamped the unstable *Central America*. Despite the crew's heroic efforts, the ship went down on the 12th. Several passing ships rescued around 150 people, including all the women and children, but 423 people were lost. Only floating debris remained from the wreck, far out at sea.

RIGHT: Gold bars sparkle on the seabed around the wreck of the *Central America*. She went down in 1857, carrying the wealth of many prospectors who had struck lucky in the California Gold Rush.

RIGHT: Gold coins recovered from the wreck of the *Central America*, which sank off South Carolina in 1857, lie on the insurance register recording the ship's original loss.

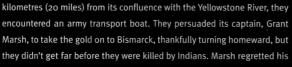

TODAY'S UNFOUND TREASURES

GOLD AT LITTLE BIGHORN

Transporting gold through hostile territory was never easy but in June 1876 the situation was desperate. The discovery of gold in the Black Hills of Dakota, a Sioux sacred site, had attracted swarms of white prospectors, bringing already tense relations with the native inhabitants to flashpoint and culminating in the massacre of General Custer and his troops at Little Bighorn. Gill Longworth was conveying £30,000 of raw gold from the Montana gold fields to Bismarck, North Dakota. The country was alive with hostile Sioux, and Longworth and his two companions began to fear for their safety. To their relief, when they reached the Bighorn River, some 32 kilometres (20 miles) from its confluence with the Yellowstone River, they encountered an army transport boat. They persuaded its captain, Grant Marsh, to take the gold on to Bismarck, thankfully turning homeward, but they didn't get far before they were killed by Indians. Marsh regretted his

decision almost at once: the gold might exacerbate an already difficult situation. He therefore buried it for safe keeping. For years it was too dangerous to retrieve the gold. Eventually Marsh tried to contact the freight company for whom Longworth had worked, but it had gone out of business. Marsh and his crew did not return to retrieve the gold, so theoretically it is still there.

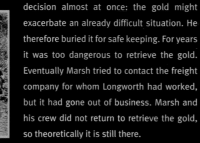

Salvage disputes

Until recent decades it was impossible to locate and recover such deep-sea wrecks. As the technology developed, however, several attempts were made to find and salvage the *Central America*. In 1987 the Columbus America Discovery Group (CADG) located the wreck 320 kilometres (220 miles) off South Carolina at a depth of 2,500 metres (8,200 feet). The vessel's contents were remarkably well preserved and the salvage company even recovered newspapers from a leather trunk. Using a remotely operated vehicle, they removed some of the ship's cargo of gold as well as luggage, the ship's bell and even cigars. They made a television film of their work and published a book and school material on the wreck. The responsible and sensitive attitude they adopted in their recovery operations stood them in good stead later.

The CADG reported its finds to the relevant authorities and in the summer of 1989 all the interested parties came to court to determine the ownership of the gold and other salvaged material. The main question was whether the original owners – or rather the insurers who had paid out after the disaster – still had a legitimate claim to the gold. After more than a century the insurers no longer had the relevant documents and the lower court, where the case was first heard, decided that they had effectively abandoned ownership. This decision was overturned by the United States Courts of Appeal in 1992: the insured portion of the cargo was still the property of the insurers, although the uninsured cargo and the ship itself were now the property of the salvors, and the insurers owed the CADG something substantial for its salvage efforts. The case returned to the lower court for amounts to be determined. In view of the considerable expense and difficulty of the salvage, and of the salvors' responsible approach to the operation, it was decided that their share should be 90 per cent of the value of the recovered gold: a vast fortune.

THE *SS REPUBLIC*

COLLISION IN FOG

On January 22, 1909 the White Star Line's luxury liner the *SS Republic* left New York with many wealthy passengers, bound for Alexandria in Egypt. She was to call at Genoa, as she was carrying relief supplies for the victims of a terrible earthquake in Italy in which more than 85,000 people had died. On the same day the Italian steamship the *Florida* was approaching New York with more than 800 Italian emigrants aboard,

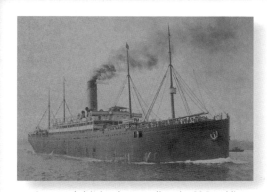

A postcard showing the ocean liner the *SS Republic*.

many of them fleeing homes ruined by the earthquake. As both ships approached Nantucket Island, a thick fog descended, blanketing out all visibility and nearly all sound. Both ships proceeded with caution, regularly sounding their foghorns, but neither knew of the other's presence until the *Florida* ran straight into the *Republic,* crushing her own bows and tearing a great hole in the *Republic*'s side.

The *Republic*'s heroic young wireless operator, John Binns, began sending out distress signals – almost the first time that the wireless had been used in sea rescue. The *Florida,* though damaged, was in no immediate danger and the crew of the *Republic* managed to seal off the holed section from the rest of the ship. The *Republic*'s passengers were transferred to the *Florida* and both ships awaited the arrival of the *Baltic,* which had answered the distress call. The fog was still thick and it was with great difficulty that the *Baltic* located the *Republic*. After doing so she took off the crew, the passengers of both ships, the mail and probably some of the cargo. She and the *Florida* now headed for port. An attempt was made to tow in the *Republic,* but she proved too badly damaged and eventually she sank.

MYSTERY OF THE CARGO

The *Republic* lies in difficult and dangerous waters and it was not until 1981 that she was relocated by diver Martin Bayerle. By 1987 he and his company, Sub Ocean Salvors Inc, had managed to raise the $1.5 million needed to attempt a salvage. Although there were likely to be many valuables aboard, the property of the passengers, the salvors were pinning their hopes on a rumour. In 1909 Tsar Nicholas of Russia had been struggling against revolution and it was said that the *Republic* was secretly carrying $3 million in American gold to aid him. Another rumour made the sum $250,000 and its destination the United States Battle Fleet.

The wreck proved to be in very bad shape and the task extremely difficult. The salvors recovered little apart from china and wine bottles. After three months they abandoned the attempt, though they still believe the gold is there.

A piece of china recovered from the *SS Republic*.

THE *TITANIC*

The unsinkable *Titanic*

At the beginning of the twentieth century two great shipping lines, White Star and Cunard, were battling for dominance of transatlantic passenger traffic, each building bigger and better ships to attract potential travellers. In 1907 Cunard launched the *Lusitania,* the first ship to make the Atlantic crossing between Britain and America in just five days. White Star decided to commission the shipbuilders Harland and Wolff to construct three huge vessels that were to be the very last word in comfort, while completing the journey in very little more time than the *Lusitania.* The first of these, the huge *Olympic,* was completed in 1910, and the following year the even more vast *Titanic* was finished.

Immense excitement grew as the *Titanic* was readied for her maiden voyage. Her creators' optimistic words that she was "virtually unsinkable" had soon been popularly translated into "unsinkable" without qualification. The passengers who boarded the ship at Southampton on Wednesday April 10, 1912 included people from many walks of life: from millionaires, like John Jacob Astor and his new second wife Madeleine, accompanied by servants, to third-class passengers like Minnie Coutts and her two sons. Also on board were Bruce Ismay, the Managing Director of the White Star Line, and Thomas Andrews, the Managing Director of Harland and Wolff, both intensely interested in how the ship would perform on her maiden voyage.

Steaming ahead

As the monstrous *Titanic* began to pull out of Southampton harbour, the *New York,* a smaller ship moored at a berth along *Titanic*'s route down the River Test, was

BELOW: Passengers on the *Titanic* dined in style. Those in second class enjoyed food cooked in the same kitchens as the food served in the first-class dining room.

sucked out into her path. Quick thinking by the *Titanic*'s captain, Edward Smith, averted disaster as he reversed his ship's engines, and the *New York* was towed to safety.

That evening the *Titanic* arrived in Cherbourg in France, where more passengers joined her, and the following day, April 11, she reached Queenstown (now Cóbh) in Ireland, her last port of call before her destination, New York. Here some passengers disembarked, having briefly tasted the luxuries of the magnificent ship, and the final travellers boarded. The historic voyage had begun.

The first-class passengers found themselves in the lap of luxury. Sportsmen like the tennis star Norris Williams could work out in the gymnasium or take a swim in the pool or a Turkish bath. A smoking room for the gentlemen was matched by a comfortable reading and writing room for the ladies. Elegant cafés and a luxurious dining saloon allowed them to eat in splendour, while a magnificent staircase under a glass and wrought-iron dome gave them access to the boat deck and an enclosed promenade deck. Luxuriously furnished staterooms were available for the most wealthy passengers, and even the third-class accommodation on the lower decks was comfortable though not spacious. Third class too had its dining room, lounge and smoking room, while those in second class could also enjoy a walk on their own promenade.

The voyage was scheduled to take a week, but progress was so good that Ismay and Captain Smith felt it should be possible to knock a day off the journey time by increasing the speed at which the ship was steaming along. So far the engines had been performing wonderfully.

Hazard warnings

The normal route across the Atlantic went into cold northerly waters where there was generally much ice in the spring. To avoid the risk of icebergs, which were reported unusually far south that year, Captain Smith

The massive bulk of the *Titanic* dominated the harbour where she awaited her first – and last – voyage. Although she was not the fastest vessel of her time, she and her sister ships were intended to be the most luxurious.

ABOVE: A salvor examines a pottery vessel recovered from the wreck of the *Titanic*. As she lies outside the territorial waters of any modern state, the right to salvage her contents has sparked bitter controversy.

laid a course farther south than was customary. Nevertheless, his wireless operators received a number of messages from other shipping in the area, warning of many icebergs and fields of ice in the vicinity. Although the general message was widely circulated, not all the specific warnings were relayed to the bridge – a fatal mistake.

The sailors on lookout duty were told to keep a careful eye open for ice. The pair who were on duty on the night of Sunday April 14 were having a hard time with this. A slight haze had developed and the sea was quite calm, so no telltale line of foam betrayed the presence of the iceberg that was directly ahead of the ship in the darkness. Suddenly, around 11.30, Frederick Fleet spotted the dark mass immediately before them. An iceberg! He rang the bell furiously to sound the warning, which he confirmed on the telephone to the wheelhouse. The officer in charge there, William Murdoch, ordered the ship's head to be swung round, but also set the engines in reverse, fatally reducing the speed at which she could turn. With a horrible sound the iceberg scraped her side.

Abandon ship!

Although the iceberg did not penetrate the ship's hull, the pressure it exerted on her caused some of the plates to open up and the rivets, weakened by the cold, to shear. Gaps opened between the plates and the icy water began to rush in. Although separate sections of the ship were sealed off, initially preventing the water from flooding throughout the hold, a dangerous amount of water had entered the ship and she soon began to list. Inexorably, the water filled the lower decks and the situation became increasingly serious.

But few people initially understood that the *Titanic* was doomed. Many wandered on to the boat deck for a good view, a lot of them clad in their dressing gowns. Within half an hour, however, Captain Smith had realized that the ship would sink. He ordered the wireless operators to put out a distress call; it was answered by several ships but none that could arrive in less than a few hours. However, flickering lights in the distance suggested that a ship that was not responding was much closer, within 16 kilometres (10 miles).

Several of the lifeboats were launched. Uncertain of the reliability of the mechanism for lowering them into the sea, the officers at first dispatched them with only a handful of passengers, instead of the full complement of 65. The lifeboat crews were told to make for the unknown ship, unload their passengers and return.

But time was running out fast. The remaining lifeboats were launched, now fully loaded. Despite the desperate situation most people stayed calm. Women and children were helped aboard the lifeboats and any man who attempted to join them was turned back, although some men were included to crew them. Many of the third-class passengers were trapped below, confused by the maze of corridors and stairs that led tortuously towards the boat deck. And eventually there were no more lifeboats. Reliance on the ship's theoretical strength and safety had led to its being equipped with far too few, enough for less than half the people aboard, even if each boat had been fully loaded.

Just after 2 a.m. the end came. The *Titanic*, already half submerged, broke in two and sank beneath the surface. Miraculously some of those still aboard were able to climb on to floating wreckage or to survive in the icy waters long enough to be pulled aboard some of the less crowded lifeboats – although many of their passengers were reluctant to help others less fortunate in case their vessel became swamped and everyone went down.

Rescue

The crew of the *Carpathia* had received the *Titanic*'s distress call and had immediately altered course towards her. But they were many kilometres away and it was not until around 2.30 a.m. that they reached the scene of the disaster. They helped the cold, wet and desperate survivors aboard, wrapped them up and gave them hot drinks, and the ship's doctors attended to those who were injured. But, of the 2,222 people who had been aboard the *Titanic*, only 705 had survived.

Among these was Bruce Ismay, who had entered a lifeboat at a late stage in the disaster. He and many other male survivors suffered for the rest of their lives from the public opinion that they ought not to have lived when so many women and children had gone down with the ship. Ismay was also one of those who had had responsibility for the ship and he was subjected to the ordeal of two legal investigations of the causes of the disaster, one in America and one in England, to establish whether there had been negligence. The conclusion was that there had not.

Nevertheless, the disaster had far-reaching consequences. Regulations were tightened so that it would never again be possible for a vessel to go to sea inadequately supplied with lifeboats. Improvements in the design of ships were also made. Ships were required to man their wirelesses 24 hours a day. And a regular ice patrol was instituted, to monitor the movement of icebergs and issue warnings.

Rediscovering the wreck

Although there is no firm evidence of treasure carried aboard the *Titanic*, many of the passengers were wealthy. And the scale of the disaster has gripped the popular imagination ever since the ship went down. So there were always hopes that the *Titanic* would be raised again. As she lay at such a depth in icy

waters, however, it was impossible for many years for anything to be done about tracing and investigating the wreck.

By the 1980s the technology to investigate the depths was beginning to be developed. Several attempts to locate the *Titanic* failed, but in 1985 Dr Robert Ballard, a geologist from the Woods Hole Oceanographic Institute in Massachusetts, began to search the area with a submersible and an underwater robot that he had devised. Initially he worked with a French team using side-scan sonar to search for the

wreck, but his efforts went unrewarded. Eventually he started using an underwater camera and in 1986 he spotted one of the ship's boilers.

Elated, he began a programme of filming her remarkable remains. She had broken up further when she hit the seabed, her bows coming to rest nearly 610 metres (2,000 feet) from the stern. Rust had attacked much of the ship's metalwork, creating great pendant pieces like yellow icicles. Some parts of her still gave a glimpse of her former glory while others lay scattered in a thousand fragments. Pieces of furniture also survived, as did many of the objects on the ship.

In 1987 salvors descended on the wreck and began to remove material from it. This gave rise to many legal battles between rival salvage companies and other interested parties, such as the insurers who had paid out on the original losses in the disaster – a can of worms that once opened has been writhing ever since.

Tairona ●

Muisca ●

Tolima ● ● Lake Guatavita

Pirate ship

Sipán ●

Nevado Ampato ●

SOUTH AMERICA

6

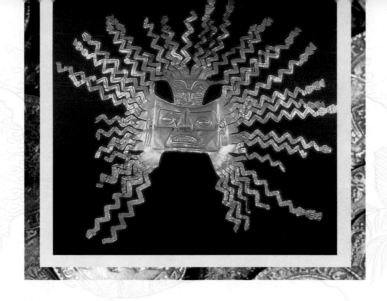

THE SPANIARDS WENT TO THE AMERICAS DREAMING OF RICHES UNTOLD. WHEN THEY REACHED SOUTH AMERICA THEY FOUND THEIR DREAMS FULFILLED. FOR CENTURIES AFTERWARD SPAIN WAS TO IMPORT VAST QUANTITIES OF GOLD AND SILVER FROM THIS REGION, ALTERING THE WORLD'S ECONOMY.

SOUTH AMERICAN TREASURES

Lands of gold

Much of the gold came from the alluvium of rivers flowing down from the Andes, while some was extracted from quartz veins. After the conquest the mines at Potosí became the main source of silver.

To the native peoples of South America, precious metals and stones had a deep religious significance. The Incas regarded gold as the sweat of the sun and silver as the tears of the moon. Metalworking began in South America as early as 2100 BC, and from early times metal objects were placed in the burials of important individuals and served as signs of rank associated with supernatural

ABOVE: The people of the Cordilleras (in modern Ecuador and Colombia) made a variety of fantastic gold figures and faces of humans and gods (top), while the Incas made beautiful naturalistic objects like this llama (centre).

LEFT: Clad in a perfect miniature set of woman's clothing, this silver figure of an Inca goddess was buried as a votive offering on the peak of Cerro Copiapó in the Andes.

power. Gold's life-giving association with the sun was often emphasized by alloying it with copper to produce a metal, called tumbaga, of a richer colour. The civilizations of Peru and adjacent regions developed sophisticated metallurgical techniques, including the beaded effect known as granulation. The goldwork of the Moche was particularly fine. To the north in Ecuador and Colombia, smaller chiefdoms flourished, each developing its own style of goldworking. For example, the Muisca produced flat figures with details added in thin wire, the Tolima specialized in a strange half-human figure with a tail like an anchor, while the Tairona cast larger figures using the lost-wax technique and added elaborate details afterward.

Inca realms

The most recent civilization to emerge in the Andes region was that of the Incas.

ABOVE: Calmly seated as if asleep, this Inca boy was offered as a sacrifice to the gods of the Andes mountains. Victims were drugged and often died of exposure without ever regaining consciousness.

land and coastal regions. Magnificent roads linked all quarters of the empire and along these there were frequent waystations and government outposts to collect taxes and administer conquered lands. Some taxes took the form of compulsory labour on government projects while others were collected as goods. Pre-eminent among these were textiles made from cotton and alpaca wool. The Incas had hierarchical sumptuary laws governing the grades of cloth to be worn by people in different levels of society. The emperor himself wore cloth of the finest vicuña wool woven by specially chosen beautiful virgins housed in a nunnery in the capital, Cuzco.

Goldworkers also resided in the capital; many of them were Chimu from the northern coast, whose metalworking skills were highly prized. Gold and silver were used in circumstances of particular sanctity. The great temple of the Sun at Cuzco, the chief Inca shrine, had doors and walls coated with sheet silver and gold. Small figurines made of gold, silver or spiny oyster shell (another highly valued material, symbolizing water) and representing people or llamas were used as offerings, placed in stone boxes in the holy lake of Titicaca or with sacrificed children among the mountain peaks.

Mountain shrines

The Incas venerated mountains as gods and constructed high mountain platforms as shrines where offerings were regularly made. In times of crisis, such as drought, earthquake or volcanic eruption, unblemished children were selected as offerings, bringing honour to their families and sending them to eternal paradise. In recent years a number of these children have been rediscovered, their bodies often perfectly preserved by the freezing conditions. Sometimes there were a pair of them, a boy and a girl, brought together in a symbolic ritual marriage. The children had been finely dressed in beautiful robes and were probably drugged before being killed by a blow to the head or stran-

Around AD 1410 the small southerly highland state of the Incas began to expand, conquering its neighbours. Under Pachacutec and his son Tupac Yupanqui the Inca Empire reached to the borders of Ecuador in the north and a considerable distance through previously unconquered lands to the south, controlling both high-

gled. With them were placed offerings such as fine pottery and small figurines dressed in miniature textiles.

One sacrifice discovered in 1995 aroused particular excitement among archaeologists. This was a girl in her teens who was exceptionally well preserved. An avalanche on Nevado Ampato had disturbed an Inca platform in which she had been buried. Part of the platform and the frozen body of the girl had tumbled down the mountainside, where they were discovered by chance by Johan Reinhard. He has spent many years investigating these mountain shrines, but he happened on that occasion to be out on the mountain to admire an active volcano. In order to ensure that the "ice maiden", as they called her, did not thaw in the sun, he and his companion had to carry her down from the mountain: a daunting task. But eventually they got her to safety and refrigeration. Since her discovery and rescue, she has been subjected to a battery of tests, including a CAT scan, which revealed the blow on her forehead that had killed her, and analyses establishing what she last ate.

Destructive plunderers

In 1525 the Europeans indirectly began the destruction of the Incas. Smallpox brought from Europe swept through South America, decimating the Incas and their subjects and killing both the emperor, Huayna Capac, and his heir. Civil war between two of his sons ensued, from which Atahualpa emerged as victor.

But he had no time to consolidate his rule. In 1532 Francisco Pizarro, drawn by rumours of the golden riches of this region,

ABOVE: The Incas made many figurines of gold and silver. Elongated earlobes show that the figure above represents a member of the élite.

landed with a small force of around 200 men on the northern coast at Tumbes. There he was met by friendly envoys and marched inland, climbing the gruelling mountain paths into and over the Andes. At Cajamarca Atahualpa was waiting for him with a vast army; to demonstrate his good faith, he accepted an invitation to meet Pizarro unarmed in the centre of the town. Pizarro, however, had no compunction about using treachery and, when the unarmed Inca forces were in place, the Spanish soldiers attacked them, massacring perhaps as many as 10,000 of them and capturing the emperor.

Atahualpa offered to buy his freedom with a vast quantity of treasure: enough gold to fill a room. Pizarro accepted this easy way of collecting the Inca gold and messengers were sent throughout the Inca realms to gather the ransom. Huge quantities of gold were brought, but again Pizarro failed to keep his side of the bargain: he executed Atahualpa for "idolatry" – his failure to embrace Christianity – and set up a puppet ruler.

TODAY'S UNFOUND TREASURES

PIRATE TREASURES OF COCOS ISLAND

Four hundred and eighty kilometres (300 miles) south-west of Costa Rica lies Cocos Island, a place inextricably linked with pirates. Captain Edward Davis, an English privateer, used the island as his base and may have buried treasure here before he vanished in 1702. The pirate Benito Bonito certainly did so in 1819: it was found in 1932. But the most intriguing cache has still to be rediscovered. In 1821 revolution threatened Lima. The treasures of the cathedral seemed particularly at risk, so they were taken to Callao, to be transported to Panama. Only one ship was available but her captain willingly accepted the commission. Once at sea he knocked the treasure's guards on the head and sailed for Cocos Island. Here he shared some of the treasure with the crew and hid the rest. Many desperate adventures followed but he was never able to return. On his deathbed he handed a map locating the treasure to his friend, John Keating. It seems Keating recovered part of the hoard, but much remained. However, Keating seems to have moved it, and although he in turn passed on a treasure map, no one has yet located the missing treasures, which are said to include a 2-metre (7 feet) jewelled gold statue of the Virgin Mary.

ELDORADO

THE GILDED MAN

Pizarro's rapacious expedition was followed by others as Spaniards' appetites were whetted by what had already been found. Many Indians were tortured to reveal where further gold – and silver and jewels – might be hidden. A curious story began to gain wide circulation: the legend of the gilded man.

Among the goldworking chiefdoms in the north were the Muisca. Although they themselves had no local gold source they were able to gain substantial quantities of gold dust by trade. Some they made into golden figures but some they reserved for the investiture of their kings. The new king would be stripped naked, coated with sticky mud and then covered from head to foot with gold dust. Seating himself on a raft and accompanied by his principal lords, he would be taken out to the centre of a lake, where he would bathe, washing off the gold, which became an offering to the gods. Large quantities of gold and emeralds would be offered at the same time.

Conquistadors, including Pizarro, on an Inca wooden beaker.

The story grew in the telling: instead of an investiture once in a ruler's lifetime it became an annual event and then a daily ritual. Expeditions were mounted to seek the location of this gold-filled lake, which indeed turned out to exist: it was identified as Lake Guatavita. (One theory suggests that as the lake was formed by a meteor the golden offerings of the Muisca were to imitate the fiery appearance of its creation.) Now the problem for the Spaniards was how to retrieve the gold. The lake, which is situated in the mountains near Bogotá, is 4 kilometres (6½ miles) around and 37 metres (120 feet) deep. Could the lake, large as it was, perhaps be drained?

An expedition led by Jiménez de Quesada made a first attempt. In the dry season of 1545 one of his captains organized a team of Indians furnished with gourds and got them bailing. He succeeded in lowering the water level by about 4 metres (13 feet) and in the exposed mud he recovered a small amount of gold.

Some years later an assault was mounted on a much larger scale. Antonia de Sepúlveda, a rich merchant, obtained a royal licence to drain the lake and began work with a labour force of 8,000. They excavated a notch in the edge of the lake and the water began to drain out, reputedly lowering the lake's level by 20 metres (66 feet). But again the finds were meagre: a mere 232 pesos of gold and one large emerald.

UNDEFEATED

Perhaps discouraged by the lack of success or perhaps infected by persistent rumours of golden treasures in unlikely corners of the continent, the Eldorado legend changed. The gilded man faded from popular memory, to be replaced by the notion that Eldorado was a city of gold. Nevertheless, Lake

Guatavita never lost its association with gold and attempts continued to be made to recover its treasures.

In 1823 a consortium was formed to attempt to drain the lake completely. They made another cutting in its edge and significantly lowered the water level, but after running way over budget they were forced to abandon the attempt without having recovered anything. An English friend of the consortium's leader suggested using a siphon to perform the drainage, but he withdrew his suggestion when he visited the lake and saw the scale of the problem.

Lake Guatavita, sacred place of the ancient Muisca people.

Another group decided that the wrong lake was being investigated. In 1856 they attacked Lake Siecha, somewhat to the south of Guatavita, and succeeded in lowering the water level by several metres. They were rewarded by the discovery of a fabulous object: a gold model of the raft from the ceremony of the gilded man, complete with the imposing figure of the chief and the smaller figures of ten of his lords.

After a while attention returned to Lake Guatavita. In 1899 the most ambitious scheme to drain the lake was begun, with the formation of a company, Contractors Limited. The plan was to drain the lake's waters out through a tunnel. Armed with quantities of equipment, including a steam pump, the company began work. In 1910 it was still hard at work, but the task was nearing completion. Indians employed by the company searched the mud at the lake's edge and occasionally turned up objects, but it was virtually impossible to explore the lake bed thoroughly. When first exposed, the mud was soft to a considerable depth and would not bear a person's weight, while it turned as hard as concrete after it had been in the sun for a day or so. The residual waters accumulated in the centre, creating a hollow, and the company suspected that this was where the bulk of the treasure must lie. It recovered enough material to mount a public auction, but nothing like the amount it had hoped to find. The lake was abandoned and allowed to refill.

Other attempts were later made, but eventually the Colombian government stepped in to ban treasure-hunting in the lake. Although many still believe that great treasures lie in its bed, it is unlikely.

A gold pendant made by the Tolima.

GOLD FOR THE LORDS OF SACRIFICE

Tomb robbers

Ever since the Spaniards discovered the Inca civilization, Peru has drawn treasure-hunters mad for gold. Huge mounds of sun-dried brick, constructed by the Moche people in the early centuries AD, particularly attracted their attention; when these were excavated, tombs were found, rich in gold and silver. Looters in the seventeenth century even diverted the River Moche to undermine one of the largest of the mounds, known locally as *huacas*. Among the people of the region an illegal industry has grown up, plundering these tombs. The *huaqueros* (*huaca* robbers) dig deep into the mounds, destroying everything in them except for the valuable objects

that they can sell. They themselves receive relatively small sums for these treasures but the middlemen who resell them to international collectors can make vast fortunes.

Working precariously at night to avoid the eyes of the law, in 1987 a group of *huaqueros* dug a pit 7 metres (23 feet) deep in one such mound at Sipán, in the Lambayeque Valley in northern Peru. On the night of February 16 they struck lucky, breaking into an intact royal tomb filled with unimaginable riches. However, a tip-off soon sent the police to the house of one of the looters, where they found discarded fragments of gilded copper: unsaleable rejects from the plunderers' haul. They set an ambush and in the ensuing confrontation one of the robbers was shot dead.

The police began surprise raids on the mound to discourage further looting as it was now being besieged by gold-fevered villagers. They called in Walter Alva, director of Peru's Brüning Archaeological Museum, to inspect

the objects they had seized. Realizing that the looted grave had been exceptionally rich, Alva organized a rescue excavation, beginning in April, to investigate what remained of the grave. He hoped to find out a little about the person buried there and, with luck, to recover any objects that the looters had missed or discarded, such as pots. The Moche made elaborate pottery, some painted with scenes from their lives, other pieces moulded into portraits, models and scenes. Usually ignored by tomb robbers, these pots provide a valuable picture of how the Moche lived, and in particular of their violent wars and human sacrifices.

Once Alva started work the site had to be guarded night and day. Not only were the local villagers angry at being prevented from continuing to plunder this and other local *huacas*, they were also extremely resentful about the death of the *huaquero*. Several times Alva was startled to hear shots, as the police fired over the heads of prowling looters.

Although the grave had been thoroughly plundered, Alva did find a few objects left in it, such as a copper sceptre. He also found traces of the wooden beams of the burial chamber. Their arrangement told him that this chamber had been added after the mound was built. If this royal tomb was a late addition, perhaps there were other, earlier burials within the mound. A close examination of the mound's surface revealed a disturbance, a pit that had been dug and filled with sand and stones in Moche times. Could this be the entrance to an intact tomb? The excavators hardly dared to hope so.

A royal grave

It was. Digging down into the old pit, they came upon the wooden beams of a burial chamber. Among a mass of pottery, including figurines arranged in scenes, they found the contorted body of a man who had probably been sacrificed. Farther down they found another body, wrapped in a cotton shroud and armed with a club and shield: the guardian of the tomb, whose feet had been removed, perhaps to stop his spirit leaving its post. Below him lay the main chamber. Four wooden coffins surrounded a larger main one and these contained four more sacrificed people: two women who may have been the concubines or wives of the deceased, another warrior and a servant with the royal dog. One woman and the warrior, like the guardian, had had their feet removed.

In the main coffin lay the Lord of Sipán, a warrior priest like those who were so often shown on pottery vessels seated on a throne and receiving a goblet of blood taken from the throat of a sacrificed prisoner. He had been buried clad in astounding wealth. Beside him lay a golden crescent-shaped headdress while the lower part of his face was wrapped in a gold mask. From his nose hung another ornament in gold and from his ears two magnificent ear ornaments of gold and turquoise. These were decorated with a tiny figure, about the size of a thumb, lavishly attired in gold like the ruler and clutching a

shield and war club. More representations of this warlike figure appeared on two banners of gilded copper mounted on cloth and on another headdress.

The rest of his body was just as sumptuously dressed. Round his neck were two necklaces of peanuts fashioned in gold and silver and a massive necklace of gold discs. Bracelets of tiny gold and turquoise beads adorned his arms, while 11 chest ornaments of white coral and red shell beads had been placed in various parts of the coffin. On his feet were ornamental copper sandals – he could never have walked in them.

Like the warriors so often seen fighting on the Moche pots, the Lord wore a flap to protect his abdomen; it was of solid gold and weighed 0.9 kilograms (2lb). A matching one was made of copper. They were decorated with the figure of a sinister deity that archaeologists call "the decapitator", a ferocious figure who in one hand holds a *tumi* (sacrificial knife) and in the other a severed head. A small symbolic war club lay at the bottom of the coffin, along with many darts for use with an *atlatl* (spear-thrower). In his hand the Lord held a gold rattle with a

ABOVE: The Lord of Sipán was richly provided with pottery and with servants to tend his needs, placed in wooden coffins around his central burial in all his golden finery.

TOP LEFT: Among the looted objects recovered by the police were two gilded copper faces of snarling jaguars, their bared fangs made of inlaid pieces of shell.

copper handle – very similar to one recovered from the looted chamber, which seems likely to have held an equally lavish burial. Both were decorated with a scene in which a warrior is holding a victim by his hair and brandishing a war club in his face. The Moche fought battles not to kill their enemies but to capture them for later sacrifice.

Alva continued to work at Sipán, uncovering the burial of a priest and, in the lowest levels of the mound, another royal grave that was, if anything, even more richly furnished. Dubbed the "Old Lord", the man buried here died around AD 100, about 200 years earlier than the Lord of Sipán. On his face was placed a funerary mask of gilded copper and beneath this he wore nose and ear ornaments. The nose ornament was an astounding work of craftsmanship: a tiny gold figure armed with shield and club and itself wearing a moveable gold nose ornament, a turquoise necklace and a golden skirt. On its head was a magnificent gold headdress with an owl in the centre.

Like the later lord, this ruler was buried with a mass of jewellery, including thousands of beads that had spilled over everything. Six necklaces of gold and silver hung round his neck. Some were made up of snarling feline heads but the finest was assembled from intricate gold beads in the shape of spiders poised above their webs. These held three tiny gold beads that would have rattled when the lord moved. On the back of each spider was a human face.

A huge gilded copper figure of a crab with a human face and legs originally decorated a banner that was covered with metal plates. The Moche were highly sophisticated metalworkers who had developed several ways of gilding metal, including one technique that used chemicals to electroplate the gold on to the copper. With the banner were ulluchu fruit, believed to have produced an anticoagulant substance. The Moche may have added this to the goblets of blood they collected from their sacrificed prisoners so that it would stay fluid long enough for the ruler to drink it.

7

TREASURE HUNTING TODAY

Reading about other people's finds is exciting but finding your own treasure is even better. How do you set about it? There are various things to consider.

In many countries, the laws require that any antiquities discovered be handed over to the local authorities, often in return for a reward. Here Israeli antiquities' officers examine a hoard of Byzantine coins discovered in the northern Israeli town of Beit Shean.

TREASURE-HUNTING TODAY

Introduction

Treasures fall into several groups. There are those that are known to have existed and which have disappeared – like the famous Amber Room (see p.135). There are once-lost treasures which have been located but which are difficult to get at, like the contents of many sunken treasure ships. And there are unknown treasures, buried or lost long ago and now forgotten, like the contents of ancient tombs or hidden hoards whose owner never returned. And of course there are the innumerable small personal treasures that have been casually lost, just waiting for the treasure-seeker to find them again: things like coins and personal jewellery dropped as people were out walking or small hoards of coins saved for "a rainy day" and forgotten when a family moved house.

Treasure-hunting and the law

Lost or hidden treasures await the determined treasure-hunter but it is important to bear in mind that many valuables have an owner, even now. Sunken ships may belong to the heirs of the original owners – such as the government of the Netherlands, the heir to the VOC (Dutch East India Company), many of whose ships went down in eastern waters – or ownership may have been transferred to the insurers who paid the owners at the time the ship was lost. There may also be local laws that make the ship the property of the country in whose territorial waters it lies. Recovering the remains of lost ships is expensive, so the current owners are often willing to enter into a contract that splits the proceeds of a successful salvage operation. Accidental discovery of a wreck carries the duty of reporting it to the proper authorities, and in some countries, including Britain, this goes not only for wrecks but also for anything found below the tideline.

Individual wrecks or wreck sites may be protected by law, as are many historical sites on land, and investigation of these is illegal – another piece of information that the would-be treasure-hunter needs to know. In every case it is important to obtain permission from the proper authorities and from the owners before salvaging material from a wreck or undersea site.

Complex local laws govern the ownership of buried treasure on land. Like wrecks, known treasures have known owners with whom an agreement has to be reached on how the recovered material should be shared. Unknown treasures may be the property of those on whose land they lie or of the state or national government. The hopeful treasure-hunter must obtain permission from the landowner and the proper authorities before searching on land or in buildings, and at this point it can be established who gets what share of any finds that are made. The sensible treasure-hunter will investigate the laws in advance and adhere to them strictly, for this is in everyone's interest. Someone starting out in treasure-hunting might feel wary of declaring their finds to the proper authorities, thinking that they

ABOVE: Spectacular discoveries can attract illicit plunderers. The Peruvian archaeologist, Walter Alva, had to work with armed guards when he excavated the fabulous burials at Sipán, to prevent tomb-robbers raiding the site.

BELOW: Finding and salvaging lost wrecks can be difficult and can cost a lot. Physical problems restrict the time that individual divers can work underwater. Often expensive equipment is needed to locate and excavate wrecks.

might lose what they have recovered. But experienced treasure-seekers are unanimous in agreeing that it is in everyone's interests to play by the book. Finds handed over to the proper authorities are usually returned to the finder, and when they are not, a reward is generally paid instead.

A cautionary tale

Two similar cases with contrasting end-results illustrate this. In England finders of gold or silver objects are obliged by law to report the discovery immediately. At a coroner's inquest it is decided whether these precious objects had been lost or hidden. If lost they are the property of the landowner and whatever agreement the finder has made with the landowner comes into force. If, on the other hand, it is decided that the objects were hidden with the intention of being recovered, then they are deemed the proper-

ty of the Crown. In this case objects of historical interest are retained by the state to be displayed in a museum, and the finder is paid a reward equivalent to the full market value. If the objects are deemed not interesting enough historically, they are returned to the finder, who may then dispose of them as they wish. This is what happened recently when Eric Lawes found a hoard of Roman silver at Hoxne in Suffolk, England (see p.114) and immediately reported it. His action enabled a team of archaeologists to investigate the site and recover not only the hoard but also details about how it had been hidden. Mr Lawes earned a substantial reward. In contrast, in the 1940s a plough-man accidentally turned up a hoard of Roman silver at Mildenhall, in the same county, but was persuaded by an unscrupulous acquaintance that it was pewter. This character kept the material, a series of magnificent dishes and cups, and did not report the find. Sometime later the find became known to others and the authorities stepped in. The silver was confiscated and the two men were investigated. Not only did they not receive the substantial reward they might have reaped had they reported the find at once, but they were lucky not to be fined for concealing it.

Established treasure-hunters strongly advise you to be very careful to sort out the legalities in advance and to make binding agreements with all interested parties. These include state or local authorities, the owners of the land, wrecks or buildings in which the treasure-hunter wishes to work, and the known owners of known lost treasures. Contracts should be drawn up in advance making it quite clear who benefits and how, if any valuable finds are made. If several people are collaborating in a treasure-hunt, watertight contracts are also essential: many a friendship has been soured by disputes over the division of the spoils after a valuable find is made.

Archaeological sites are protected by law in almost every country, so the treasure-seeker should steer clear of these. Archaeologists are not looking for treasure, though very occasionally they find it. They are searching for information that will enable them to reconstruct a picture of what took place in the past. Every scrap of evidence provides some clue, not only from the finds themselves but from the details of where they were found. Holes dug into the remains of the past destroy this evidence for ever. For example, Alva's excavations at Sipán in Peru (see p.173) have revealed a fascinating wealth of information about the Moche people as well as amazing the world with the richness of the objects buried with the two lords. But we know nothing about the people in the looted tomb at the same site and, because looters destroyed the evidence, we will now never be able to find out anything about them.

Before you start on a treasure-hunt the first thing to do, therefore, is find out the rules. Whose permission will it be necessary to obtain in order to undertake the search and what will you be able to keep if it proves successful?

Research

The next step is to look for clues and find out relevant details. Sometimes treasure-seekers are pursuing known or suspected lost treasures: galleons known to have been wrecked, for example, or hoards known to have been buried by individual pirates. At other times the search is more general, such as seeking the hoards of highwaymen or looking for hidden savings. Or it can be even broader: for example, hunting for recently dropped money and valuables.

In every case the successful treasure-hunter is the one who has obtained appropriate information on where to look. Old official records give details of the routes and cargoes of ships lost at sea, together with information that may help pinpoint where the vessels went down. They will also give details of original salvage attempts and what, if anything, was recovered. A thorough study of the pattern of where ships have been lost in the past may also lead you to unknown wrecks, ships caught by the same shoals, rocks, reefs or cliffs that caused known losses at sea. Treasure-seekers can save themselves a lot of time, effort and expense by making their investigations as thorough as possible. For example, the Spanish galleons wrecked off the Florida Keys in 1733 (see p.149) were almost entirely salvaged at the time, yet many modern treasure-hunters have picked over the wrecks, finding nothing, of course, but often irrevocably damaging the historic wrecks – a loss to everyone.

Records are similarly important when looking for treasure on land. Old newspapers, land deeds, wills, parish records, journals and other such documents give information on specific property, perhaps allowing you to trace the disappearance of particular treasures and giving clues that may put you on their trail. Old maps and

ABOVE: Finding out precise details of where a ship went down and where its cargo and other valuables were stored is of great importance when searching for wrecks and recovering their treasures.

other land records may give useful clues to features of the landscape, now often vanished, that could have had links to treasures in the past. For example, river fords were a popular place for highwaymen to operate and many a small valuable could have been dropped there in the struggles and drama of the robbery. Woods were a popular place for highwaymen to conceal their loot. Many other people also thought woods a good place to choose when concealing hoards in times of trouble, for trees both offered the owners privacy while concealing their treasure and gave them excellent markers to enable them to return to the same spot to recover it.

Old houses, often now demolished, may have had their owners' treasures hidden within the structure or grounds. Not everyone succeeded, of course, in relocating such hiding places, since many hoards were never recovered. The seventeenth-century English diarist Samuel Pepys gives a vivid account of the difficulties he experienced when attempting to recover valuables he had buried in his garden not long before. Clearly it is easy for treasure to be lost even if the person who concealed it returns to look for it.

Simple searching on land

Armed only with a simple metal detector and a trowel, you are likely to be successful in finding recently lost valuables if you search in the right spots. Metal detectors are, of course, not choosy in what they locate and you must put up with finding many other objects of little interest, such as tin cans, ring-pulls and silver paper. It is a good idea to pick these up and dispose of them as you go along, since not only are they untidy but they also present a continuing nuisance if you decide to search the same area repeatedly, as professional treasure-hunters often do. The most successful treasure-seekers are those who are systematic in their searches. Having determined where they intend to search, they cover every bit of the ground in an orderly fashion so that nothing is missed. Where appropriate, they mark the area to be searched with pegs and string.

Before there were banks, and even into recent times, people often hid small stores of valuables within their houses. If there is a chance to explore a disused building or an old house, these may be rediscovered. Attics and cellars are promising places to start looking. Other good places to pursue this search are under floorboards and in chimneys.

Places where people pass through in large numbers are excellent locations to investigate. Footpaths, particularly overgrown or muddy ones, are ideal places to search for modern coins, jewellery and other lost goods, since people out walking often drop things and often do not find them again. Town and village streets are also possible locations, though less likely, since things that are dropped are more visible against the pavement or road.

Beaches are a trap for small valuables, since once dropped they rapidly become hidden in the sand. The area between the

RIGHT: Count Alexander Zu Lynar-Redern displays his family collection of silver and porcelain which he and his mother, Princess Victoria, had buried in 1945 when the Red Army was approaching east Germany.

BELOW: Even when the location of buried treasure is known, finding it again can still be difficult. Here men are digging for Count Lynar-Redern's family treasure buried in these woods fifty years earlier.

high and low tidelines is the best zone to hunt in, since here the waves turn over the sand and may wash clean some of the objects that lie hidden in it. The determined treasure-hunter should choose a time when holiday-makers are not around, preferably toward the end of the season, and should take note of relevant information such as the times of tides and the places where pebbles the size of coins have been deposited, since these are often the best spots. Sometimes more ancient material may turn up, washed ashore in stormy conditions, perhaps from an old shipwreck: like the coins from the Spanish treasure fleets that were sometimes deposited on the Florida beaches. These, unlike modern coins, take a sharp eye to spot, since they are generally tarnished and blackened and may

be encrusted with undersea material.

Rivers and streams are similarly productive zones if you are looking for lost coins and other small objects. Whereas things lost on beaches are generally either recovered in a short time or irretrievably lost to the sea, those that end up in watercourses may lie there for several hundred years before being rediscovered. Information about the high and low water levels in the river is useful to the searcher, since this will provide clues to where objects dropped into the water may be deposited. Places where people cross the watercourse, such as bridges or fords, are also good spots to search; follow the eddies downstream to see where things have been deposited by the water. Wharves, jetties and other riverside locations where people

congregate or goods are loaded and unloaded are likely places to recover coins and other objects. Areas downstream from riverside pubs are particularly fruitful, and pub grounds are also a good place to search.

More ambitious treasure-hunts

While modern valuables can readily be recovered from such places as paths, beaches and streams and are likely to turn up in old houses or gardens, treasures from the past are mostly discovered by chance – when ploughing a field, for example, landscaping a garden or building an extension – and such discoveries are rare. Nevertheless, some treasures have a documented history that can be the starting point for a treasure-hunt. Your search may last a lifetime, cost all your savings and go

ABOVE: Nicknamed 'WASP', this revolutionary underwater submersible allows a diver to explore arctic waters and recover material from wrecks like the 19th century *Breadalbane* that were previously inaccessible.

LEFT: Modern technology has made underwater treasure seeking much easier. Remote sensing devices like side-scan sonar can be used to locate wrecks, while individuals can scour the seabed with hand-held metal detectors.

unrewarded, but it might just lead to success. Down the ages, there have always been people who mounted hopeful treasure-seeking expeditions – from Jason's search for the Golden Fleece to such doomed quests as those for King Solomon's Mines or the legendary city of Eldorado.

Searches for shipwrecks are less likely to be unsuccessful than those on land, since they have two important ingredients: good documentation of the loss and difficulties in immediate recovery. Ships that went down in deep water could neither be located nor dived on in the past, while those near the coast might have been too hazardous to investigate or, once they had broken up, it may have proved too difficult to locate the scattered remains.

Over the past few decades the development of highly sophisticated diving and reconnaissance equipment has made the salvage of many such shipwrecks possible. Devices such as sonar can be used to detect wrecks even if they are buried quite deep within the seabed. Diving equipment is now extremely sophisticated, allowing people to penetrate some areas themselves, while robots and other remotely controlled devices can now be used in more inaccessible localities.

Although this sounds very encouraging, these searches are generally extremely expensive. Such famous salvors as Kip Wagner and Mel Fisher (see p.149) invested very great amounts of time, energy and money in their searches before they struck lucky – and for every success story there are thousands of failures. Often the cost of such ventures is borne by selling shares in an enterprise intended to locate a particular wreck. Like buying lottery tickets, such expeditions should be regarded as gambling with the remote possibility of success rather than as a safe investment.

And even ventures that succeed can be fraught with difficulty. Salvors working on wrecks, like the *Titanic*, which went down in international waters that are outside the jurisdiction of any government, have frequently had trouble with rival salvors. Even in territorial waters, where salvage claims can be registered, it has often proved difficult to keep away illicit rivals: the modern equivalent of the pirates who hampered the recovery attempts of the original salvors at the time of the wreck. Many salvors have found themselves caught up in complicated legal cases, despite their care in apparently obtaining all the necessary authorization in advance of recovery. Such lawsuits often hinge on disputed ownership: a complex business that often does not surface until something spectacular has been found.

So be warned: treasure-hunting may be exciting and rewarding, but the more spectacular the finds the bigger the associated problems are likely to be.

RIGHT: Success! A diver smiles as he returns to the surface with a piece of silver he has recovered from the Spanish ship *La Capitana* which sank off Ecuador in 1654.

BIBLIOGRAPHY

Allen, G. & D. *Clive's Lost Treasure,* Robin Garton, 1978

Allen, J. *Glittering Prospects,* Hamish Hamilton, 1975

Alva, W. "Discovering the World's Richest Unlooted Tomb" *National Geographic,* October 1988

Alva, W. "New Royal Tomb Unearthed" *National Geographic,* June 1990

Andronicos, M. "Regal Treasures from a Macedonian Tomb" *National Geographic,* July 1978

Andronikos, M. *The Royal Graves at Vergina,* Athens, 1980

Anon "Mystery Statue Surfaces on a Bronze Age Wreck" *National Geographic,* May 1993

Antonova, I., Tolstikov V. & Treister, M. *The Gold of Troy,* Thames and Hudson, 1996

Artamonov, M. *Treasures from Scythian Tombs,* Thames and Hudson, 1969

Bacon, E. (ed.) *The Great Archaeologists,* Martin Secker and Warburg, 1976

Bahn, P. (ed.) *The Story of Archaeology,* Weidenfeld and Nicolson, 1996

Bahn, P. (ed.) *Wonderful Things,* Weidenfeld and Nicolson, 1999

Baines, J. & Málek, J. *Atlas of Ancient Egypt,* Andromeda, 1996

Ballard, R. & Michel, J.-L. "How We Found Titanic" *National Geographic,* December 1985

Ballard, R. & Tarpy, C. "A Long Last Look at Titanic" *National Geographic,* December 1986

Ballard, R. "Epilogue for Titanic" *National Geographic,* October 1987

Barnes, G.L. *The Rise of Civilization in East Asia,* Thames and Hudson, 1999 (1993)

Bass, G.F. "Oldest Known Shipwreck Reveals Splendours of the Bronze Age", *National Geographic,* December 1987

Bass, G.F. "From Bronze Age Wreck, More of Everything" *National Geographic,* May 1992

Bedoyere, Guy de la *The Golden Age of Roman Britain,* Batsford, 1999

Beresford Ellis, P. *The Ancient World of the Celts,* Constable, 1998

Bland, R. & Johns, C. *The Hoxne Treasure,* British Museum, 1993

Blunden, C. & Elvin, M. *Cultural Atlas of China,* Phaidon, 1983

Branigan, K. *The Atlas of Archaeology,* Macdonald, 1982

Bray, W., E.H. Swanson & I.S. Farrington *The Ancient Americas,* Phaidon, 1989

Brothwell, D. *The Bogman and the Archaeology of People,* British Museum, 1986

Bruhns, K.O. *Ancient South America,* CUP, 1994

Carter, H. *The tomb of Tutankhamen,* Sphere, 1972

Carver, M. *Sutton Hoo: Burial Ground of Kings?,* British Museum, 1998

Caso, A. "Monte Alban, Richest Archeological Find in America" *National Geographic,* October 1932

Ceram, C.W. *Gods, Graves and Scholars,* Alfred A. Knopf, 1967

Champion, T., Gamble, C. Shennan, S. & Whittle, A. *Prehistoric Europe,* Academic Press, 1984

Coe, M. *Mexico,* Thames and Hudson, 1994

Coe, M., Snow, D. & Benson, E. *Atlas of Ancient America,* Facts on File, 1986

Collis, J. *The European Iron Age,* Batsford, 1984

Cunliffe, B. (ed.) *The Oxford Illustrated Prehistory of Europe,* OUP, 1994

Cunliffe, B. *Iron Age Britain,* Batsford, 1995

Cunliffe, B. *The Ancient Celts,* OUP, 1997

Dahl, Roald *The Mildenhall Treasure,* Jonathan Cape, 1999

Daniel, G. *A Short History of Archaeology,* Thames and Hudson, 1981

Darville, T. *Prehistoric Britain,* Batsford, 1987

Davalos Hurtado, E. "Return to the Sacred Cenote" *National Geographic,* October 1961

Davidson, B. *The Story of Africa,* Mitchell Beazley, 1984

Delgado, J. (ed.) *British Museum Encyclopedia of Underwater and Maritime Archaeology,* British Museum Press, 1997

Desroches-Noblecourt, C. *Tutankhamen,* Penguin, 1965

Deuel, L. *Testaments of Time,* Secker and Warburg, 1966

Dixon, P. *Barbarian Europe,* Phaidon, 1976

Donnan, C.B. "Iconography of the Moche: Unravelling the Mystery of the Warrior-Priest" *National Geographic,* October 1988

Donnan, C.B. "Masterworks Reveal a Pre-Inca World" *National Geographic,* June 1990

Evans, A.C. *Sutton Hoo Ship Burial,* British Museum, 1986

Feather, R. *The Copper Scroll Decoded,* Thorsons, 1999

Fenwick, V. & Gale, A. *Historic Shipwrecks,* Tempus, 1998

Forte, M. & Siliotti, A. (ed.s) *Virtual Archaeology,* Thames and Hudson, 1997

Foster, S. *Picts, Gaels and Scots,* Batsford, 1996

Franzen, A. "*Kronan*: Remnants of a Warship's Past" *National Geographic,* April 1989

Furneaux, R. *On Buried and Sunken Treasure,* Puffin, 1973

Godard, P. *The First and Last Voyage of the Batavia,* Abrolhos Publishing, 1993

Graham-Campbell, J. (ed.) *Cultural Atlas of the Viking World,* Facts on File, 1994

Groushko, M. *Treasure,* Apple Press, 1990

Gryaznov, M. *Southern Siberia,* Nagel, 1969

Hall, Alice J. "A Lady from China's Past" *National Geographic,* May 1974

Harding, D. *Prehistoric Europe,* Elsevier Phaidon, 1978

Harris, N. *Hamlyn History of Imperial China,* Hamlyn, 1999

Harris, R. *The World of the Bible,* Thames and Hudson, 1995

Hemming, J. *Philip's Atlas of Exploration,* Philip's, 1996

Hemming, J. *The Search for Eldorado,* Michael Joseph, 1978

Hills, C.A.R. *The Destruction of Pompeii and Herculaneum,* Dryad Press, 1987

Hunter, J & Ralston, I. (ed.) *The Archaeology of Britain,* Routledge, 1999

Huntington, S. *The Art of Ancient India,* Weatherhill, 1985

James, S. *Exploring the World of the Celts,* Thames and Hudson, 1993

James, P. & Thorpe, N. *Ancient Inventions,* Michael O'Mara Books, 1995

Jettmar, K. *Art of the Steppes,* Methuen, 1964

Johnson, S. *Hadrian's Wall,* Batsford, 1989

Kenoyer, J.M. *Ancient Cities of the Indus Valley Civilization,* OUP, 1998

Lerici, C. "Periscope on the Etruscan Past"

National Geographic, September 1959

Littlehales, B. "Treasure Hunt in the Deep Past" *National Geographic,* October 1961

Lyon, E. "*Atocha,* Tragic Galleon of the Florida Keys" *National Geographic,* June 1976

Lyon. E. "Treasure from the Ghost Galleon: *Santa Margarita*" *National Geographic,* February 1982

Lynch, D. *Titanic. An Illustrated History,* Hodder and Stoughton, 1992

Maiuri, A. "Last Moments of the Pompeians" *National Geographic,* November 1961

Martin, C. *Scotland's Historic Shipwrecks,* Batsford, 1998

McCormick, F. "China's Treasures" *National Geographic,* October 1912

MacInnis, J.B. "*Titanic:* Tragedy in Three Dimensions" *National Geographic,* August 1998

McQueen, E.I. *Diodorus Siculus: The Reign of Philip II,* translated, Duckworth, 1995

Madden, R. "China Unveils her Newest Treasures" *National Geographic,* December 1974

Mazzatenta, O.L. "A Chinese Emperor's Army for an Eternity" *National Geographic,* August 1992

Mazzatenta, O.L. "China's Warriors rise from the Earth" *National Geographic,* October 1996

Millett, M. *Roman Britain,* Batsford, 1995

Moorehead, C. *The Lost Treasures of Troy,* Weidenfeld and Nicolson, 1994

Montet, P. *Lives of the Pharaohs,* Weidenfeld and Nicolson, 1968

Moseley, M. *The Incas and their Ancestors,* Thames and Hudson, 1992

Nelson, S.M. *The Archaeology of Korea,* CUP, 1993

Norvill, R. *The Treasure Seeker's Treasury,* Hutchinson, 1978

O'Brien, P. *Philip's Atlas of World History,* Philip's, 1999

O'Kelly, M.J. *Early Ireland,* CUP, 1989

Parker Pearson, M. *Bronze Age Britain,* Batsford, 1993

Parker Pearson, M. *The Archaeology of Death and Burial,* Sutton, 1999

Peterson, M. "Graveyard of the Quicksilver Galleons" *National Geographic,* December 1979

Petrie, A. *An Introduction to Greek History, Antiquities and Literature,* 2nd edition, OUP, 1962

Phillips, E. *The Royal Hordes,* Thames and Hudson, 1965

Phillipson, D. *African Archaeology,* 2nd edition, CUP, 1993

Platt, C & Wright, J. *Treasure Islands,* Michael O'Mara, 1992

Pickford, N. *The Atlas of Shipwrecks and Treasure,* Dorling Kindersley, 1994

Piggott, S. *Early Celtic Art,* The Arts Council, 1970

Postgate, N. *Early Mesopotamia,* Routledge, 1992

Potter, T. *Roman Britain,* British Museum, 1983

Prag, J. & Neave, R. *Making Faces,* British Museum, 1997

Pritchard, J. (ed.) *The Times Atlas of the Bible,* Times Books, 1989

Quirke, S. & Spencer, J. *The British Museum Book of Ancient Egypt,* British Museum, 1992

Rawson, J. (ed.) *Mysteries of Ancient China,* British Museum, 1996

Rawson, P. *Indian Asia,* Phaidon, 1977

Reinhard, J. "Sacred Peaks of the Andes" *National Geographic,* March 1992

Reinhard, J. "Peru's Icemaiden: Unwrapping the Secrets" *National Geographic,* June 1996

Reinhard, J. "Sharp Eyes of Science Probe the Mummies of Peru" *National Geographic,* January 1997

Reinhard, J. "Research Update: New Inca Mummies" *National Geographic,* July 1998

Renfrew, C. "Ancient Bulgaria's Golden Treasures" *National Geographic,* July 1980

Renfrew, C. & Bahn, P. *Archaeology,* Thames and Hudson, 1996

Richards, J. *Stonehenge,* Batsford, 1991

Roaf, M. *Cultural Atlas of Mesopotamia,* Facts on File, 1990

Robertshaw, P. *A History of African Archaeology,* Heinemann, 1990

Rolle, R. *World of the Scythians,* Batsford, 1989

Roux, G. *Ancient Iraq,* 2nd edition, Penguin, 1980

Rudenko, S. *Frozen Tombs of Siberia,* Dent, 1970

Sacks, D. *Encyclopedia of the Ancient Greek World,* Constable, 1995

Sayer, I. & Botting, D. *Nazi Gold,* Granada, 1984

Scarre, C. *Past Worlds. The Times Atlas of Archaeology,* Times Books, 1988

Scarre, C. *Exploring Prehistoric Europe,* OUP, 1998

Shaw, I. & Nicholson, P. *British Museum Dictionary of Ancient Egypt,* British Museum, 1995

Smith, M. *The Aztecs,* Blackwell, 1996

Stein, M.A. *On Ancient Central Asian Tracks,* University of Chicago Press, 1964

Stenuit, R. "Priceless Relics of the Spanish Armada" *National Geographic,* June 1969

Stenuit, R. "The Sunken Treasure of St. Helena" *National Geographic,* October 1978

Topping, A. "China's Incredible Find" *National Geographic,* April 1978

Villiers, A. "Sir Francis Drake" *National Geographic,* February 1975

Wagner, K. "Drowned Galleons Yield Spanish Gold" *National Geographic,* January 1965

Townsend, R. *The Aztecs,* Thames and Hudson, 1992

Wagner, K. & Taylor, L.B. *Pieces of Eight,* Longmans, 1966

Watson, W. *The Genius of China,* Times Newspapers, 1973

Whittle, A. *Europe in the Neolithic,* CUP, 1996

Williams, M.O. "At the Tomb of Tutankhamen" *National Geographic,* May 1923

Wilson, D. *The World Atlas of Treasure,* Collins, 1981

Wilson, I. *Undiscovered,* Chancellor Press, 1987

Woolley, L. "Archeology, the Mirror of the Ages" *National Geographic,* August 1928

Woolley, L. "New Light on Ancient Ur" *National Geographic,* January 1930

Woolley, L. *Ur 'of the Chaldees',* revised edition by Moorey, P.R.S., Herbert Press, 1982

Wright, J. *Encyclopedia of Sunken Treasure,* Michael O'Mara, 1995

INDEX

PICTURE CREDITS